STOLEN

ALSO BY RICHARD BELL

*We Shall Be No More: Suicide and Self-Government
in the Newly United States*

Buried Lives: Incarcerated in Early America
(Coedited with Michele Lise Tarter)

STOLEN

FIVE FREE BOYS
KIDNAPPED INTO
SLAVERY AND
THEIR ASTONISHING
ODYSSEY HOME

Richard Bell

37 INK

SIMON & SCHUSTER

NEW YORK • LONDON • TORONTO • SYDNEY • NEW DELHI

37 INK

SIMON &
SCHUSTER

An Imprint of Simon & Schuster, Inc.
1230 Avenue of the Americas
New York, NY 10020

First 37 INK / Simon & Schuster trade paperback edition December 2020

37INK / SIMON & SCHUSTER and colophon are trademarks of
Simon & Schuster, Inc.

For information about special discounts for bulk purchases, please
contact Simon & Schuster Special Sales at 1-866-506-1949 or
business@simonandschuster.com.

The Simon & Schuster Speakers Bureau can bring authors to your live
event. For more information or to book an event, contact the Simon &
Schuster Speakers Bureau at 1-866-248-3049 or visit our website at
www.simonspeakers.com.

Interior design by Dana Sloan

5 7 9 10 8 6 4

Library of Congress Cataloging-in-Publication Data is available.

ISBN 978-1-5011-6943-4
ISBN 978-1-5011-6944-1 (pbk)
ISBN 978-1-5011-6945-8 (ebook)

For Ruby and Rosie

For Ruby and Rose

CONTENTS

CONTENTS

STOLEN

THE REVERSE UNDERGROUND RAILROAD

CORNELIUS SINCLAIR WAS ten years old and he was trapped. He was stuck in the belly of a small ship bobbing in the middle of the Delaware River, a mile south of Philadelphia. A man had grabbed him from a spot near that city's market an hour ago, shoved a black gag across his mouth, tossed him into a wagon, and hauled him here.

It was dark below the waterline, but Cornelius could see enough to know that he was not alone. Four pairs of eyes stared back at him—four other black boys.

Yesterday they had all been free. Today they were slaves, prisoners of a gang of child snatchers who planned to sell their lives and labor, most likely to plantation owners in the Deep South. If the boys' abductors got away with this, Cornelius would spend the rest of his life as someone else's property somewhere very far away. He would never see his family again.

❖

Cornelius disappeared from Philadelphia in late August 1825, about eleven months short of the fiftieth anniversary of the signing of the Declaration of Independence in that city in the summer of 1776. So much had changed since then. The new nation's population had tripled, topping ten million, its land area had more than doubled, and the number of states in the union had jumped from thirteen to twenty-four, all of them now latticed together by ever-expanding networks of roads, canals, and steamboat routes.

Slavery in America was changing too. In 1776, there had been enslaved people in every rebel colony, but by 1825, slavery was dead or dying in the North. Fewer than twenty thousand black northerners remained in bondage, most of them in rural parts of New Jersey and New York where slavery was on its last legs. In the South, it was a different story. Slavery remained profitable and popular there, and more than 1.75 million black southerners lived as slaves. Assuming office in March 1825, John Quincy Adams, the sixth president of the United States, presided over a union equally divided between free states and slave states, twelve of them apiece. The Mason-Dixon Line, which separated Pennsylvania—a free state—from Maryland and Virginia—two slave states—seemed to split the nation in two. It served, in the words of its recent biographer, as "the closest thing to a modern international border anywhere in North America."[1]

Situated just forty miles north of that border, Philadelphia was one of the nearest free cities to the slave South. That proximity made its many free black residents attractive targets for professional people snatchers from the slave states. They preyed on the members of the city's black community relentlessly, putting bull's-eyes on their backs and prices on their heads. Cornelius Sinclair was one of dozens of

African American children to vanish from Philadelphia in 1825 alone. By then, the city was without question the hub of American slavery's newest and blackest market. Its gridded streets and tangled alleys were hunting grounds for crews of professional kidnappers who made their livings turning free black folk like Cornelius into southern slaves. Philadelphia had long had a reputation as a safe haven for people of color, and was home to the headquarters of the American antislavery movement. But it was probably one of the most dangerous places to be a free black person anywhere in the United States.

The people these kidnappers stole could each fetch anywhere from $400 to $700 ($9,000 to $15,000 today) in Louisiana, Mississippi, and Alabama, three of the new territories and states rising up along the Gulf Coast. The American settlers swarming into that region demanded a bottomless supply of slave labor to cut sugarcane and pick cotton and would take almost anyone—including children as young as ten-year-old Cornelius. Buying some of their slaves from kidnappers may not have been their first choice, but planters in the Deep South had few other options. They had been forced to look to sources within the United States for their labor needs ever since 1808, when lawmakers in Washington had outlawed slave imports from Africa and the Caribbean—a major turning point in the history of slavery in America. Interstate slave traders worked hard to satisfy these settlers' demand for black labor, bringing them thousands of American-born slaves each year from states like Maryland, Delaware, and Virginia, but planters across the Deep South always wanted more.

The more settlers were willing to pay, the more tempting and profitable it became for unscrupulous entrepreneurs to kidnap free people from northern cities, smuggle them into the legal supply chain, and sell them in this vast new southern slave market. These incentives left Philadelphia's large and dynamic black community

dangerously exposed, and by 1825 the city had become the center of
an interregional kidnapping operation, the northern terminus of
what we might usefully call the Reverse Underground Railroad.

⁜

This Reverse Underground Railroad and its better-known namesake, the Underground Railroad, ran in opposite directions but
were mirror images of each other. On the Underground Railroad,
enslaved people abandoned southern plantations and trekked
northward, dreaming of new lives and opportunities in freedom.
On the Reverse Underground Railroad, free black people vanished
from northern cities like Philadelphia and were made to trudge
southward and westward to be sold into plantation slavery. On the
Underground Railroad, conductors like Harriet Tubman risked
their lives and liberty to help black fugitives make these epic journeys. On the Reverse Underground Railroad, the conductors were
kidnappers and human traffickers motivated by money.[2]

The volume of traffic on the two railroads was roughly the
same. Each one carried hundreds of black adults and children
across state lines each year. Both networks roared to life in the early
nineteenth century to exploit what by then had become major dif-
ferences in the legal status of slavery in the North and the South.
Both were loosely organized and opportunistic. Both ran on secrecy
and relied on small circles of trusted participants, forged documents,
false identities, and disguises. Whether traveling from the slave
states into the free states or vice versa, black voyagers had to hide in
stables, barns, cellars, and attics. The direction of travel was different, but the routes taken by freedom seekers and victims of kidnapping like Cornelius Sinclair were often the same. They might
even have passed one another on the roads from time to time.[3]

Most Americans know something about the Underground Railroad. Scholars have spent decades studying the strategies and tactics that Harriet Tubman and her fellow conductors and station agents used to help freedom seekers escape from slavery. Accounts by former passengers and biographies of former participants have spurred immense interest not only in Tubman but also in her many comrades and collaborators. Their achievements saturate popular culture. There are walking tours, television shows, and museums dedicated to celebrating the men and women who, in the words of the National Underground Railroad Freedom Center in Cincinnati, "created the secret network through which the enslaved could escape to freedom."[4]

We know far less about the Reverse Underground Railroad. Its conductors and station agents worked tirelessly to remain untouchable, and the identities of all but a handful still remain a secret. Unlike Harriet Tubman, they never gave public lectures about their work or went on fund-raising tours. Only rarely do their names and crimes appear in surviving police files or trial transcripts, their low profiles the result of the years they spent in the shadows, protected by bribes, avarice, and indifference. Unlike legal interstate slave traders who sometimes bequeathed their papers to southern colleges and historical societies, the outlaws who built the Reverse Underground Railroad left no business records or bundles of private letters for historians to read and examine. They did not write memoirs or pose for paintings or photographs. Their homes and warehouses no longer stand.[5]

Yet these professional kidnappers left their mark everywhere. They stole away many thousands of free black people in the first six decades of the century, many of them children like Cornelius who were under the age of eighteen. Most of those kidnapped could not read or write and were never heard from again. Their families and friends searched, advertised, and petitioned. They waited in earnest for news, but usually nothing came. Beyond the meager ranks of a few Quaker-led antislavery societies, free black people in northern cities like Philadelphia had few white allies. White employers openly discriminated against African American job applicants, while city constables generally ignored people of color's complaints and turned a blind eye to most white-on-black street violence. So when children like Cornelius went missing, their parents could rarely persuade mayors and magistrates to get involved. It was rarer still for anyone to be able to gather enough evidence to compel authorities to issue arrest warrants, search property, and interrogate suspects. Even then, experienced members of kidnapping crews knew what to do and what to say to talk their way out of trouble and get back to work.

Solomon Northup was one of only a few legally free people to experience the Reverse Underground Railroad, escape from southern slavery, and then return home to write about it. In *Twelve Years a Slave* (1853), Northup explains how, in 1841, a pair of well-dressed white con men lured him—a well-educated and prosperous musician in his midthirties—into New York City from his home upstate. In Manhattan they wined, dined, and drugged him, then sold him to an interstate slave trader in Washington, DC. Northup was forced onto a slave ship bound for New Orleans and sold in one of the city's infamous slave marts to a planter who put him to work in his cane fields. Though the 2013 Oscar-winning film based on Northup's extraordinary autobiography drew overdue attention to his ordeal, both the memoir and the movie offer distorted and perhaps misleading views of who the agents of the Reverse Underground Railroad were, whom they usually targeted, and how they made money.[6]

Northup's experience was actually not at all typical. Most kidnappings were committed not by smartly dressed confidence men, but by poorer people who had never set foot in a fancy bar or restaurant.

Most of the kidnappers active on the Reverse Underground Railroad were men, though some were women. Most were white, but a surprising number were black. They rarely approached highly literate, middle-aged men like Northup. They preferred instead to lure away poorly educated children with ruses that could swiftly separate them from their families. Very few of their captives traveled by ship to New Orleans. Instead, kidnappers forced most boys and girls to trek southward on foot in small, specialized overland convoys known as *coffles*, after the Arabic word for "caravan." Their prisoners rarely ended up in showrooms or on the auction block, and were vastly more likely to be sold off in ones and twos to planters in the Mississippi and Alabama Cotton Belt who could not afford big-city New Orleans prices.[7]

❖

Unlike Northup's experience, the full story of what happened to Cornelius Sinclair and the four other boys who went missing from Philadelphia in August 1825 has never before been told—and for understandable reasons. Cornelius was a child at the time and came from a hard-up family that was not the sort to leave behind traces in libraries and archives. This is a problem, of course, because historians need sources—and lots of them—to reconstruct past lives in ways that are fair and true. The stories and struggles of the many people who did not leave rich troves of papers, diaries, or memoirs often remain untold and unstudied as a result.

I have reconstructed the basic outline of this single episode in the long history of the Reverse Underground Railroad from a small packet of letters written to or from the mayor of Philadelphia and from coverage of later events in a single antislavery magazine, the *African Observer*. Historians have known about these modest sources for some time, but there is a lot more that is new here too. I've unearthed all sorts of treasures, buried within thirty-five archives in fourteen states and the District of Columbia. Among them: a plaintive missing-persons notice written by Cornelius's grieving father; the handwritten notes of a trial that took place in Tuscaloosa, Alabama, to decide the boy's fate; and a pair of letters in which one of his kidnappers asserted his innocence. Together, this patchwork of new sources makes it possible at last to properly illuminate the experiences of these five young riders on the Reverse Underground Railroad. Still, the tale told here has holes, and I hope readers will notice those moments when I have taken the liberty to speculate because the paper trail has run dry.

Any story about free children ripped from their families and swallowed up by slavery is worth telling for its own sake, but the

Boy Lost.

THE Subscriber's son, Cornelius Sinclair, a coloured Boy, about 11 years old, left his friends yesterday, and as he had no cause, and never before absented himself, it is feared he has been seduced away, by some evil minded person ; he is a very dark mulatto, pretty stout built, thin long fingers, his eyes weak, left eye smaller than the right. Any person hearing of him, will confer a favour on his afflicted parents, by giving information to Wiggin & Whitney, No. 19 South Front-street, and all persons are forbid harbouring him under penalty of the law.   JOSEPH SINCLAIR,
     aug 13—3t Crab-street, below the Old Theatre.

Cornelius Sinclair's parents rushed a missing-persons notice into the pages of the city's most popular paper within three days of their son's disappearance. Joseph Sinclair directed readers with tips to call at his place of work, a merchant house near the docks, where he was employed as a porter. Poulson's American Daily Advertiser, *August 13, 1825. (Courtesy of the American Antiquarian Society.)*

remarkable ordeal that Cornelius and his four fellow captives endured demands attention for many other reasons. It serves as a pointed reminder that child snatching was frequent, pernicious, and politically significant in the first half of the nineteenth century, and that black freedom in northern towns and cities was achingly fragile. It demonstrates too the important role that the traffic in kidnapped free people played in spreading slavery into the Deep South and in fueling the American economy over the same period.

The dogged efforts of all those involved in trying to save these boys and others like them from the horrors of Southern slavery also had profound consequences. That campaign and its aftermath would radicalize black communities across the free states, emboldening African Americans to embrace violence in the cause of self-defense and mutual protection as never before. The case would reshape the rest of the antislavery movement as well by encouraging white abolitionists to focus the public's attention on the suffering of black families forcibly separated by slavery. Most immediately, outrage over the abduction of these five boys forced lawmakers in Pennsylvania to pass tough new antikidnapping measures. Those laws enraged southern slaveholders and set in motion a chain of retaliations that culminated in the passage through Congress of the Fugitive Slave Act of 1850, a bonanza for slaveholders that put the country on a collision course with civil war.

The events that unfold in these pages were the product of massive economic and political forces and would usher in a new chapter in the history of slavery and freedom in the United States. Yet this lasting legacy must not be allowed to obscure the urgent and elemental stakes of this particular story.

A ten-year-old boy and four other free children were dragged into slavery in 1825.

They would have to fight like hell to try to escape.

Chapter 1

SANCTUARY CITY

Sam Scomp woke early. He was a runaway from one of the last remaining slave plantations in New Jersey and had been bedding down in doorways all over Philadelphia for the last seven nights. The summer had been scorching, but a smart dash of rain overnight had finally, mercifully, cut the August heat. Hungry and stiff, Sam figured that an hour or two spent lugging barrels and boxes up from the docks would warm him up, dry his clothes, and earn him enough to buy a bun for breakfast.[1]

Most of the city was still asleep. The only real activity was down by the Delaware River, where a scrum of men and boys crowded the wharves looking for a day's work. Clustered around one or another of the dozen or so oceangoing vessels wedged side by side along Philadelphia's clogged waterfront, they hustled and hollered to try to catch each first mate's eye. Only when they got his nod could they board and begin heaving heavy crates from a ship's slippery wooden decks down onto sturdy carts bound for the city's central market.[2]

Just fifteen years old, Sam was young and strong. He was used to hard work, but had been in Philadelphia for only a week. He did not have his own wagon or wheelbarrow, and he barely knew anyone. Finding work, even on the docks, turned out to be harder than he had expected, and white men seemed to be catching most of the breaks. One by one, each crew chief sent Sam packing, preferring to deal with experienced cartmen who had their own wheels, or with other dock boys who had already proven themselves on hundreds of other mornings just like this one.

So it seemed like a blessing when a light-skinned black man strolled over to Sam and offered him work. The boy's benefactor said his name was John Smith. He told Sam that he had a delivery of "Peaches, Oranges, Water Melons &c" that he needed to unload from a small sloop at anchor out by the Navy Yard and then haul back to a

Dockwork was a major source of employment for unskilled laborers in Philadelphia in the 1820s. This image shows young black and white haulers jockeying for work near the Arch Street ferry several blocks north of Market Street in 1800. William Russell Birch, Arch Street Ferry, Philadelphia. *Hand-colored engraving, 1800. (Courtesy of the Library Company of Philadelphia.)*

stall at the market. The job would take no more than two hours, and they could use a wagon already waiting for them down by the ship. Could Sam help him out? How did twenty-five cents sound?[3]

Sam did not hesitate. As the two of them set off on the brisk mile-and-a-half walk to the Navy Yard, he might have begun to calculate what his morning wages could get him back in town. A quarter dollar could buy an armful of buns, and beer too, and who knew what else. Philadelphia's market had it all, not just fruit sellers hawking melons, peaches, and oranges. If you knew where to look—if you poked around on the fringes of that grand outdoor bazaar on the high street—you could usually find food vendors hawking hominy and pepper pots, even roasted possum or squirrel, all of them selling for pennies.[4]

Sam was distracted and daydreaming, and his walk to the Navy Yard passed quickly. He was typically on his guard around strangers, especially white people, but he was hungry, and the prospect of easy money for light work had disarmed him. And besides, his new employer's brown skin was only a little lighter than his own. John Smith was a decade older than his new assistant, yet slight and boyish looking. Sam could probably have bested him in a scrap, though a fight did not seem to be in the cards.

Smith was actually quite charming. If he had seemed a bit skittish when he'd first sidled up to Sam down by the docks, he had grown ever more at ease as they walked together down Front Street, leaving the city behind them. Anyone who came upon them that morning might have assumed they were longtime friends, or cousins, or half brothers out for some sort of dawn lark.

Not that anyone saw them. The riverbank was deserted as Sam and Smith hiked along, skirting scrublands and flower-filled meadows not yet swallowed by Philadelphia's southward sprawl. They walked together for nearly half an hour, until finally several huge wooden sheds loomed ahead. This was the Philadelphia Navy Yard. Though small by European standards, this complex of dry docks housed several massive ships—all men-of-war—in various stages of construction and repair. As Sam and Smith approached, a rowboat scuttled out from a little cargo vessel bobbing in the middle of the yawning river and tied up to a small pier that jutted out into the water on one side of the yard.[5]

The man who now scrambled ashore to hail them was about twice Sam's age, thirty or so, strong and sinewy. He and Smith obviously knew each other. He told Sam his name was Joseph Johnson, and he chatted idly with his two passengers as he rowed them out to the *Little John* to collect the fruit from the ship's hold. Two minutes later, all three had clambered aboard, and Johnson introduced Sam to the *Little John*'s crew: Thomas Collins, a deckhand, and Bill Paragee, the captain. Paragee told Sam and Smith that he had set out refreshments for them belowdecks and beckoned them all to follow him and "take a drink" before setting to work.[6]

At the bottom of the stairs the four men's friendly faces suddenly hardened to stone. Johnson shoved Sam to the floor and knotted the boy's hands with rope. Sam began to howl for help, pausing only long enough to hear Johnson tell him that he was going to be shipped back to his master in Maryland. Sam roared at that lie—he was from New Jersey and had never once been to Maryland. You're wrong, he told his captors, wrestling against the cords that now dug into his wrists. You've made a terrible mistake.[7]

Johnson was unmoved. He waited while the boy proceeded to shout himself hoarse. Then he moved closer, taking a "large Spanish knife" from his belt. For that brief moment Sam might have thought that Johnson was about to cut him free and release him. Instead, Johnson thrust the blade close to the child's face and "threatened to cut his throat if he resisted or made a noise."[8]

Sam swallowed the urge to scream, and watched, silently now, as his kidnappers went to work. Smith, the man who had baited Sam and brought him here, tied the boy's feet. When he was done, Johnson told him to be off. Smith did as he was told, taking the rowboat back to shore and disappearing in the direction of the city. Johnson, Paragee, and Collins then hustled Sam into the depths of the ship's hold, farther below the waterline. Using irons and locks, the men chained the boy's legs to a pump there before returning to the deck and closing the hatch behind them. Sam was left in darkness.[9]

When the sound of the men's footfalls receded, the whispers around him began. As Sam's eyes slowly adjusted, he realized he was not alone. He could make out the shadows of two other boys, both shackled like him. He could tell from their voices that they were younger than he was, and he could hear them stifle their sobs as they told him who they were and what had happened. The older child was Enos Tilghman. He was ten years old. He seemed to be darker skinned than Sam, and said he worked as a sweep, cleaning chimneys in the city. The younger boy was lighter skinned and about eight years old. He had curly hair and said his name was Alex Manlove.[10]

Both of them had been stuck in this floating dungeon for many hours already. They could not be sure, but they guessed that a full day and night had passed since they had been lured to the *Little John* by the man who called himself John Smith. They were friends and had been playing together before falling for Smith's promise to pay quarters for unloading fruit that didn't exist.[11]

The next few hours passed slowly. The boys' talk started and stopped, punctuated by fear-stricken silences whenever they heard noises overhead. Then, quite suddenly, they heard scuffling above as someone roughly opened the hatch. In the half-light, Sam caught a glimpse of John Smith's face as he and Joseph Johnson pushed another boy down the stairs and tied him up in a corner of the hold. An hour or two later, sometime in the early evening, the same thing happened again and another boy arrived.

One of the new arrivals looked to be only a bit younger than Sam, maybe fourteen or just recently turned fifteen. He was so upset he could barely speak. Haltingly, he told Sam, Enos, and Alex that his name was Joe Johnson—coincidentally, the same name as one of their captors—and that he too was a sweep. The other new inmate was much younger, though a bit more composed. He told Sam that his name was Cornelius Sinclair, that he was ten years old, and that he knew Alex from school.[12]

Cornelius had been sitting outside in the city center earlier that afternoon when Smith had sauntered up to him full of talk about money to be made hauling peaches. Cornelius's parents, both former slaves, had warned him to be wary of strangers like Smith. So at first he had refused the unsolicited offer of work, but for some reason that he could not now explain, Cornelius let Smith keep talking and eventually agreed to follow him to a back alley. There Smith overpowered him, fixing "a black sticking plaster" across the boy's mouth and dumping him into the back of a small covered wagon, which took off toward the distant silhouette of a ship floating in the middle of the river near the Navy Yard.[13]

❖

Sam Scomp was the oldest of the five boys chained in the hold of the *Little John*. He was not on the run from a master in Maryland as Joseph Johnson had claimed, but it was true that he was a fugitive slave. He was actually on the run from a slaveowner in New Jersey. On the day John Smith kidnapped him, August 10, 1825, Sam had been, by his own account, "but a few days in Philadelphia," having fled across the Delaware River from his New Jersey master just a week earlier. New Jersey was still a slave state in 1825, home to the largest population of enslaved people anywhere north of Delaware. While slavery was nearly extinct in every other state north of the Mason-Dixon Line, New Jersey's five thousand or so enslaved workers remained a vital part of its agricultural economy.[14]

Sam was born in Readington Township in late 1810 or early 1811, one of the 25 percent of black New Jerseyans who still worked as bound laborers. The name Scomp was Dutch and quite common in the state at the time, and Sam's father and mother, Samuel and Rose, had likely worked for someone of that name at some point. By the time Sam was born, they were owned by John Kline,

Sam's first master was John Kline, a German American tannery owner from Reading-ton, New Jersey. Kline was forty, married, and childless in 1824, the year he sold Sam to David Hill, a resident of nearby Amwell. James P. Snell, comp., History of Hunterdon and Somerset Counties, New Jersey, with Illustrations and Biographical Sketches of Its Prominent Men and Pioneers (Philadelphia, 1881). (Courtesy of the American Antiquarian Society.)

who was of German extraction. Kline was the owner of a prosperous tanners' yard and a one-hundred-acre homestead in Hunterdon County, a farming community tucked away in the northwest corner of the state. A lifelong member of Readington's Lutheran congregation, he was known by many as a modest and charitable man of "simple, child-like faith . . . who exerted a widespread influence for good."[15]

Like many pillars of this rural community, Kline owned at least half a dozen slaves. Several, including Sam, were technically his apprentices. In America, children born to enslaved women were typically condemned to a lifetime in bondage, but the Gradual Abolition Act passed by New Jersey state legislators in 1804 had moderated this matrilineal curse. Rather than serve as slaves for life, children born to enslaved mothers after 1804 were designated as slaves "for a term," bound laborers whose legal status was more akin to that of indentured servants. Sam was one of these term slaves, required by law to labor for Kline until his twenty-fifth birthday. The same was true for Sam's younger brothers, Frank and Peter.[16]

In practice, events cut short Sam's quarter-century-long apprenticeship. In the fall of 1824, Kline decided to trade the remaining years of Sam's term of labor to a neighbor named David Hill in exchange for a black woman "named Ebey and a two year old bull." That winter, Kline sent the boy to live on Hill's grain farm in Amwell Township, ten miles from Readington. It was close enough that Sam might still visit his parents and brothers from time to time, but far enough away for the separation to be painful, if not deeply wounding. At the time, Sam still had a decade of his indenture left to serve, and so had little choice except to do as he was told.[17]

Sam now belonged to David Hill, a young man not yet thirty.

His father, Paul Hill, had come to the colonies from Scotland in the 1780s and had slowly built his first small farm into a modest but profitable estate. Deciding to use slave labor to grow corn, wheat, barley, and other cereals for sale at markets in New York or Philadelphia had made all the difference. This was not at all unusual in West Jersey. As one visitor to Hunterdon County noted in a diary entry in 1824, "almost every farmer has from one to half a dozen slaves."[18]

Sam came to Amwell soon after Paul Hill died. Paul's will, executed in July 1824, divided the little farm between his two eldest sons, Asher and David. Neither had inherited their father's head for business, and the purchase of Sam's labor from John Kline that fall was one of several extravagant early investments that David Hill made shortly after taking possession of his part of the property. With a rapidly expanding family of his own to feed and clothe, Hill found that his bills soon began to exceed the farm's income. His debts mounted, and by the summer of 1825, just months after purchasing Sam's labor, Hill and his wife, Maria, were looking for ways to trim their expenses.[19]

Sam must have begun to suspect that his new master might one day decide to sell him to someone else. Hill needed cash ever more urgently, but the local resale value for a young flight risk like Sam was limited. An out-of-state sale would be much more profitable, and there were always interstate slave traders passing through— enslaved people called them "Georgia men"—willing to buy a prime hand and then sell him to cotton growers setting up in the Deep South. The terms of an 1818 New Jersey law prohibited Hill from selling term slaves like Sam into lives of perpetual slavery beyond the borders of the state. And yet it happened all the time. Unscrupulous owners often colluded with corrupt county judges to produce fraudulent evidence that term slaves had given their consent to be sold out of state. Hill considered himself a law-abiding Christian man: he had been baptized and born again just five years earlier at the Baptist church six miles down the road from his farm. The Baptists took no formal position on the selling of slaves, however, and Hill needed money.[20]

Sam did not wait to discover his fate. He took to his heels, fleeing David Hill's farm on August 6, 1825. With ten more years of bound labor on his indenture and a growing suspicion that Hill was preparing to sell him into lifelong slavery in Georgia or perhaps even Alabama or Mississippi, Sam saw no better option. But where to go? If he ran home, back to his family and his former master ten miles away in Readington, Hill would surely find him before the week was out.[21]

Sam knew he could not stay in New Jersey, much as he might have wanted to. The state's free black population was small and lacked powerful white allies who could advocate for their interests. New Jersey's only antislavery organization had disbanded back in 1809, a casualty of infighting and apathy. In the fifteen years since then, the free black communities scattered across this still largely rural state had lived under siege, deprived of voting rights by local lawmakers who seemed intent on making their lives miserable.[22]

Where else could Sam go? Most fugitive slaves ran north, but Sam's nearest refuge lay to the south in Philadelphia, fifty miles from Amwell. A free city in a state in which slavery was in its final death throes, Philadelphia sat on the far shore of the Delaware River, a natural boundary and freedom line no less potent in the imaginations of West Jersey's bound laborers than the Ohio River would later become for enslaved people fleeing northward from Kentucky in the 1840s and 1850s.[23]

Sam set out for Philadelphia. Countless runaways from New Jersey had made the same southward journey across the Delaware

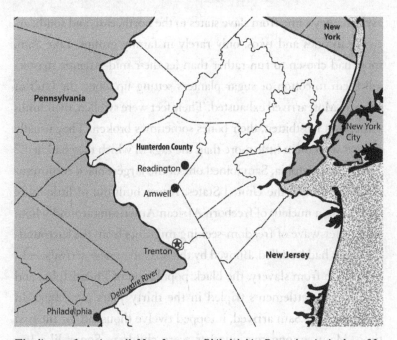

The distance from Amwell, New Jersey, to Philadelphia, Pennsylvania, is about fifty miles. Sam's most likely route followed the path of the Delaware River, which divides these two states. (Digital cartography by Caitlin Burke. Courtesy of the GIS and Geospatial Services Center, University of Maryland.)

River in recent years. Sam had likely been to the city himself on trips with Kline or perhaps Hill to deliver wagonloads of produce to its market, but he had never been there alone and never on foot. The fifty miles from Amwell to Philadelphia was a vast distance without a horse. It took Sam several nights to dash and dart his way from Hunterdon County to Pennsylvania's largest, grandest city, keeping out of sight as much as possible and searching for food wherever he could.[24]

Sam arrived in Philadelphia alone, his face now perhaps a little more hollowed and angular than before. He was one of perhaps a thousand runaways who found their way to the city in 1825. Seeking asylum, they came from slave states to the north, east, and south, arriving in ones and twos, only rarely in family groups. Like Sam, most had chosen to run rather than let their mid-Atlantic masters sell them to cotton or sugar planters setting up along the Gulf of Mexico. Most arrived exhausted. Their feet were swollen, their limbs sometimes frostbitten, their bones sometimes broken. They usually carried with them little more than the rags in which they had fled.[25]

In Philadelphia, Sam joined one of the largest black communities anywhere in the United States. It was built out of little more than hope, a nucleus of freeborn African Americans around whom wave after wave of freedom-seeking migrants from the surrounding states had huddled. Buoyed by this stream of new arrivals seeking refuge from slavery, the black population of Philadelphia and its adjacent settlements tripled in the thirty years after 1800. In 1825, the year Sam arrived, it topped twelve thousand for the first time. Many among this number were children. Some, like Joe, Cornelius, Enos, and Alex, were free, native-born Pennsylvanians. Many more, like Sam, had fled plantations on their own initiative, usually to avoid being sold. As a result, the city seemed to teem with young black people. The 1820 census, which likely undercounted the transient segments of Philadelphia's African American population, found that roughly one in three black people were under the age of fourteen.[26]

Young fugitives like Sam thought that these demographic facts made the city an ideal place to hide in plain sight. The 1793 Fugitive Slave Act empowered owners of slaves to cross state lines to hunt their human property wherever they might be hiding, and some slaveholders did not think twice before dispatching bounty hunters to recover their escaped chattel from Philadelphia. But others evidently regarded it as hostile territory, a sanctuary city in which their legal property rights would be vigorously contested.

George Washington, himself the owner of dozens of slaves, once told a friend that recovering fugitives from Philadelphia "is not easy to do [as] there are numbers [there] who had rather facilitate an escape than apprehend a run-away."[27]

In 1825, that was truer than ever. Many New Jersey and Maryland masters knew that paying to place runaway-slave ads in the city's newspapers was akin to throwing money into the wind. David Hill seems to have reached the same conclusion. Sam must have looked over his shoulder a dozen times an hour during those first days in Philadelphia, but there is no evidence that Hill ever gave chase or hired slave catchers to try to hunt him down.[28]

❖

Free from a master for the first time in his life, Sam spent seven days and nights in the city trying to find his footing. Over the years, many black refugees had made their way to the lanes and side streets "mostly inhabited by colored people." Some struck up friendships and romances there, joined black churches, and landed jobs. Sam's best bet was to do the same, to seek out other black faces quickly, and to try to find cover and company as soon as possible. He was an outlaw, after all.[29]

Things did not go as planned. If Sam knew of friends or family members who lived in Philadelphia, he had no luck finding them that first week. No one took him in. If Sam had once imagined the city as a land of milk and honey, reality soon began to bite. It did not take him long to realize that for all their advantages compared to bound laborers in rural New Jersey, free black Philadelphians still struggled mightily for even the most basic resources. No one except John Smith ever took him aside to ask him how they could help.

Sam's most immediate challenge was to find shelter. Black people lived in every corner of the city, but most tended to cluster in the rough-and-tumble communities within or adjacent to the four poorest wards, a warren of dimly lit courts and blind alleys bounded by Pine, Fitzwater, Fifth, and Tenth Streets. These roads marked the boundaries of the first urban ghetto in the United States, and it was stuffed nearly to bursting. More than a hundred people could live on a single block. The poorest among them, like Sam, slept out on the streets, while those with more cash on hand might find spots in a cramped boardinghouse, which they paid for by the night. Slightly better-off residents, like Cornelius Sinclair's parents, did only marginally better and got along by splitting monthly leases with extended family or friends in order to rent out rooms in shabby, foul-smelling tenements.[30]

There were few other options. Saving money was nearly impossible given the scarcity of good jobs open to black people. Women like Hester Tilghman and Amy Douglass, the mothers of Enos Tilghman and Alex Manlove, usually found themselves confined to grueling and prospectless drudgery as washerwomen or seamstresses. A few others secured positions as cooks or scrubbers in wealthy white households. Still, as one 1829 municipal report concluded, the wages these women earned in such occupations were "utterly inadequate to their support . . . particularly if they have children."[31]

Their husbands fared even worse. A tiny minority of black men, perhaps one in ten, started their own businesses, socking away enough to eventually purchase their own homes and claw their way into the city's black elite. A few more, perhaps one in five, snagged skilled work as blacksmiths or barbers, preachers or teachers. Most, though, were not so fortunate. They spent their waking lives hauling carts, sawing wood, picking rags, whitewashing walls, and digging wells and graves. These were unskilled, highly seasonal, ill-paid, and thoroughly unsatisfying jobs, some so awful that white men refused to do them at all.[32]

The other alternative was the sea. Elijah Tilghman, the father of ten-year-old Enos, was one of hundreds of black Philadelphians who took leave of their families to try to make their way as sailors on cargo ships in the 1820s. This was not a decision to be taken lightly. Laboring aboard the coasters that plowed up and down the Atlantic seaboard on trading voyages to Charleston, Savannah, New Orleans, or beyond was dangerous work, especially for black seamen. Most southern states barred black mariners like Tilghman from setting foot on their shores. Facing arrest, imprisonment, sale, and enslavement if they stepped off their ships, most had to remain aboard for weeks at a time. Black husbands and fathers like Tilghman chose to shoulder such risks anyway. There were few other options.[33]

Like Sam, most black Philadelphians were industrious and ready to work but lacked the opportunities to do so. The city's shipbuilding and manufacturing industries were in the midst of a decade-long depression, while openings in other sectors were constrained by white "negrophobia," motivated by fears about labor competition and interracial sex and marriage. A study conducted in 1823 found that "prejudice and pride" among white crew bosses prevented black applicants from breaking into 75 percent of occupations in and around Philadelphia. "Turnpikes, Canals, Coal-Mines, Brick-Making, Street Paving and Cleaning, which engage so many thousands give no employment to them, no relief," the report concluded.[34]

Beyond the workplace, black children and their parents had to navigate a city that, for all its vaunted freedoms, was bitterly divided by racism. With each passing year, white working people grew ever more enamored of schemes to deport to Liberia or Haiti black neighbors they regarded as idle and worthless. At the same time, white juries, consumed by rumors in the press that the city was in the grip of a black crime wave, convicted African Americans accused of poverty crimes like theft and burglary at disproportionate rates. The same discrimination continued behind bars. According to one 1825 report, white prisoners in the Philadelphia jail refused to even sit on the same benches as black inmates.[35]

On the streets, the atmosphere in which Joe, Cornelius, Enos, and Alex grew up was thick with insult and injury. Attacks against black people and their property occurred almost daily. In 1819, three white women stoned a black woman to death, while in 1825, several white youths burst into a black church on Sixth Street and threw an exploding pepper mixture into its stove as the minister delivered his sermon. The smoke and fumes spread quickly, choking the two thousand worshippers and sending them rushing for the exits. In the panic, two church members were trampled to death and many others injured. These were not isolated events. Throughout the early 1820s, white thugs beat, robbed, or otherwise molested many black residents, knowing full well that city authorities were unlikely to prosecute them.[36]

❖

Until they became targets for terrorists, black churches had served as important sanctuaries for their members. They were one of the few places in Philadelphia where this besieged community could gather, and chances are that one or more of the kidnapped boys had been among the congregants who worshipped regularly at Mother Bethel or one of the half dozen other black churches built in the city since the Revolution. Each week, parents brought their children into these sacred spaces to hear ministers like Mother Bethel's Richard Allen preach against racism and oppression and to hear messages that stressed virtue, industry, and charity above all else. Over time, these all-black churches also took on other functions. They fed, clothed, and hid fugitives from slavery like

Sam, and their premises also served as soup kitchens, employment agencies, and community centers.[37]

Black families like the Sinclairs and the Tilghmans were also responsible for establishing other anchors of black community life such as masonic lodges, schools, and mutual-aid societies. They joined groups like the Sons of Africa, the Benezet Philanthropic, the Benevolent Sons of Zion, the African Insurance Company, and the Female Granville Society (the latter named in honor of a British abolitionist). The members of these organizations did their bit for the cause of collective uplift, paying out dozens of small grants each year to help other struggling black households rise above poverty and degradation. Their efforts were not merely charitable. They were also avowedly political, designed to transform a group of refugee migrants fresh from slavery into a cohesive and self-supporting community of respectable citizens.[38]

Education was essential to these efforts, and Cornelius Sinclair and Alex Manlove, two of the boys John Smith would later lure away, were among the early students at the Adelphi School on Gaskill Street. Self-conscious of their own illiteracy, many African American parents believed that teaching their children to read and write was the surest path to prosperity, dignity, and respectability. So they competed ferociously to secure spots in the few charity schools for free black students that dotted Philadelphia's neighborhoods. As a result, most were overcrowded. At the Adelphi School, sixty-five children of color packed into its single schoolroom before it moved to larger premises in May 1825.[39]

Cornelius seems to have thrived at Adelphi, though the instruction he received at this Quaker-funded free school was rudimentary at best. Adelphi's curriculum followed the Lancastrian system, a low-cost British model that employed only one salaried instructor for dozens of children and that required older students in the class to monitor and mentor youngsters like Cornelius. They learned to write by copying the letters of the alphabet over and over—first in sand, then in chalk, and finally in ink.[40]

This rote work could be stultifying, and Caleb Kimber, the white man who served as Adelphi's lone paid instructor, spent a good deal of his day writing up punishments for truancy, tardiness, and poor behavior in class. Expulsions from schools like his were common and many children simply drifted away before completing the curriculum. Cornelius was not one of them. Despite the tedious daily schedule and acute lack of resources, he proved himself a quick study. By the day of his disappearance, Cornelius knew the basics of both reading and writing, a rare set of skills among the city's free black population, and skills that his own father, Joseph, a porter for a merchant house, likely lacked.[41]

By contrast, Alex Manlove was one of Kimber's problem students. Eight years old when John Smith stepped into his path, Alex had taken classes at Adelphi when he was small, but grew restless and distracted and had quit after only a few months. At the time, Alex was living with his mother, Amy Douglass, in a rented property next to a burial ground on the southern edge of the city. His father, a white laborer named Solomon Manlove, had died in 1821, and Alex's problems at school seem to have stemmed from his difficult relationship with his new stepfather, John Raymon. Alex detested Raymon and often acted out. When asked to describe his missing stepson, Raymon remembered Alex as a "bad boy" and expressed little regret when he recalled how city officials had taken this tall and scrawny child from his care sometime in 1824 and sent him to the almshouse.[42]

Philadelphia's almshouse served purposes broadly equivalent to modern-day foster care. Its staff specialized in placing disadvantaged children like Alex in the custody of local craftsmen who could teach them a trade and perhaps some manners. In October

1824, almshouse officials indentured Alex to Caleb Carpenter, a mat maker who kept a workshop on Market Street. As Philadelphia's racial divisions deepened over the years, these sorts of placements had become very hard for young black boys to come by, but Carpenter himself was African American and was willing to give this "cunning," "uncommonly smart" boy a chance. Things did not go well. Alex did not want to make mats six days a week. He lied to his new master repeatedly and also stole from him, earning a flogging every time Carpenter caught him. When Alex disappeared in August 1825, Carpenter first assumed that the boy had finally decided to run away.[43]

Alex might not have admitted it, but making mats was not so bad. Most other black youths Alex's age had to settle for dead-end jobs that required harder work in worse conditions. The largest, strongest boys might spend their youth fetching and carrying in Philadelphia's lumberyards or brickyards. The only other alternative was sweeping chimneys for a living, arguably the dirtiest and most dangerous work in the city.[44]

Enos Tilghman and Joe Johnson, two of the other boys kidnapped by John Smith in August 1825, were both apprentice sweeps. Mockingly nicknamed "lily whites" because they were always covered in the blackest grime and were typically African American, climbing boys like Enos and Joe were familiar figures on the streets of Philadelphia. Master sweeps usually had two or three boys like them in their employ at any one time, the younger and slimmer the better. At dawn each morning, these boys would scour the city for sweeping jobs, hollering "Sweep O!" as they rounded corners. Clothed only in rags and the roughest secondhand garments, Enos and Joe, who worked for different masters but likely knew each other, would have been indistinguishable from beggars, save for the singing and the soot.[45]

Enos Tilghman and Joe Johnson worked as apprentice sweeps before their abduction. Chimney sweeping was dirty and dangerous work that white laborers largely refused to do. Alexander Anderson, Alexander Anderson Scrapbooks. *Wood engraving, n.d. (Courtesy of Print Collection, Miriam and Ira D. Wallach Division of Art, Prints and Photographs, the New York Public Library, Astor, Lenox and Tilden Foundations.)*

Each sweeping job Enos or Joe found would have been pretty much the same as the last. Inside each house, young sweeps would tack up a blanket over the fireplace, strip down to their underclothes, and pull on a coarse cloth cap to protect their eyes. They would grasp the brushes and an iron scraper in one hand and then try to scramble up into the flue. The zigzag chimneys popular in fancier homes were surprisingly narrow, some as tight as one square foot. In a city still made mostly of wood, these chimneys had to be swept regularly to avoid causing fires, though the muck that Enos and Joe scraped out each day was almost as deadly. The soot itself turned young soft skin into hardened leather and left eyes red and raw. A few months spent working up chimneys was often enough to bring on a lifetime of breathing problems and significantly raise the chances of cancer and sterility.[46]

Enos and Joe had no choice but to put up with it. Unlike the many climbing boys who fled this slave-like drudgery by running away from their masters, Joe, who was about fourteen on the day he disappeared, worked for his father, a master sweep who lived on Elizabeth Street on Philadelphia's south side and had done so for years. Enos, four years younger than Joe and very "slim built," was serving out a seven-year-long apprenticeship to Samuel Murray, an African American master sweep who lived just around the corner from him and his mother. There was no getting away from either man, so they both stuck it out as best they could.[47]

Like most climbing boys, Enos and Joe lived in their imaginations. They spent their working hours fantasizing about the fun they would have when the workday was done and their time was their own. In the summer, the first order of business after any apprentice sweep knocked off for the day was to get clean and get cool. By late afternoon you could usually find a gaggle of them down by the Delaware River, horsing around in the water, looking for mischief and adventure—and for food. Used to begging for scraps from the cooks they met in the big houses they cleaned, Enos and Joe were exactly the sort of lads to jump at a stranger's invitation to earn twenty-five cents in return for a little light work and a jaunt in a rowboat.[48]

Chapter 2

BLACK HEARTS

J OHN SMITH, the man who abducted Sam, Joe, Cornelius, Enos, and Alex, was a phantom, a conjuring trick, and a chameleon. Smith was one of his aliases, a convenient, generic, and forgettable disguise. His real name was John Purnell, and he made his living separating children from their parents and trafficking them into slavery. While some of the other kidnappers who stalked Philadelphia's streets in the 1820s targeted adults and children in roughly equal numbers, Purnell preferred to prey solely on boys under the age of sixteen. Their size, age, and marginal status made them perfect marks. While young girls typically worked indoors, their brothers were more often out and about unsupervised, and Purnell, surely found "slim built" or "slim made" boys like eight-year-old Alex easier to overpower or choke into silence than full-grown men or women. His snarled threats or the flash of a blade were more likely to intimidate children. Besides, if they owned freedom papers confirming their legal liberty, they rarely carried them with them.[1]

Youngsters were also more trusting. Although kidnappers still carried off dozens of men and women each year in the mid-1820s, most black adults had long since grown wise to their ploys. Children, even those with their wits about them, had shorter memories and less life experience. And the city was full of them. Some buzzed about on their way to and from work and school. Others loitered on street corners, or wandered the wharves begging for work and food. Runaways like Sam, who had no one looking out for them, were especially vulnerable. They were broke and hungry, used to living on filched vegetables, stale bread, and scraps. It did not take much to lure them away.[2]

Sometimes, all it took was the prospect of a full stomach. More often, con artists like John Purnell baited their traps with the promise of a few silver coins. They pledged handsome rewards to lads who could help fetch wood from across the river or pilot a vessel to some nearby wharf. On one occasion, a man posing as a ship's captain coaxed a black girl aboard his craft "under the pretence of giving her some clothes to wash." Likewise, in 1824, another child snatcher, a "yellow woman who called herself Tilly James," succeeded in abducting Isaiah Sadler, a seventeen-year-old orphan, by inviting him to come live with her on an isolated country farm that she said her uncle owned. Highly skilled in what one antislavery activist described as the "arts of dissimulation," Tilly James, John Purnell, and traffickers like them spun lies for a living, trading on false claims of authenticity to exploit anyone naive enough to take them at their word.[3]

Purnell, then, was one of the nation's first professional con men. Philadelphia was teeming with strangers in the 1820s, and grifters seemed to be everywhere. They dabbled in every possible variety of confidence trick, though the fundamentals were always the same. Cunning, conviction, and a silver tongue were necessities. So too was the ability to size up someone quickly and project the illusion of shared identity and common cause. Purnell was a master at this, able to disguise his intentions behind an air of amiable harmlessness that was powerful enough to persuade people he had just met to follow him down quiet side streets and out of town.[4]

John Purnell's greatest professional asset was, of course, his dark complexion. Black parents regularly pleaded with their children to be on the lookout for white "Georgia-men" and to stay away from corrupt white constables who might be in the pay of slave catchers, but most were loath to suspect someone who looked like Purnell of conspiring with white-led kidnapping collectives. That blind spot cost many black children their freedom. In 1815, for instance, two brothers, Peter and Levin Still, about six and eight, accepted a ride to church from "a tall dark man, with black and glossy hair." They never arrived. Three years later, Philadelphia Judge Richard Rush sentenced an African American man named William Young to pay a large fine and serve "three years at hard labor" for kidnapping two black men and a little black girl and selling them to "merciless Task-Master[s]" in Georgia and the West Indies. The following year, 1819, a black man "decoyed another man of colour" from the city. "It is said he knocked him up at the dead of night," *Relf's Philadelphia Gazette* reported, "pretending that he wanted him to go and pray with a sick friend! The man is since missing."[5]

Black women sometimes worked as traffickers too. When Pennsylvania authorities arrested Mary Brya and Ann Brown "on a charge of selling, or attempting to sell" a pair of young people into slavery in 1818, the two black women admitted "they have been engaged in this kind of traffic for several years." The same longevity characterized the careers of three Baltimore women: Rachel Jones, Fanny Parraway, and Nanny, "an old black woman who lives on Fell's Point." According to an 1821 newspaper report, all three women had long been "in the habit of kidnapping other colored people" and then selling them to interstate kidnapping crews, one of which was led by Joseph Johnson, John Purnell's employer.[6]

That longevity was a testament to the obvious advantages of black and mixed-race kidnappers. Boys like Sam, Joe, Cornelius, Enos, and Alex were more likely to trust an adult of the same race— or at least, to give that person the benefit of the doubt—than they were to believe the tall tales of a white stranger. They were also less likely to question unsolicited offers of work, food, or shelter when those offers issued from the lips of people who looked and sounded like their uncles and aunts. In fact, if white bystanders happened to witness a boy being beaten or dragged away by someone like Purnell, they might assume that they were simply watching an unruly child receive necessary discipline from a parent or family relation.

White witnesses who came upon kidnappings committed by black confidence men like John Purnell may not have realized that they were witnessing a crime in progress. John Lewis Krimmel, "Worldly Folk" Questioning Chimney Sweeps and Their Master before Christ Church, Philadelphia. *Watercolor and graphite on white laid paper, 1811–13. (Courtesy of the Metropolitan Museum, Rogers Fund, 1942.)*

John Purnell was good at his job, and it is not hard to understand why Joseph Johnson hired him. Without people of color like Purnell to lure victims to isolated locations where they could be confined and overpowered, abduction attempts could easily go awry. White kidnappers acting on their own risked drawing excessive attention from bystanders or family members and all too often had to use violence to subdue their prey. When that happened, things could quickly get out of hand, and those operatives sometimes had to cut their losses and run. On May 22, 1822, for instance, *Relf's Philadelphia Gazette* reported that one white "scoundrel [had] attempted to carry off a small negro girl on Sunday evening. [But] before he had time to secure her, she alarmed [the neighbors] by her cries and he fled."[7]

Eager to avoid those sorts of spectacles, Joseph Johnson relied on John Purnell and a few other black collaborators to do his dirty work for him. The tight job market worked in Johnson's favor. Recruitment must have been difficult, but the money was good, and Purnell used the cash he made by selling out street kids to feed his own children, pay his bills, and stifle his conscience. If caught, black kidnappers usually pleaded poverty as their excuse. In private, they were more candid. Believing he was speaking in confidence to a friend, Purnell once bragged that he could earn "from fifty to an hundred dollars in a Week" hustling boys like Enos and Alex aboard schooners like the *Little John*, a massive payday compared to the ten or fifteen dollars per week he might hope to make sawing wood or pulling a handcart.[8]

Men like John Purnell and women like Tilly James prowled Philadelphia's streets almost daily during the 1820s, turning the city's broad avenues and narrow lanes into hunting grounds. They made no distinction between those like Sam, who were fugitives from slavery, and those like Joe, Cornelius, Enos, and Alex, who were legally free. No one who might conceivably fetch a price as a slave in the Deep South was ever truly safe from their ruses and scams. Because of the furtive nature of their business, it is impossible to make an accurate count of the number of abductions in any given year. It is clear, however, that fear of kidnapping was ubiquitous, the one thing every person of color in the urban North had in common. The daily threat posed by white and black kidnappers alike haunted their neighborhoods, a constant and existential reminder of the limits of African American freedom in postrevolutionary America.

❖

Philadelphia's embattled black community lacked reliable protection from local constables, so their only hope to thwart predators like John Purnell lay in taking matters into their own hands. Families formed the first line of defense. Husbands and wives reminded each other to carry their freedom papers at all times and to keep them up to date. They also begged their children to stay safe when out on their own. At home each night before bed and again over breakfast the next morning, parents pestered their sons and daughters to stay in large groups, to read body language, to steer clear of certain streets, and to be wary of promises too good to be true. Out in the world, black adults tried to look out for the safety of the children in their community as best they could, forming de facto neighborhood-watch networks that shared information and intelligence. When they saw suspicious-looking white men who possessed the familiar "gallows appearance" of kidnappers and slave catchers, word spread quickly. Parents would hurry their children inside, while some brave soul crossed the street to inquire after the stranger's business in the area.[9]

One summer's day, Reuben Moore, "an orderly respectable colored man," was walking down Market Street when he saw two white men dragging a black man along the road "by the collar." Moore demanded to know what was going on. The men told him that they were legal slave catchers empowered by the 1793 federal Fugitive Slave Act who had apprehended a runaway. Their prisoner, however, said otherwise. He insisted that he was no slave and that he "had no knowledge of the persons who had arrested him." Moore took the latter at his word and turned to go find a magistrate. As he did so, one of the kidnappers fired at Moore, shooting him in the chest and knocking him to the ground. It took emergency surgery to remove the ball and save Moore's life. Another intervention, this time by a husband trying to prevent his wife's abduction, was likewise thwarted when one of the kidnappers "drew from his side pocket a short bludgeon or loaded mace," swung it at the would-be rescuer, and "at one blow . . . laid the poor fellow prostrate."[10]

In the absence of courageous witnesses like these, most victims of kidnapping had to defend themselves as best they could. When two men started to batter down John Read's front door, he managed to barricade it with a barrel of cider. This simple blockade bought him a little time, and when his pursuers finally forced their way inside, they found Read armed and waiting. He shot one man dead and pistol-whipped the other, leaving him unconscious. Lacking access to firearms, the vast majority of black Philadelphians fought back in other ways. Some clutched at doorjambs and handles as kidnappers dragged them from their beds into the back of curtained carriages and away into the night. Others bit and kicked. When one young woman's captor leaned in to blindfold her, she "seized his cheek with her teeth, and tore a piece of it entirely off," causing the man to scream and curse, though he did not let her go.[11]

The most effective way to free yourself from the clutches of a kidnapper like John Purnell was not to bite or spit but to shout and yell. Such howling usually drew attention, creating witnesses and alerting neighbors. That was why Purnell stuck a black rag in Cornelius's mouth when abducting him. It was also why Benjamin Clarke's wife ran "out of the house and screamed as loud as she could, 'Kidnappers! Kidnappers!'" when a slave catcher came to her home to seize her husband. Within a minute, a dozen or more black people "prepared for war" filled the alley outside the Clarke home, blocking the only way out. The women inside neighboring tenements then flung open their windows "and let fly a general volley of brickbats" upon the head of the slave catcher, a corrupt city constable named Richard Hunt. Once Hunt "fell to the ground, bruised and cut," Clarke ran for his life.[12]

Black people used violence to defend their liberty whenever necessary, but reserved their harshest treatment for kidnappers of color like John Purnell. In June 1825, just two months before Sam, Cornelius, and the three other boys vanished, black residents of York, Pennsylvania, got word that two "traitorous brethren" suspected of decoying fugitives were living among them. Unable to locate one of the men, a crew of "between 20 and 25" black people surrounded the other villain's house and battered it with stones until they burst its windows and broke down the door. "Finding that his house would not answer as a castle," the kidnapper inside was forced to surrender. His neighbors then "stripped and tied him, and gave him one of the most severe lashings ever laid on the back of man."[13]

While rare, these acts of vigilante violence against kidnappers (and collaborators) of color served several important purposes within the black community. They were clearly punitive, designed to dole out a measure of justice to people who might otherwise evade it. They were deterrents as well, designed to make men like

John Purnell think twice. And they were also markers of collective identity, public displays of the belief that antislavery solidarity should be a core principle of black life in freedom.[14]

❖

In all but a handful of cases, the efforts of vigilante neighbors to tackle traffickers and intercede in kidnappings fell tragically short. Skilled operatives like John Purnell knew what they were doing. They had learned by experience how to operate in the shadows, how to do their work quickly and quietly, and how to hustle their captives away before anyone could save them. Usually, the only help that friends and relations could offer was after the fact. When intruders snatched Aaron Cooper from his Delaware home in 1811, all his wife could do was dispatch a posse of her neighbors to try to track him down. They came back empty-handed. Likewise, when Stephen Dutton's ten-year-old granddaughter went missing from nearby Wilmington in 1824, his only recourse was to place a missing-persons ad in a local paper. In it he implored readers to look for young Eliza Boyce among "the droves of slaves" leaving the state each week for the Deep South and to get in touch with him, though no one did.[15]

Had either of these kidnapping victims lived in Philadelphia, their family members would likely have brought their misfortunes before the Acting Committee of the Pennsylvania Abolition Society (PAS), the region's only significant antislavery organization. In a city in which interracial cooperation was typically rare and fleeting, relations between black Philadelphians and the all-white, Quaker-led membership of the PAS were surprisingly robust, the result of many years of close collaboration.[16]

Isaac Hopper, a Quaker, had been one of the first PAS members to earn the trust of Philadelphia's African American residents.

As a boy, Hopper had counted among his friends "an old colored man named Mingo," who had often described his own experience as the victim of kidnapping and forced migration from Africa to America decades earlier. Mingo remained haunted by that ordeal and "wept like a child" when he told young Hopper how he had been "hurried away from mother, father, brothers and sisters, and sold into slavery, in a distant land, where he could never see or hear from them again." Mingo's tale came to haunt Hopper too. As a young man, he volunteered to teach black children in the city's charity schools, and soon after chose to dedicate his life to preserving the personal liberty of Philadelphia's black community.[17]

Over the next twenty-five years, Isaac Hopper helped, by his own estimates, about a thousand black men and women to evade or escape enslavement. He harbored hundreds of runaways, giving them meals, money, a place to sleep, and a wealth of practical and legal advice. He also fought to recover dozens of other black Philadelphians who fell victim to kidnappers, pouring his own time and money into rescue missions that were often dramatic and dangerous. Ruffians on board one departing sloop once attempted to throw Hopper overboard rather than reveal to him the contents of their cargo hold. As a Quaker, Hopper was committed to nonviolence, and on that occasion he avoided drowning only by grabbing at their coats. By such work, Hopper earned a reputation as an enemy of kidnappers, catchers, and slave traders. As a result, the city's beleaguered black community came to regard him as a steadfast ally. "I will be your friend," Hopper told one young fugitive who came to him for help, "and come what will, you may feel certain that I will never betray you."[18]

Under pressure from black residents to follow Hopper's example, his colleagues in the PAS agreed to investigate more and more disappearances and unlawful seizures in the first three decades of the nineteenth century. They began comparing the names of all the men, women, and children apprehended as fugitives within city limits against published lists of people in possession of freedom papers and launched legal proceedings to try to extricate those they thought had been wrongfully detained. At the urging of black people, these Quaker activists also lobbied state officials to enforce antikidnapping statutes and to empower law enforcement to pursue traffickers across state lines. There was always more to be done. In 1816, PAS officers set up a subcommittee on kidnapping to handle the growing caseload, and in 1821 they began recording the names of missing residents like Joe, Cornelius, Enos, and Alex on a master list.[19]

In the wake of almost every new abduction, black Philadelphians ran to Hopper and to other PAS officers to plead with them for assistance. Minutes mattered, so the boldest parents and spouses wasted no time knocking on members' doors. Maria Jacobs interrupted Thomas Shipley, the chairman of the PAS Acting Committee, in the middle of dinner on a Sunday evening in August 1820 to beg his help finding her ten-year-old daughter. She told him she had seen a woman hustle the child onto a schooner two hours earlier. The ship had since departed the docks, and her daughter's rescue now "depended upon [your] using dispatch." Shipley's dinner could wait, Jacobs told him. After describing her daughter's physical appearance down to the last remembered detail, she insisted that Shipley ride downriver in an ultimately unsuccessful attempt to intercept the vessel before it could clear the estuary.[20]

Standing before members of the PAS Acting Committee in fury and in grief, people like Maria Jacobs demanded that this lawyerly organization engage in direct and immediate action to protect the rights of Philadelphia's most marginal residents. The same men and women also pushed PAS officers to pursue longer-term lobbying efforts at the state capitol to assert a moral boundary between Pennsylvania and the slaveholding states that surrounded it. So insistent were they that in 1820 Pennsylvania legislators passed a new personal liberty law that agreed "to increase the penalties and forfeitures, for the crime of man-stealing."[21]

On rare occasions, statutes like these could make all the difference. One morning in September 1822, a professional slave catcher named Jason Clark barged into a black family's home on Arch Street and seized Ann Chambers, "a colrd [sic] girl," as a suspected runaway. He shoved her into a carriage and sped off to find a judge who would issue him the necessary paperwork to legally remove her from the state. In the meantime, Ann's parents tracked down two PAS lawyers who, in a hasty appeal before the same judge, challenged Ann's detention and proved her freedom and right to remain under the terms of the 1820 personal liberty law. Hours later, Clark returned Ann to her home on Arch Street where the sobbing child collapsed into her parents' arms.[22]

Happy endings like this were, of course, few and far between. The complexities of pursuing predators like Jason Clark and John Purnell across multiple jurisdictions ensured that successful rescues remained a rarity. Antikidnapping work was very dangerous—especially for unarmed Quaker pacifists like Isaac Hopper. It was also time-consuming and hugely expensive. The PAS required almost bottomless funds to support its investigators and pay sheriffs' fees, registration charges, postage, and travel expenses. As its kidnapping caseload mounted steadily throughout the 1810s and 1820s, accounting for at least a third of all PAS business in this period, the society found itself stretched thin. In 1821, an internal report privately conceded that "the low state of the Funds" prevented PAS members from pursuing all of the "cases of Persons kidnapped from this City [that are] now under the Care of the Society."[23]

PAS officers reluctantly closed the book on dozens of unsolved kidnappings in the decade before 1825, sometimes noting with regret that "justice cannot be done." The parents, spouses, friends, and neighbors of these vanished persons found no such closure. Their sorrow was sharp and piercing, and it never went away. "PARENTS! FATHERS! MOTHERS! You know how to feel for those who have children," Stephen Dredden, the father of two kidnapped youngsters beseeched the readers of *Poulson's American Daily Advertiser* in 1817. "Although I am black, I have a heart like you, and they have pierced it thro' with sorrow—they have stolen my children!"[24]

By 1825, despair like Dredden's had become a condition of life that bound together Philadelphia's twelve thousand black residents. Despite its reputation as a sanctuary from slavery, the city was a dangerous place to be African American. Professional traffickers like John Purnell treated it as a human stockyard to plunder at will. These ruthless men and women baited their prey with the prospect of easy money unloading ships, picking cherries, or clearing brush, ensuring that the freedom of young black people was in constant jeopardy.

The five boys in the hold of the *Little John* realized their own fate too late to escape it. When the ship in which Purnell had sequestered them slunk away from the Navy Yard and out into the Delaware River on the evening of August 10, 1825, they were quiet as mice. Over the years, a few abductions had been stopped when folks on nearby wharves heard children's muffled cries issuing from the holds of departing schooners. But not this time. Terror had snuffed out any natural bravado or courage that Sam, Joe, Cornelius, Enos, and Alex might have possessed—at least for the time being. So too had the sight of Joseph Johnson's knife and another snarling threat, this time from his crewmate Thomas Collins, to "make no noise or I'll cut your throats."[25]

✥

The first missing-persons notice turned up in the pages of *Poulson's* three days later, sandwiched between an ad selling a horse and a note asking after some mislaid spectacles. Cornelius's father, Joseph Sinclair, had scraped together enough money for the ad to run three times that week, hoping it could jog some memories and produce some leads. "Boy Lost," his ad read, telling readers his son's age ("about 11 years old"), build ("pretty stout"), face ("left eye smaller than the right"), and complexion ("very dark mulatto").[26]

When Cornelius had not come home that first night, his parents had assumed he was just acting out, sleeping over at a friend's place perhaps. But now, after three days, the Sinclairs were frantic—"afflicted," Joseph said. They were finally beginning to admit to each other that their dear son, their only child, was gone, "seduced away, by some evil minded person."[27]

Chapter 3

MIDNIGHT LAND

It was after dark on Wednesday, August 10, 1825, when Bill Paragee and his deckhand Thomas Collins took in the lines, hoisted the mainsail and jib, and steered out into the central shipping lanes of the Delaware River with Sam, Joe, Cornelius, Enos, and Alex stashed in the hold below. The *Little John* did not have the river to itself. The wind was light that night, and all the vessels trying to leave Philadelphia had to push against the flood tide that was moving in the opposite direction.[1]

The *Little John* cut one of the smaller silhouettes in this drifting flotilla. The port of Philadelphia was the busiest in the new nation and attracted hundreds of cargo ships each year from Europe, West Africa, the Caribbean, South America, and China. These transoceanic behemoths dwarfed the *Little John*. Unsuited to long voyages in open seas, Paragee's modest single-masted sloop was one of the scores of regional coasters commonly used to shuttle timber products and dry goods back and forth between the city and Delmarva, the peninsula just south of Pennsylvania that is home to most of Delaware, and to slivers of Maryland and Virginia.[2]

The traffickers aboard the *Little John* hoped to hide their human cargo by maneuvering out into this idling convoy of other freighters. Yet the risks of discovery and disaster were still considerable. After midnight, the clouds came in and cloaked the moon, increasing the likelihood of a collision in crowded waters, even at these low speeds. A few years earlier, a small craft with a well-known black preacher named Jarena Lee aboard had narrowly escaped "from being run down by a large ship" on this same stretch. And the Delaware River presented its own challenges. In the "Horse-Shoe," a natural bowl at a bend just four miles south of the Navy Yard, inexperienced captains often ran aground, causing pileups and traffic jams.[3]

Bill Paragee had no shortage of experience. The *Little John* had made this journey before, spiriting away other kidnapped school-boys and sweeps at least four times since the start of spring. Still,

This 1840 oil painting of daytime traffic on the Delaware River contrasts the size of small sloops similar to the Little John *with larger schooners, naval warships, two rowboats, and the* Robert Morris, *a paddle steamer built in 1830. The twin ship sheds of the old Philadelphia Navy Yard are also visible. Thomas Birch,* Philadelphia Harbor from the South. *Oil on canvas, ca. 1840. (Courtesy of the Library Company of Philadelphia.)*

Paragee knew to keep his wits about him. Crews on board passing ships had sometimes forced ashore sloops like his when they heard muted cries coming from holds that were meant to be filled with things and not people. So he, Thomas Collins, John Purnell, and Joseph Johnson plowed on as unobtrusively as they could. To keep their five young captives quiet, they made repeated threats to kill them and likely forced them to choke down enough liquor to dizzy them and drive them to sleep, a common tactic among professional traffickers in this period.[4]

For hours, the *Little John* crept on in darkness. As the Delaware River yawned wider, the dense forests on the sloop's port side gradually grew distant. Hewing closer to the shore on the starboard side, Paragee steered the sluggish vessel past Wilmington, Delaware's commercial hub, then onward toward the dim shapes and shadows of New Castle as dawn broke. Beyond New Castle, there were few signs of life. The post road that had run alongside their route since the Navy Yard disappeared, replaced by an endless matrix of wheat fields hedged by great swaths of white arrowhead blossoms. Every hour or so, as the ship shambled on through Thursday morning and into Thursday afternoon, that vista was broken by an inlet or a long stretch of brackish marshland that buzzed with the sound of mosquitoes.[5]

It took Bill Paragee almost a day and a half to pilot the *Little John* out to Cape Henlopen, where the olive-green mouth of the Delaware River meets the Atlantic Ocean. By then, most other vessels had set off in other directions; only a few remained within signaling distance. Using the beam from the Henlopen lighthouse as his guide, Paragee spent the early hours of Friday morning weaving through the treacherous shoals of the lower estuary, a shallow, sandbanked maze that had wrecked dozens of ships over the years. Finally clear of them, he plotted a course that took the craft southward for a dozen miles before turning it sharply to starboard and slipping between two sand spits and into Rehoboth Bay. Following a familiar route, he navigated the *Little John* upstream against the current, tracing the Indian River's winding course through a cypress forest. An hour or two before sundown on Friday, August 12, the *Little John* came to a full stop in a cove not far from the town of Millsboro, Delaware.[6]

Chained belowdecks, Sam, Joe, Cornelius, Enos, and Alex had no idea how long they had been at sea, or where Paragee and his three-man crew had taken them. Darkness, terror, liquor, and seasickness had left them disoriented. Sam, for one, believed that he had been "on the water about a week." In truth, it had been less than two days. In that time, they had sailed no more than 120 miles. With good winds, the *Little John* could have made this trip in just eight or nine hours. This time, though, it had taken more than forty hours. It would have been almost as quick to walk.[7]

No wonder, then, that Purnell and Johnson were in a hurry. With practiced efficiency, the two men descended the stairs into the sloop's cramped hold and unshackled the five boys from their leg irons. By now, even Enos and Alex, the two youngest boys, had likely figured out why Purnell and Johnson had kidnapped them and where they might be headed. With their limbs free for the first time in two days, the boys' impulse to try to fight or flee must have been strong, especially for Sam, who had a history of running away. So Purnell and Johnson took no chances and kept their knives in hand as they tied fresh ropes around the boys' necks, linking one to the other. Bound together in a coffle, they could do nothing except hobble forward on command, gingerly climbing up to the main deck and then down again into the ship's little rowboat.[8]

Leaving Paragee and Collins aboard the *Little John*, Purnell and Johnson rowed their five young captives to a nearby landing under cover of nightfall. On previous stops at this isolated cove, the two men had locked prior victims in a derelict oyster house while they went off in search of a cart to carry them to their next destination twenty miles inland. This time they wanted to keep moving, so they ordered the boys to start walking. With Joseph Johnson

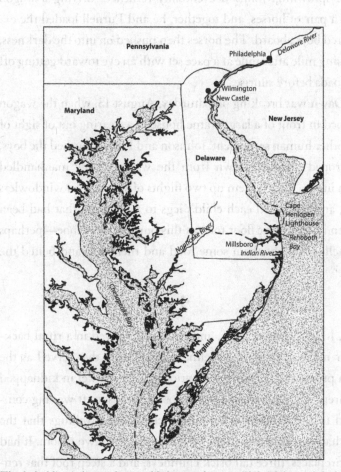

The dashed line indicates the most likely route between Philadelphia and the kidnapping gang's safe houses near the state line that divided Sussex County, Delaware, from Dorchester County, Maryland. (Digital cartography by Caitlin Burke. Courtesy of the GIS and Geospatial Services Center, University of Maryland.)

sprinting on ahead and the Atlantic Ocean at their backs, the prisoners spent the next few hours trudging westward, deep into the peninsula's interior, through marshes, cornfields, and brushwood. John Purnell stuck close to their side, goading them on when their pace slowed or when one or another child tripped and sent the coffle sprawling. Johnson eventually returned, driving a wagon with a pair of horses, and together, he and Purnell loaded the exhausted boys aboard. The horses then pushed on into the darkness, covering mile after mile at a pace set with an eye toward getting off the roads before sunrise.[9]

Dawn was breaking on Saturday, August 13, when the wagon stopped in front of a large frame house in a clearing out of sight of any other human settlement. Johnson and Purnell pushed the boys, still roped together, down from the wagon. They manhandled them inside, jostled them up two flights of stairs into a windowless attic, and manacled each child's legs to a metal tie that had been driven into the attic floor for just this purpose. Someone—perhaps Purnell—brought them some food and then shut and bolted the door.[10]

❖

Sam, Joe, Cornelius, Enos, and Alex had arrived in a rural backwater midway down the Delmarva Peninsula that served as the main processing center of the nation's black market in kidnapped children. The house belonged to Joseph Johnson. It was big compared to the handful of low-slung clapboard dwellings that the boys had rumbled past in the wagon in the predawn gloom. It had five fireplaces, three tall brick chimneys, and a steep roof that rendered its two attic rooms just high enough to stand in upright without stooping. It sat on a large, three-quarter-acre plot near a quiet crossroads three miles north of the Nanticoke River, on the far eastern edge of Dorchester County, Maryland, just a few hundred yards from the Delaware border.[11]

Slavery flourished in this part of the peninsula. Despite the presence of a large and growing free black population, the peninsula's central counties were still slave country. More than five thousand enslaved people lived in Dorchester County, Maryland, in 1825, and two thousand more labored in fields and workshops just across the state line in Sussex County, Delaware. Frederick Douglass (b. 1818) and Harriet Tubman (b. 1822) were among the many enslaved people to grow up around here, on one or another of the jumble of sizable plantations and small farms within a half-day's ride of the Johnson place.[12]

Most of Joseph Johnson's white neighbors were struggling wheat planters. Twenty years before, they had farmed tobacco, but had retooled after the Napoleonic Wars (1792–1815) cut off their markets in Europe, causing the bottom to fall out of that business. The switch to wheat brought its own problems. Margins were lower and the region's farmers had to fight new threats like cutworms, caterpillars, and Hessian flies. And because raising wheat required fewer hands than tobacco cultivation, they had to slash their labor costs quickly to stave off bankruptcy. During the 1820s, planters on the peninsula were in the midst of getting rid of the slaves they thought they could do without, selling some to interstate traders in return for hard cash, and reluctantly freeing others.[13]

The many enslaved families in and around Joseph Johnson's Nanticoke River neighborhood were devastated by these sell-offs. Each new sale to professional flesh dealers like Baltimore's Austin Woolfolk cut into enslaved households like a scythe, sundering husbands from wives, parents from children, and grandparents, aunts, uncles, and cousins from their kin. Growing up on Maryland's Eastern Shore, Frederick Douglass lost at least fifteen members of his own family to slave traders in these years, and he later recalled having nightmares about Woolfolk and other "imps, in human shape . . . that gather in every country town of the state, watching for chances to buy human flesh, (as buzzards to eat carrion)."[14]

Those black men and women freed by their cash-strapped masters during these years—the technical term was "manumission"—fared little better. The free black population of the peninsula's central counties roughly doubled in the two decades before 1825, but most of those newly freed people found that happiness remained far beyond reach. Because planters rarely manumitted slaves as family groups, most freed people could not leave Delmarva without abandoning partners or children who remained enslaved. So they had little choice but to live on there in limbo. In the words of one historian, they were "half in and half out of slavery."[15]

The majority of white residents had no sympathy for their African American neighbors' predicament and regarded the peninsula's growing free black population with suspicion and disdain. Only one in five white households here owned slaves in the 1820s, but a great many more made their living in slavery-dependent occupations such as storekeeping, warehousing, and shipping. Conditioned by custom and culture to regard the liberty of African Americans as unnatural, many white residents worried that free blacks were a dangerous influence upon those who remained enslaved. Others saw them as imbeciles unsuited for freedom. "You can manumit the slave, but you cannot make him a white man," Robert Goodloe Harper, a former US senator from Maryland, wrote in 1817. Harper wanted these free blacks gone and was one of many white Marylanders and Delawareans—including Francis Scott Key, author of the poem that became the national anthem—to take leading roles in the African colonization movement, a patchwork of groups committed to deporting "back to Africa" people who had been in the United States for generations.[16]

Joseph Johnson had built his home in a place where free black people found their paths to prosperity and autonomy blocked at every turn. Typically illiterate, many manumitted men had to work as day laborers on the plantations of their former masters. State law prohibited them from owning weapons, buying liquor, or preaching without a license. They were not allowed to operate boats without white supervision or to go within half a mile of polling places on Election Day. In Maryland, statutes barred them from testifying in any and all court proceedings, while across the line in Delaware they could testify in criminal cases only when no competent white witnesses could be found. These same laws effectively encouraged local constables to ignore all but the most egregious violence against black residents, ensuring that they lived in constant fear of attack.[17]

Coordinated antislavery activity in and around Joseph Johnson's Nanticoke River neighborhood was almost impossible in this political climate. Delaware's only significant activist group, the Delaware Society for Promoting the Abolition of Slavery, made its headquarters in Wilmington, in the far north of the state, and had only a handful of members from the counties farther south. Quakers had founded antislavery groups across the mid-Atlantic region, but very few Friends, as they were known, ever settled in central or southern Delmarva. Instead, the people who populated this part of the peninsula tended to shun all forms of radical theology, especially if peddled by outsiders. The Nanticoke River watershed seemed particularly stuck in time and set in its ways. Despite the local economy's reliance on its commercial ties to Wilmington, Philadelphia, and Baltimore, visitors often remarked on how close-minded and clannish the area felt.[18]

Frederick Douglass shuddered when remembering his own up-bringing here during the 1820s. Writing in 1855, Douglass described the district where these five black boys were now sequestered as a dangerously secluded twilight zone "where slavery, wrapt in its own congenial, midnight darkness, *can*, and *does*, develop all its malign and shocking characteristics, where it can be indecent without shame, cruel without shuddering, and murderous without apprehension or fear of exposure." This was a place where slaveholding and slave trading were common and unremarkable, and where free black people suffered daily indignities and menaces. This was the place where Joseph Johnson built his center of operations.[19]

❖

The men and women who hoped to make a living trafficking black people regarded the close-knit and target-rich Nanticoke River region as the perfect place to set up shop. In the fifty years following American independence, many professional kidnappers and enslavers built businesses here, Joseph Johnson and John Purnell among them. In 1789, for instance, a Wilmington newspaper announced the discovery of "a nest" of traffickers who had recently borne away six free black people from Cambridge, Dorchester's county seat, in hopes of selling them as slaves in Georgia. The provincial press reported a steady trickle of similar outrages over the following decades, and opportunistic residents of eastern Maryland and southern Delaware committed almost all of them.[20]

The scale of this black-market business surged after 1808, the year in which the Jefferson administration's ban on importing enslaved Africans from overseas took effect. Closing US borders to international slave traders at the same time that settlers were setting up new slave plantations in the Deep South created extraordinary new opportunities for anyone with access to domestic sources of black labor. Legal interstate traders found they could make substantial profits buying the "surplus" slaves of wheat farmers in

Maryland and Delaware and reselling them to sugar and cotton planters in Louisiana, Alabama, and Mississippi. The same economic forces—squeezed supply and swollen demand—also multiplied the incentives for anyone sufficiently cold-blooded to kidnap free people and sell them into slavery in the Deep South.

Operating in the shadow of the much larger, legal domestic slave trade, kidnappers like Joseph Johnson and John Purnell found they could make small fortunes in this line of work. The barriers to entry were temptingly low. Unlike legal traders, kidnappers did not have to scrape together the capital to purchase the men, women, and children they hoped would fetch a price in the Deep South. If they could broker a sale for a dollar amount that exceeded their transportation and carrying costs, any cash left over was pure profit. For some struggling heads of households in the depression-stricken central counties of the Delmarva peninsula, the prospect of making quick and easy money was more than enough to offset the obvious risks. In fact, the more people who took those risks, the less risky the work became. As members of a Delaware grand jury put it in 1817, "The pecuniary advantages to be derived from this iniquitous traffick are now so great and it enlists in it so many, that they are able to evade the vigilance of the existing laws, or set them at open defiance."[21]

In the two decades after 1808, more and more area residents began kidnapping free people and selling them to out-of-state buyers. Between 1812 and 1819, for instance, records from the Delaware governor's office detail charges brought against James Perkins, John Hukill, Joseph Stampfer ("otherwise called Joseph Reynolds"), William Perry, Dennis Minner, John Porter, William Nelson, James Welsh, James Lackey, Joseph Jacquitt, and John McKee. These were just the amateurs. As the members of the grand jury had pointed out, the shrewdest traffickers typically eluded law enforcement.[22]

Nor was arrest any guarantee of conviction and punishment. While antikidnapping laws were on the books across the peninsula, most white residents considered those statutes to be too strict, and juries refused to enforce them, ensuring that many violators evaded justice. In Delaware, for instance, the prescribed penalties for those convicted of kidnapping free people included a fine of at least $1,000, thirty-nine lashes on the bare back, and an hour in the pillory, nailed there by the ears, the soft parts of which the sheriff would cut off afterward. This was all for a first-time offense. The same 1793 statute required that those convicted a second time face the death penalty. Most jurors winced at the thought of imposing such biblical corporal and capital punishments upon their neighbors, however guilty they might judge them to be. Even Benjamin Lundy, an outspoken antikidnapping activist based in Baltimore, decried the Delaware statute as an ineffective "relic of the barbarous practices of former years."[23]

In Johnson's Nanticoke River neighborhood, rampant racism also contributed to low rates of conviction. Judging by the frequency of acquittals, many white jurors thought that man stealers and child snatchers were doing valuable service by carting away "a great many rogues and vagabonds who were a nuisance." For that, some reasoned, men like Johnson and John Purnell should not be rebuked but rather rewarded. According to the author of a letter to the editor of Delaware's *American Watchman* newspaper in 1825, "every kidnapper who will convey a free Negro, or mulatto, to the southern states, [deserves to] be exempted from taxation for five years." Many elected officials did not disagree, and on the rare occasions when juries on the peninsula did convict kidnapping suspects, the governor typically stepped in to spare the felon from being maimed or hanged. In fact, eight of the eleven convicted kidnappers named in records kept by the Delaware governor's office between 1812 and 1819 (the eleven men mentioned above) appear in those documents because they received gubernatorial clemency of one kind or another.[24]

Kidnappers like Johnson were also shielded from the full force of the law by other actors in the peninsula's legal system. Rumors flew that dozens of local constables took kickbacks from kidnappers in return for tip-offs when their homes and hideouts were about to be raided. Activists in Philadelphia likewise repeatedly alleged that attorneys and judges around the Nanticoke watershed colluded to fix trials in return for bribes, and that keepers at lockups on both sides of the Maryland-Delaware line sometimes looked the other way during jailbreaks. Even the most scrupulously honest county sheriffs struggled to do the right thing. Badly paid and lacking the legal authority to pursue suspected kidnappers across state boundaries, sheriffs could not always secure the warrants they needed to search homes like Johnson's, and also found themselves repeatedly hamstrung by laws across the slave states that prohibited black testimony against white suspects.[25]

Professional criminals like Johnson and Purnell also put up all sorts of additional roadblocks to avoid capture and conviction. They deliberately cultivated reputations for savagery and violence, and, according to antislavery activist Jesse Torrey, when challenged "by the messengers of law," they were "generally found armed with instruments of death, sometimes with pistols with latent spring daggers attached to them!" Most local sheriffs and their agents trembled at the thought of confronting suspects who were armed to the teeth. "The constable dare not take them," another antislavery activist reported following a failed attempt to serve a pair of warrants.[26]

On the rare occasions that experienced kidnappers found themselves in serious legal jeopardy, they were quick to produce forged documents of sale to account for the black people in their possession.

The longer they had been in the business, the more likely they were to know their legal rights and be able to confidently rebuff attempts at search and seizure that lacked the proper paperwork. Even if arrested, professional kidnappers typically refused to admit wrongdoing and instead made sure to hire talented and well-connected lawyers and pay off witnesses when they thought they could get away with it.[27]

By the early 1820s, the sparsely populated counties around the Nanticoke River had gained a reputation as the central hub for several child-snatching crews active across the mid-Atlantic states. Writing from Baltimore in 1822, Benjamin Lundy told readers of his newspaper, the *Genius of Universal Emancipation*, that "the horrid practice of kidnapping, [has] increased so rapidly in [Maryland] and in some of the adjoining states." In his mind's eye, Lundy imagined a human chain of black-market mercenaries linked arm in arm, stretching from the streets of Baltimore and Philadelphia down to Dorchester and Sussex and "with branches in every county on the Eastern Shore."[28]

The scale of kidnappers' operations through the peninsula's central counties was, by 1825, difficult to exaggerate. "To enumerate all the horrid and aggravating instances of men-stealing, which are known to have occurred," Jesse Torrey wrote, "would require a heavy volume. In many cases, whole families of free coloured people have been attacked in the night, beaten nearly to death with clubs, gagged and bound, and dragged into distant and hopeless captivity and slavery, leaving no traces behind, except the blood from their wounds."[29]

Torrey was one of a small cadre of amateur activists who devoted their adult lives to thwarting Joseph Johnson and kidnappers like him. In Wilmington, Delaware, the members of the peninsula's only active antislavery organization did all they could.

They set up a special committee to produce press releases "on the subject of kidnapping," and they petitioned the region's legislatures to reform relevant statutes to make them more enforceable and effective. Still, they got no traction with most elected officials from these constituencies and repeatedly reproached themselves for only being able to stand by as men like Johnson were "roving at large in the spirit of wickedness, untouched by the hand of justice."[30]

Knowing that sheriffs and activists posed only modest peril to their livelihoods, many kidnapping collectives continued their trade undaunted, prospering throughout the 1810s and 1820s. With each passing year, the threat they presented to the liberty of the larger region's free black community intensified, a brute fact of which people of color were only too keenly aware. In 1822, for instance, one white activist reported overhearing a free black woman tell a bridge operator in Wilmington that she had cut short a journey to the peninsula's central counties that day "for fear of being caught on the road by the kidnappers." Those who lived in Sussex and Dorchester did not have that luxury, and the youngest black residents of the Nanticoke River watershed were at particular risk. As a white householder there explained in a letter to a Quaker friend in Philadelphia in July 1825, "The most frequent instances of kidnapping has [sic] been of children, who from the circumstances of their being less able to make their escape, or capable of making a statement of their case, have made them more the objects of this species of lawless violence."[31]

✤

Sam, Joe, Cornelius, Enos, and Alex were captured in August 1825, less than a month after that letter was written, and would discover the truth of that remark for themselves. Free in Philadel-

phia just two days earlier, they were now chained to a stout metal
tie that had seen a lot of prior use. So as soon as the footfalls on the
other side of the bolted attic door died away, the boys surely struggled to pry it loose and free themselves. It would not budge. After
a time they likely turned their frantic, exhausted attention to the
iron locks that cuffed their calves. Clenching their teeth in agony,
scraping skin and bone, and drawing blood, they must have tried
repeatedly to force the shackles over their swollen ankles. It was no
use. They were stuck.[32]

Saturday passed. Then Sunday. Did anyone return to feed
them again, or did they go hungry? Did they howl for help, or cry
silently, inconsolably? Did they sleep? Did they dream? The
waiting—the knowing and not knowing what would happen
next—must have been almost too much to bear. Finally, on Sunday
evening, August 14, two men barged through the door, unlocked
the boys from the metal tie, and told them they were leaving. The
boys did not recognize these men, but were so tired and terrified
that they did as they were told, stumbling down the lamp-lit lad-
der and another flight of stairs and out into a bright night. Above
them was a vast tracery of stars. Their captors had not bothered to
hood them. What was the point? None of these children knew
where they were. They had never been there before, and, if things
now went as they usually did, they would never be there again.[33]

Chapter 4

IN-LAWS AND OUTLAWS

THE MEN WHO burst into the attic and seized the five boys were Joseph Johnson's deputies. The elder of the pair was his brother, Ebenezer, while the younger man was Johnson's brother-in-law, Jesse Cannon Jr. They had instructions from Johnson to move the children to a safe house two miles away. This was his usual practice. Johnson was notorious in this neighborhood and preferred to get the proof of how he made his living off his property as quickly as possible. So the five boys and their two salt-hearted escorts headed east toward a smaller, less ostentatious dwelling just across the state line, a few hundred feet inside the western boundary of Sussex County, Delaware. Whether Sam, Joe, Cornelius, Enos, and Alex covered the distance on foot or as freight in the back of a wagon, they were not on the road for long.[1]

Like the Johnson place, this second safe house sat at a quiet crossroads, half-buried from view by trees on two sides. It too had a large attic on its second floor. Ebenezer Johnson and Jesse Cannon Jr. prodded their five captives up there, into what a visitor once described as "a small room or rather closet, about seven or eight feet square." They shoved their prisoners down onto a set of low stools crowded around the attic's empty fireplace, bound them with heavy chains, and then bolted the door behind them as they left. The boys would remain warehoused there until Joseph Johnson could find a slave trader willing to buy them and carry them out of state. Failing that, some of Johnson's accomplices could smuggle the boys southward and look for buyers themselves, just as soon as he gave them the signal.[2]

⁜

Whether the boys knew it or not, these two isolated houses were the control and command centers of the Reverse Underground Railroad's most vicious group of conductors and station agents. Joseph Johnson's gang was a family business, begun by his father-in-law soon after 1808, the year the federal government closed the nation's borders to further shipments of slaves from overseas. Since then, this operation had steadily grown, adding personnel and extending its reach year after year. Operatives were good at their jobs and had developed all sorts of strategies to maximize their profits and minimize their chances of arrest. In 1825, Johnson's crew had a half dozen core members, most of them related to one another by blood or by marriage, and many more freelance suppliers and hired hands. Those tangled family ties were crucial to the gang's longevity, the glue that bound these in-law outlaws together and helped them keep law enforcement at bay for so long.

The two-story homestead that would serve as the boys' new slave pen belonged to Joseph Johnson's mother-in-law, Patty Cannon. She had lived there, in the company of a handful of enslaved people, for nearly thirty years, and was now the warden of this makeshift prison. According to later legend, Cannon was not merely a kidnapper and human trafficker but also a highway robber, a cross-dresser, and a serial killer—a female precursor to Jack the Ripper.

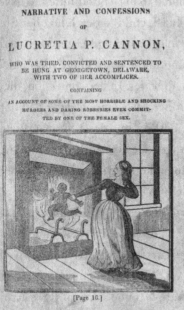

NARRATIVE AND CONFESSIONS
OF
LUCRETIA P. CANNON,
WHO WAS TRIED, CONVICTED AND SENTENCED TO
BE HUNG AT GEORGETOWN, DELAWARE,
WITH TWO OF HER ACCOMPLICES.

CONTAINING

AN ACCOUNT OF SOME OF THE MOST HORRIBLE AND SHOCKING
MURDERS AND DARING ROBBERIES EVER COMMIT-
TED BY ONE OF THE FEMALE SEX.

[Page 16.]

NEW YORK:
PRINTED FOR THE PUBLISHERS.
1841.

Renderings of Patty Cannon from John Clayton's 1841 pamphlet and a 1954 men's magazine depict her as a "female fiend," a monstrous Amazon whose lack of maternal instincts, overabundant sexuality, and extraordinary physical strength upended gender conventions. Since the pamphlet's publication, there has been no end of magazine features, plays, and novels about Cannon, all of them drawing on Clayton's misleading claims to a greater or lesser degree. Left: [John M. Clayton], Narrative and Confessions of Lucretia P. Cannon . . . , *New York, 1841. Right: William Hartley, "The Case of the Sobbing Owl," Cava-*lier Magazine, *April 1954. (Left: Courtesy of the Library Company of Philadelphia. Right: Courtesy of the American Art Archives.)*

the case of the
Sobbing Owl

By day beautiful Patty Hanley killed her guests
with kindness. By night she just plain killed them.
Her final score was 24—a record that still stands

by William B. Hartley
Illustrated by Howell Dodd

In a written confession long attributed to her, she admitted to having once scorched a five-year-old black child to death in a hot fire and to having killed ten other people, including her husband and one of her own children "by strangling it when three days old." Her parents had apparently been no better. In her confession, dictated from a jail cell at the end of her life, Cannon described her father as a drunkard, smuggler, and ax murderer from upstate New York who was eventually hanged for his crimes. Her mother, she said, was a brothel keeper who had made young Patty and her several sisters peddle their own flesh to survive.[3]

Most of this was lurid nonsense made up by a Delaware pamphleteer named John Clayton. He authored Patty Cannon's so-called confessions in 1841, sixteen years after the five boys arrived in her attic, in hopes of cashing in on the emerging market for tales of sensational female fiends. In truth, Cannon's origins were actually quite different, though only a bit less scandalous. She was born in Dorchester County, Maryland, in 1765 to Levin and Sally Handley. Her birth name was Martha, though no one ever seems to have called her that. Her father's family had deep roots on Maryland's Eastern Shore and could trace their ancestors back to English migrants who had arrived there a hundred years earlier. She grew up on Handley's Regulation, a 550-acre tobacco and livestock plantation. Her uncle ran the place while her father, Levin Handley, indulged his obsession for breeding and racing horses.[4]

Levin's income was irregular during his daughter's childhood. Several times, when money got tight, he turned to pawning stolen property, including the occasional slave. Property rights were sacred on the peninsula, and stealing a slave from his or her legal owner was a capital crime. So when the Dorchester County sheriff threw Levin Handley in jail in 1781 for abducting an enslaved man known as "Negro Ben," Patty's father found himself on trial for his life. He had no cash to hire a lawyer, but eventually succeeded in persuading a local attorney to accept the gift of a stallion named Masron as payment. It was not enough to save him. The jury soon found the suspect guilty as charged, and Sheriff John Stevens hanged Levin Handley a few days later outside the tiny brick jail on Locust Street, in Cambridge.[5]

Patty Handley was sixteen on the day in 1781 when her father swung. She had black hair and dark eyes, and several authors have since speculated that her upbringing working with horses imbued her with unusual physical strength. After Levin's death, she retreated to her uncle's house. A few years later, when she was in her early twenties, she caught the eye of Jesse Cannon, a distant relative. They married in 1787. Within twelve months, she gave birth to their first child, Jesse Jr. A second child, whom they named Mary, was born sometime later.[6]

Her new husband, Jesse, had trained as a carpenter and cabinet-maker, but his father's death in 1789 forced him to take charge of the family's Eastern Shore tobacco plantation, something he had long hoped to avoid. Newly married with two young children, Jesse and Patty took over the Cannon plantation house, but struggled for years afterward to establish themselves as planters. In the 1790s, tobacco prices fell sharply, and the couple doubted that shifting to wheat would solve their problems. So in 1808—the earliest date allowed under the terms of his father's will—Jesse Cannon began selling off parcels of his patrimony to cousins and neighbors, using the cash proceeds to cover his household's mounting debts.[7]

That same year, the federal government outlawed imports of enslaved people from overseas. Jesse Cannon recognized the opportunity. That year marks the first time his name appears in legal records in connection with the suspected kidnapping of free black people. On July 28, 1808, a woman named Hester Craig and her several children disappeared from Lewes, in eastern Delaware. Acting on an anonymous tip, the sheriff there issued arrest warrants for five men, including Jesse Cannon.[8]

Under questioning, Cannon tried to shift blame to one of the other suspects, a free black man named Cesar Rhoads, who was the estranged father of one of Hester Craig's children. Cannon claimed Rhoads had hired him and three other white men to stage the abduction and enslavement in order to relieve him of the burden of monthly child support. On the basis of Cannon's claims, an outraged all-white jury swiftly convicted Rhoads, who was barred from testifying in his own defense. The judge directed that he be sold into slavery out of state. With a black perpetrator now punished (or at least plausibly scapegoated), the attorney general abandoned the case against Cannon and the three other white mercenaries and let them walk free.[9]

Lawmen linked Jesse Cannon to a string of other kidnappings over the next fifteen years, each one a little bolder than the last. In 1811, for instance, Sussex County constables arrested him for his role in kidnapping a family of black Delawareans who had since escaped and raised the alarm. However, the sheriff could find no white witnesses to corroborate their story, and he was forced to drop the charges as a result.[10]

Each time this happened, Cannon's sense of his own invincibility grew. So too did his ambitions. By the early 1810s, he had begun to send raiding parties of trusted associates as far afield as Philadelphia and Baltimore to prospect for prey. One of these accomplices was Henry Brevington, his daughter Mary's new husband. Brevington worked for Cannon on multiple occasions before a murder charge sent him to the gallows in 1813.[11]

This stipple engraving by Alexander Rider depicts four white men abducting a widow and her young child from a garret in Delaware. Rider based the scene upon the woman's later testimony to the Philadelphia physician Jesse Torrey. Her testimony emphasized the kidnappers' ready use of brutal violence, her struggles to raise the alarm and avoid seizure, and the pair's subsequent delivery into the hands of a "Man-Dealer" across the line in Maryland, most likely Jesse Cannon. Jesse Torrey, Portraiture of Domestic Slavery, *Philadelphia, 1817. (Courtesy of the Library Company of Philadelphia.)*

Among the family confidants to offer comfort to Mary Brevington in her grief was Joseph Johnson. A powerfully built man who stood six feet tall, Johnson had begun doing grunt work for Mary's father two years before and had worked side by side with her late husband on at least one kidnapping mission: a scheme to steal away a Maryland man referred to in court documents as "Negro James." Johnson's courtship of the only daughter of Jesse and Patty Cannon was exceedingly brief. He married Mary in the fall of 1813, mere months after she became a widow.[12]

Like his new in-laws, Joseph Johnson had grown up on Maryland's Eastern Shore, within a few miles of the Nanticoke River. His father had made his money as a schooner captain shipping sugar, rum, and slaves between the United States and the Caribbean. Now retired, Ebenezer Johnson Sr. was trailed by a reputation as "a bully and outlaw, a man who for the smallest recompense could be hired to commit any outrage." Sussex County constables twice jailed him for assault and battery, and he died in a gun battle with a member of his own extended family in 1816. Besides Joseph, he left two other children: a daughter, Britannia, and a son, Ebenezer Jr., who married a Dorchester County woman named Sally Shehee in 1824, a matter of months before he helped move the five boys between the gang's two main hideouts.[13]

Joseph Johnson quickly made himself indispensable to his new father-in-law, Jesse Cannon, and together the two men expanded the family business. Between 1813 and 1822, they and their widening circle of collaborators carried away several dozen free people, as well as numerous slaves they had stolen. Predictably, most of Johnson's and Cannon's associates were their relatives by blood or by marriage—people bound to them by strong ties of trust, familiarity, and mutual interest. Indeed, the gang's most important guardians were two of Jesse Cannon's cousins, Isaac and Jacob Cannon. They were loan sharks who made a lucrative living offering high-interest cash advances to hard-up farmers and storekeepers in the area, only to foreclose quickly at the first signs of default. These brothers kept a warehouse near the banks of the Nanticoke River that they filled with furniture—tables and chairs, beds and cribs—from the homes they seized and the families they dispossessed. Their formidable reputation likely helped to protect Jesse Cannon's trafficking business as it took off during the 1810s and early 1820s. Certainly, few local homeowners would have dared indict or turn witness against any member of the Cannon family as long as Jacob and Isaac held the deed to their farm or controlled their line of credit. Better to mind their own business and keep their mouths shut.[14]

✦

Because so many Nanticoke-area residents stayed silent, historians know precious little about most of the kidnappings and out-of-state slave sales that Jesse Cannon and Joseph Johnson staged in this period. Usually we have only the barest details—a name, a date—to go on. Thankfully, a letter written to the officers of the Pennsylvania Abolition Society by their chief investigator fills in a great many evidentiary gaps about how this extraordinarily successful gang conducted its business.

In May 1819—six years before Sam, Joe, Cornelius, Enos, and Alex vanished from Philadelphia's streets—Sarah Hagerman, a free black girl aged eleven, disappeared from a job near the waterworks just outside that city. After her widowed mother made a public appeal for "any information," a tip led to the arrest of Sarah's employer, a woman named Margaret Ward. At her trial that October, Ward confessed to selling Sarah to a stolen-goods dealer who had then "sold the girl to a certain Jesse Cannon" out on the Eastern Shore. Two weeks later, in early November, the PAS dispatched John Willits to the peninsula to try to "rescue this unfortunate victim of avarice from the grasp of oppression and restore her to her friends."[15]

Willits, a dogged and experienced private detective, arrived in Denton, Maryland, on November 13. With him was a man named Miller who knew Sarah and hoped to identify the child by the "scar on her forehead, and one on her knees." But the pair ran into trouble almost immediately. The sheriff in Denton, who volunteered his disgust for "this detestable traffick" in kidnapped children, informed them that Jesse Cannon actually lived beyond his jurisdiction, across the state line in Sussex County, Delaware. It took Willits another full day to track down a Delaware magistrate willing to issue a warrant to search Cannon's house, and a second day to persuade a Sussex County constable to execute that order. The officer in question, a man named Robeson, was none too keen to do so. He had heard that Joseph Johnson, Cannon's partner and son-in-law, had holed up in the same house, and that both men were likely to be armed and dangerous.[16]

The three of them—the private eye, the family friend, and the reluctant local constable—arrived at Jesse Cannon's house on horseback on November 15 as the day was turning to dusk. Peering through the back door, Willits "saw three or four small coloured girls" inside, though none matched Sarah's description. Miller, a few paces behind, thought he "caught a glimpse of her" disappearing "thro' the garden" and into the woods with some men. But before Miller could follow her, Joseph Johnson "suddenly darted from behind a corner of the house, and presenting [a] pistol to [Miller's] head swore that if he attempted to advance another step he would blow his brains out."[17]

Johnson demanded to know their business. Without dropping his weapon, he peered at the search warrant Willets had in hand, declaring it void now that the sun had set and swearing to "shoot the first man who should attempt to raise a latch" anywhere in the house. Only at the detective's prodding did constable Robeson insist on the warrant's validity. Even then Johnson gave no more than an inch of ground, allowing Robeson and Miller to search the place for Sarah Hagerman only "on condition that no questions should be asked" of any other black people they might discover inside. While Willits remained at the door, Robeson and Miller ventured upstairs, with Johnson and his father-in-law, Jesse Cannon, "attending them with cocked pistols in their hands."[18]

When Johnson unbolted the door leading to the second-floor garret, Robeson and Miller came face to face with five black women "bound together by heavy chains." They sat in terrified silence around a cold fireplace. With Cannon's pistol pressed to his head, Miller hastily inspected each of them, looking for Sarah's telltale scars. As he passed among them, each person's face "became faintly illumined by a transient hope that she would be claimed," only to "immediately relapse again into the settled features of despair as she saw him pass on without the ability to save her." None of these women were Sarah Hagerman. They were all too old, "from eighteen to twenty years of age" by Miller's reckoning.[19]

They continued their house search for a few more minutes, but Sarah Hagerman was nowhere to be found. Johnson and Cannon seemed to enjoy watching this rescue mission fail and snidely insisted that their visitors examine the outbuildings as well. Inside one shack in the yard Willits found two boys and three more "small coloured girls." None of them bore Sarah's marks. By then, it was obvious that they were not going to find her. Sarah's captors had evidently heard that their posse was coming and had hustled her off the property before they had arrived. Night was falling fast, and with "no hope of finding the girl now remaining," Willits, Robeson, and Miller soon had to give up and go home. In lantern light they retreated to their horses as Johnson and Cannon jeered and hollered. The next morning, Willits and Miller returned to Philadelphia empty-handed. No one in Sarah Hagerman's family ever heard from her again.[20]

Willits's report to the PAS, which he submitted two weeks later, offered rare firsthand testimony as to the limits of law enforcement's powers. It also shined light upon the size of Jesse Cannon and Joseph Johnson's operations, and the efficacy of the tactics they used to protect their black market business and preserve their own liberty. Despite his years of experience as an investigator, Willits had struggled mightily to gain the element of surprise, to secure a search warrant, and to persuade county constables to enforce it. Evidently well connected and much feared locally, Cannon and Johnson had bested him easily.[21]

✛

Jesse Cannon, the founder of the kidnapping network responsible for the abduction of Sam, Joe, Cornelius, Enos, and Alex, died in 1822 at the age of fifty-seven. He never paid the full price for the terror and grief he caused so many free black families. Though Cannon once spent an hour in the pillory for his role in "kidnapping a certain free negro Boy named William Rop," the governor of Delaware stepped in to spare the soft part of his ears. Prosecutors brought several other cases against Cannon over the years—including charges stemming from Sarah Hagerman's disappearance. They all came to nothing, augmenting his regional reputation as a "notorious offender" who was effectively untouchable.[22]

Cannon had long been grooming his son-in-law, Joseph Johnson, to take over the business, and upon his patron's death, Johnson moved quickly to shore up control. He brought in his brother, Ebenezer, to assist him and began giving orders to his mother-in-law, Patty Cannon, and to her son, Jesse Cannon Jr. It was almost certainly Johnson's idea that the gang step up its abductions of free black children, especially young boys. On his command, subordinates subsequently stole James Wilson, age seventeen; Rachel and James Johnson, two young siblings; Charles Bryan, "a free negro boy"; and Martin Hardcastle and Patrick Williams, ages eight and twelve. According to the newspapers, all of them lived "in the neighborhood of the notorious Joseph Johnson." He also escalated the frequency of the gang's raids into Philadelphia and Baltimore, experimented with using sloops as holding pens, and expanded the use of black operatives on city streets. Despite frequent indictments, the occasional arrest, and one brief spell behind bars, Johnson quickly emerged from his father-in-law's shadow. By the time Sam, Joe, Cornelius, Enos, and Alex disappeared in 1825, Joseph Johnson was, in the words of his nemesis, Delaware Attorney General James Rogers, "perhaps the most celebrated Kidnapper and Negro Stealer in the Country."[23]

Johnson's rise to power within the gang's senior leadership did not go unchecked, however. While Jesse Cannon Jr. seems to have done as Johnson told him, his widowed mother sought an active and equal role in this blossoming criminal syndicate. In the wake of her husband's death, Patty Cannon found ways to assert ever more influence over the gang's operations. Rumors swirled in these years that she occasionally dressed as a man in order to go out hunting for victims, that she once assaulted a constable whom she caught snooping around her house, and that she and the Johnson brothers had together choked or beaten to death three black children. Prosecutors failed to prove any of this in court, though one later investigation did find that she sometimes directed Cyrus James, a hawkeyed free black man who had grown up in her household, to take her carriage and disappear into the night in pursuit of fresh targets.[24]

Warehousing black children and securing them against escape was critical work upon which this entire outlaw organization depended, and Patty Cannon proved almost impossible to pin down and prosecute. Regional law enforcement officials repeatedly struggled to build cases that could link this country widow to the disappearances of children from city streets more than a hundred miles away. It was not just that Cannon's work largely took place behind locked doors, out of sight of white witnesses. Cannon's gender likely also helped insulate her from legal retribution. In the 1820s, judges and juries were particularly reluctant to subject white women to bodily punishment, and on the one occasion when the names of Patty Cannon and her daughter, Mary Johnson, appeared among a list of gang members indicted for kidnapping, James Rogers, the Delaware attorney general, dropped the charges against both women without explanation.[25]

All the while, Cannon's notoriety grew. By 1825 she had earned a reputation as Joseph Johnson's chief co-conspirator. One planter in a neighboring county believed that "a very bad woman named Patty Cannon . . . directed" all the gang's operations, and told his six-year-old daughter as much. Most other observers understood Johnson and Cannon to be equal partners, though the latter's capacity for violence struck them as peculiarly unfeminine and unnatural. Consider, for instance, a description of Patty Cannon penned by a neighbor in Milford, Delaware, in a letter to antislavery activists in Wilmington: "The female part of the [Cannon-Johnson] family," he wrote in 1825, the year Sam, Cornelius, and the others disappeared, appears "to have lost those soft humane and peculiar dispositions which make them the ornament of society, and in their place to have caught the feelings of the lioness raging for her prey." A later newspaper retrospective of Patty Cannon's exploits as a station agent on the Reverse Underground Railroad in these years described her as "heedless and heartless, the most abandoned wretch that breathes."[26]

Patty Cannon's growing profile both within the gang's hierarchy and in the public's imagination makes it easy to overlook a second change in the group's composition that occurred at about the same time. In the wake of Jesse Cannon's death in 1822, Joseph Johnson and Patty Cannon dramatically expanded their network of collaborators, taking on several new hands. They hired Bill

Paragee, the skipper of the *Little John*, and paired him up with Thomas Collins, an illiterate waterman from Sussex County. They also strengthened their partnership with Jacob and John Purnell, a father-and-son team of traffickers, both of whom were mixed race. Jacob Purnell, John's father, was the former slave of a white doctor from a prominent Eastern Shore family. He was on the Cannon-Johnson gang's payroll as early as August 1821, when a report in the *Baltimore Patriot* named him as the bald-headed man responsible for kidnapping and selling eighteen residents of that port city "to [Joseph] Johnson & [Jesse] Cannon" over the course of a single summer.[27]

After Jesse Cannon died, Jacob Purnell began reporting to Joseph Johnson and Patty Cannon, and he led the gang's hunting trips to both Baltimore and Philadelphia for the next two years. Regional newspaper editors tracked his moves as best they could. In press reports, he appears as a master criminal possessed of foxlike cunning, with a pronounced proclivity for dragging his gagged and bound victims along by nooses tied tightly around their necks. In 1824, Jacob Purnell's luck finally ran out. When three of his accomplices botched a kidnapping, an arresting officer and a posse of forty local men laid siege to his home in Snow Hill, Maryland. Caught in the act of ripping up a floorboard and trying to hide in a crawl space, Purnell found that "he could not escape" and "cut his own throat from ear to ear."[28]

At the time of his father's suicide in March 1824, John Purnell was in his midtwenties. He was married and a new parent himself. As a child he had lived in Snow Hill, about forty miles southeast of the Nanticoke watershed. Though he had some training as a shoemaker, his real apprenticeship had been at his father's side on the streets of Baltimore and Philadelphia. There, he used his own talon-sharp skills as a confidence man to coax black street kids to accept a few quarters and walk with him out of town toward the distant silhouette of Paragee's sloop, the *Little John*.[29]

❖

In August 1825, John Purnell's newest victims would spend nearly a week in Joseph Johnson and Patty Cannon's custody. Like so many others before them, Sam, Joe, Cornelius, Enos, and Alex lived those days from moment to moment, in constant fear and danger of brutal physical abuse. Johnson, especially, was known for his hot temper, and he and Cannon did not think twice about kicking, stomping, and whipping their captives at the slightest provocation.[30]

Escape seemed impossible. Secured by heavy chains behind a bolted attic door, the boys could do little more than fantasize about breaking out and getting away. Only two children caught by these hawks had ever escaped from any of the gang's several safe houses. The first, a boy named Isaiah Sadler, did it by stashing a spoon given to him with his supper, and later using its handle to jimmy the locks and make a run for it. The second, a thirteen-year-old girl named Nancy, was tied up outside and managed to wriggle free when her guard fell asleep, heavy with drink. Even then, Nancy did not get far. The neighbors who briefly took her in quickly turned her over to one of Johnson's subordinates when he came looking for her.[31]

Patty Cannon and Joseph Johnson learned from these earlier escape attempts, and by August 1825 their security protocols were tighter than ever. They no longer chained their captives to pines and oaks outside. Nor did they keep them gagged and bound in pits dug into the sandy earth beyond the tree line, as Jesse Cannon had once done. Instead, the boys spent five endless days and broken nights sweltering in an airless upstairs room with only one door in or out.[32]

At some point on Tuesday, August 16, 1825, Ebenezer Johnson, Jesse Cannon Jr., and John Purnell burst through that door and barked at the boys that they were leaving. Despite a week's effort, Joseph Johnson had found no out-of-state trader audacious enough to buy these stolen children and then resell them farther south as legally tradable slaves. So Johnson had devised a different plan.[33]

Together, his three deputies bundled the boys out of Patty Cannon's house. It was the first time they had been outside in five days. Above them, the sky threatened rain. With his new wife, Sally, standing by, Ebenezer Johnson shoved these five wild-eyed children into a familiar wagon. It began a slow, jolting trundle down a rocky road to the banks of the Nanticoke River, about three miles away. Purnell led in the wagon, pulled by one horse, while the other gang members, including Sally and Ebenezer, followed behind in a two-wheeled carriage, called a trap.[34]

The boys did not have the back of the wagon to themselves. Chained alongside them were two adults. One was Mary Fisher, a tall, broad black woman between forty and fifty years old. Her hair was short and tightly coiled, and she had a scar on the side of her face. She sat there speechless, as fraught with fear as any of the terrified children. A few days earlier she had been a free woman. The wife of a farm laborer named Charley Fisher, and the mother of their several children, she had lived all over Delmarva, working as a domestic servant in one white household after another. Most recently she had been working for a family in Elkton, Maryland, in the peninsula's bustling northwest corner, and had been foraging for kindling when two men kidnapped her and tossed her into a cart bound for one of Joseph Johnson's holding pens. Two days later, she was in this wagon with the boys.[35]

Next to her, looking no less drawn and scared, sat Mary Neal. She was a slave from a nearby Delaware plantation. The Cannon-

Johnson gang had stolen several enslaved workers from surrounding estates over the years, but Mary Neal's situation was different.
As she later told her fellow travelers, she believed that Joseph
Johnson had purchased her legally from her master and that he
was planning to resell her in the Cotton Kingdom, perhaps using
her genuine bill of sale as a way to draw scrutiny away from the
receipts the gang would have to forge for their other prisoners if
they hoped to sell them at a decent price in the Deep South.[36]

South was indeed the direction their wagon was headed. When
the road dead-ended at the riverbank, Purnell, Cannon, and the
Johnsons turned the five boys and two women out of the wagon
and marched them toward the landing. Commandeering a little
wooden raft normally used to row paying passengers across the
Nanticoke, they ferried their seven captives out into the river's central channel, took them aboard a waiting sloop and down below its
deck, then put them back into fetters.[37]

They moved quickly to avoid discovery. John Purnell paddled
back to shore, while Jesse Cannon Jr., Ebenezer Johnson, and Sally
Johnson remained aboard. The new ship was a bit larger than the
Little John. Its skipper was an older man named Robert Dunn. As
soon as Purnell cleared the hull, Dunn got to work, adjusting the
sails to catch what wind there was. He turned the craft into the
gathering current and piloted the sloop along the Nanticoke's ser-
pentine thirty-mile path to the sea, passing Twiford's Wharf,
Vienna, and Frog Point. On they went, out into Tangier Sound,
the salty confluence where the tea-colored waters of the Nanticoke
meet the mouth of the Wicomico River. Then onward still, out
into the vastness of the Chesapeake Bay and toward its southern
horizon.[38]

Chapter 5

THE BEATEN WAY

IT TOOK ROBERT Dunn almost six days to pilot his ship to Norfolk, Virginia. A port town at the mouth of the Chesapeake Bay, Norfolk was just 110 nautical miles south of the Nanticoke watershed. A steamer could travel that distance in twelve hours, but Dunn's sloop had to rely on the wind to fill its small sails, and there was none to be had. The slow going must have been agonizing for Jesse Cannon Jr. and the Johnsons, who were keenly aware that every hour they spent idling increased the risk that crews of other ships drifting along in their vicinity might detect their trafficking voyage.[1]

This was hardly paranoia. The Chesapeake Bay was one of the busiest commercial arteries anywhere in the United States—"ever white with sails," according to Frederick Douglass. Even on still days, the massive estuary was crowded with cargo ships hauling timber toward Baltimore or ferrying legally purchased enslaved people from Alexandria and Georgetown to showrooms and auction houses in New Orleans. Dunn's cargo was different, of course. The gang had bought Mary Neal fair and square, but they had kidnapped the other six captives on board. The less Dunn did to attract attention from passing crews, the better.[2]

Revolt was another danger. To prevent that sort of trouble, Dunn, Cannon, and the Johnsons kept the five boys and two women chained belowdecks in the sloop's shallow storage area, passing down whatever food Dunn doled out from a tiny galley rather than bringing everyone up into the fresh air. Shipboard uprisings had struck one in ten transatlantic slaving voyages during the previous century. Women and children were rarely the instigators of those plots and were far less likely than men to have the physical strength to overpower their captors. Still, Dunn and his crew were taking no chances.[3]

The crew's fears were nothing compared to the agony felt by the seven souls stashed below deck. Scared and disoriented, Sam, Joe, Cornelius, Enos, Alex, and the two adult women, Mary Fisher and Mary Neal, spent hours each day in near total darkness. What they whispered about and what their imaginations fixed on when words failed are not hard to guess. Solomon Northup, who made a similar journey with another cargo hold full of stolen people in 1841, recalled filling those terrorized days by "learning the history of each other's wretchedness . . . conversing together of the probable destiny that awaited us, and mourning together over our misfortunes." To quiet their minds or to stave off tears, perhaps they also turned to prayer or doleful song from time to time. The three younger children surely sought comfort from Sam and Joe and the two older women. But, because Mary Fisher's later actions strongly suggest that she was sexually assaulted by at least one of the white men on board, she probably had little comfort to spare.[4]

The seven prisoners were exhausted and likely insensible with terror by the time Robert Dunn tied up the ship at a quiet pier on Norfolk's far fringes on Thursday, August 25, 1825. When Jesse

In this 1840 map of the Chesapeake Bay, the Nanticoke River snakes down from the middle of the Delmarva Peninsula, while the port of Norfolk, Virginia, sits bottom center. Fielding Lucas Jr., A Chart of the Chesapeake and Delaware Bays, *Baltimore, 1840. (Courtesy of the David Rumsey Map Collection.)*

Cannon Jr. and the Johnsons finally yanked them one by one from the hold and out onto the wooden wharf, the younger and more naive among them might have assumed that their ordeal was almost over. They were wrong. It was just beginning.[5]

❖

Norfolk stank. In the hot summer months, a nostril-choking stench drifted up from the city's shabby harbor area where meanly built wooden stores bulged with perishable goods that spoiled in the heat. Some of these warehouses were filled with produce earmarked to feed hungry black field hands in the Caribbean. Local slave dealers owned or rented the rest of these sheds and used them to confine "the multitude of negroes, many of them miserable creatures" they had legally purchased from across the Chesapeake region until they could secure onward passage for them to the Deep South.[6]

Cannon and the Johnsons had sailed their seven captives here in hopes of selling them. Norfolk was a major point of embarkation for slave ships making the nineteen-day voyage to New Orleans. For that reason, kidnappers regularly brought their victims here to try to peddle them to legal traders who would turn a blind eye to their origins and then work them into the larger supply chain that was slowly stocking the new Gulf States with slaves. This was often how the Cannon-Johnson gang did business. Three years earlier, "some unknown ruffian" in the pay of Joseph Johnson had kidnapped Nancy, a thirteen-year-old girl from Laurel, Delaware. According to her former employer's best information, the assailant had then "carried [her] off in a vessel from the Nanticoke river to Norfolk," to be sold and shipped out "from thence to some Southern Market."[7]

This time, the gang had no such luck. The spring slave-buying season had been strong, and most legal traders who used Norfolk as a staging ground had already bought all the Chesapeake slaves they could afford. It was almost September now and, despite their well-honed sales skills, neither Jesse Cannon Jr. nor the Johnsons could find a middleman who would offer a fair price for any of these seven people. The only flesh merchants willing to make a deal refused to cough up more than a pittance for the privilege of shouldering the risks of reselling people who would surely insist that they were legally free.

Frustrated, Cannon and the Johnsons decided that the best way to capitalize on their investments was to deliver them to the Deep South themselves. They had made this calculation several times before, in similar circumstances, and each time it had eventually paid off. Ebenezer Johnson had returned from a journey to Mississippi just three months earlier. He knew from that experience that plantation owners there, or in neighboring Alabama, were likely to pay $200 to $300 more per person (that's $4,400 to $6,600 today) than traders here in Norfolk.[8]

The fastest route south was by ship on one of the oceangoing coasters that made weekly runs down to New Orleans, the largest slave-trading center anywhere in the United States. Ships from Norfolk and other Chesapeake ports delivered about fifteen hundred slaves there each year in the mid-1820s. That volume was rising, but most enslaved new arrivals were destined for sale to sugar planters across Louisiana who had a strong preference for adult men who could shoulder a scythe and spend long days hacking sugarcane.[9]

The gang had women and children to sell and knew they could command better prices if they avoided New Orleans and instead headed overland to the bustling slave yard a mile north of Natchez, Mississippi, known as "Niggerville." Natchez, the commercial hub of the expanding cotton industry, lay just far enough inland that the majority of slave traders with business there eschewed the sea lanes entirely, opting instead for land routes through the nation's interior. Although that journey was very slow, it was no more expensive than shipping freight to the region by sea. Most important, it had the great advantage of allowing criminal traffickers to avoid the customs inspections and document checks in New Orleans that could easily expose them.[10]

Once they had decided to head for Natchez and take a land route to get there, it took Cannon and the Johnsons only a day or two to make the arrangements. They stripped Dunn's ship of rope, cuffs, and other paraphernalia they knew they would need for the journey. From Norfolk's well-equipped storekeepers they purchased two horses, a small wagon, and a light two-wheeled carriage called a gig. They also bought blankets, cookware, and enough food for at least the first week on the road. The goal was to travel light and keep transport costs as low as possible. Food, fodder for the horses, and ferry and bridge tolls were necessities, but they could eat into profits if coffle drivers did not know what they were doing.[11]

To save money, Jesse Cannon Jr. would return to Maryland's Eastern Shore, leaving the newlyweds Sally and Ebenezer Johnson to continue on without him. Legal traders typically hired small teams of guards to help them and often lodged their captives in jails or taverns each night en route. The Johnsons, however, would do it all themselves, and would force their seven captives to sleep in the open air at campsites or along the road. Legal traders also usually paid for advertising, insurance, licenses, lawyers' fees, doctors' fees, commissions, taxes, and interest payments on loans. The Johnsons would shirk all of these, and expected to pocket close to fifty dollars per prisoner (eleven hundred dollars today) in savings by being so economical.[12]

❖

Their nine-person caravan rumbled out of Norfolk on a late August day, leaving Jesse Cannon Jr. to return to the wharf where Dunn's sloop waited to take him back to Maryland. The Johnsons forced the two adult women and the three older boys, Sam, Joe, and Cornelius, to trudge on foot, though they left them unfettered—at least in daylight hours. Behind them, the two youngest children, Enos and Alex, drove a horse and a small uncovered wagon loaded with provisions and baggage. Ebenezer and Sally Johnson trailed them all in the two-wheeled carriage, never letting any of them out of their sight.[13]

In this grim formation, they trooped past Norfolk's fort, a half-moon-shaped pile of bricks, before joining a thickening stream of other travelers, all moving slowly in the direction of the new southern and western states. Many were migrant farming families trying to escape falling tobacco prices and exhausted soil in Virginia and Maryland who were headed out to the frontier, to fertile land in Alabama, Mississippi, and Louisiana. The federal government had acquired these three new states over the previous quarter century in a string of gun-to-the-head treaties and land cessions with the region's Native tribes, who found themselves confined to ever-smaller reservations. These migrant farmers may not have seen themselves as nation builders, but by turning what had once been Indian country into settled cash-crop plantations, and by stocking them with enslaved people dragged there to be worked to death, they were doing just that.[14]

The scale of their migration was unprecedented. By 1820, more than 250,000 white settlers had poured into these three deep southern states. Many more set out to follow them every spring and summer, beckoned to the region by promoters who promised homesteaders lives of ease and abundance and who downplayed the bitter, ongoing land disputes with southern Native peoples. This tide of wagons rolling southward made for busy roads heading in and out of the larger towns that studded the major routes. Israel Pickens, a future governor of Alabama, recalled the "crowd of strangers" that bustled through these bottlenecks when he and his own family made the journey there, and he took obvious pleasure overtaking "many waggons & other carriages" in between rest stops.[15]

Some of these migrant families embarked on this expedition in hopes of making their fortunes planting sugarcane, but many more set their sights on cotton. Farming its short-staple variety could be hugely profitable, thanks in part to the recent mechanization of spinning and weaving in England and the invention of the cotton gin in the United States in 1793. As promoters never tired of explaining, cotton plants thrived in the rich, black soil of the Deep South, creating near-perfect conditions for cultivation. Once confined to a chain of tidal and barrier islands along the coast of Georgia, the cotton frontier had been moving rapidly west in the past two decades. The craze for cotton reached Natchez, Mississippi, in 1820, just five years before the Johnsons and their seven prisoners set out from Norfolk in the same direction.[16]

Besides all these emigrant families, most of the people that Sam, Cornelius, and the others saw on the roads that summer and fall were other slaves in other coffles. The first white settlers in the emerging Cotton Kingdom had concluded almost immediately that cotton picking was slave work, but the US government had banned all further imports of foreign-born slaves in 1808, closing off the most obvious source of black labor. So instead, slave owners in the Chesapeake stepped in to meet the demand. Planters in Maryland, Virginia, and Delaware were grappling with a surplus of slaves caused by the collapse of the tobacco economy and the subsequent switch to wheat and other less labor-intensive grains. They were only too happy to strike deal after deal to sell men, women, and children they no longer needed to professional traders who would transport them to the Deep South where aspiring cotton growers were willing to pay record prices.[17]

The rise of this domestic trade in slaves quickly turned the region into slave country. The census reveals that 143,000 enslaved people lived in Alabama, Mississippi, and Louisiana by 1820. That number doubled over the next decade because of this forced migration. This was a torrent of humanity—or, as the writer Edward Ball has described it, "a thousand-mile-long river of people, all of them black." Some went south when their masters relocated from the Chesapeake, the Carolinas, or Georgia. Several thousand others—including these five boys—made the trek under the guard of conductors on the Reverse Underground Railroad who had stolen their freedom. The vast majority, though, tramped there in the custody of slave traders who had bought them from their previous owners, and who had broken no laws.[18]

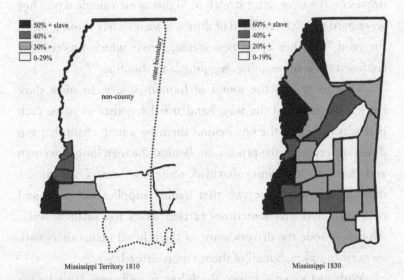

Slavery spread rapidly through Mississippi in the years before and after it achieved statehood in 1817. Maps adapted by Caitlin Burke from David J. Libby, Slavery and Frontier Mississippi, 1720–1835 *(Jackson: University Press of Mississippi, 2004).*

One out of every five enslaved people in Virginia made the journey to this new Cotton Kingdom in the 1820s. Most were strangers to one another who had been sold to traders seeking laborers with particular characteristics or demographics. Cotton picking required dexterity and stamina rather than strength, so while adult men commanded the best prices, buyers were equally interested in women and children. In these decades, children between the ages of eight and fifteen made up about a quarter of all coffle slaves. "We have a few likely girls and a choice lot of boys," one trader boasted to a colleague before setting out for Natchez.[19]

Travelers on southern roads saw these convoys of children and adults all the time. The turnpikes and paths that veined the southern states were the capillaries of a domestic middle passage more than twice the size the transatlantic slave trade to the British mainland colonies had been. One Virginia traveler saw four different droves on the same short stretch of highway on a single day. They were hard to miss. "A cloud of dust was seen slowly coming down the road," another eyewitness wrote, "from which proceeded a confused noise of moaning, weeping, and shouting."[20]

That noise was the sound of human misery. In most slave coffles, the men led the way, handcuffed together in pairs; each pair was linked to the one behind them by a long chain that ran down the center of the procession. Behind the men limped women and children, sometimes shackled, sometimes not. Then came a mule-driven wagon or two that hauled supplies like food and cookware, and that sometimes carried slaves too small to walk. Alongside rode the drivers, some of them hired men, others with ownership stakes, but all of them visibly armed.[21]

With just seven captives, the Johnson coffle was puny by the standards of the day. Most legal slave convoys topped out at between thirty and forty people. Others were much longer and reminded

Lewis Miller, a folk artist originally from Pennsylvania, depicted a slave coffle leaving Virginia and setting out for Tennessee in the 1850s. Note the composition of the coffle and the prominence of the drivers' weapons. Lewis Miller, Sketchbook of Landscapes in the State of Virginia, 1853–1867. *(Courtesy of the Colonial Williamsburg Foundation. Gift of Dr. and Mrs. Richard M. Kain in memory of George Hay Kain.)*

travelers of nothing so much as giant serpents. Whatever their size, coffles were hard to avoid. Large, wide, and slow moving, they could block the way ahead, slow traffic to a crawl, and cause frustration and sometimes rage among those stuck behind them. "All the roads . . . are crowded with troops of negroes on their way to the slave markets of the South," Basil Hall, an English visitor, complained after a visit through Virginia, the Carolinas, and Georgia in the spring of 1828.[22]

❖

Over the next four months, the seven captives and their husband-and-wife captors would travel together west and then south, into the molten new center of American slavery. They would cover more than a thousand miles, a monstrous distance—two million steps on foot.[23]

None of them kept a journal or wrote or spoke more than a few sentences about the experience later, a fact that makes reconstructing their precise route almost impossible. Fortunately, plenty of other people kept accounts of similar journeys that can fill this great gap in the record. Most legal traders and their slaves leaving Norfolk first trekked almost four hundred miles inland, disappearing into Virginia's ancient forests. It took slave coffles on these roads about a month to cover that sort of distance, hobbling past Black Water Bridge, Lynchburg, New London, and Roanoke, before crossing the foothills of the Allegheny Mountains near Blacksburg to descend into Tennessee.[24]

The western road turned sharply southward there, and if the members of the Johnson coffle followed this route, they would have spent another two weeks threading their way through Tennessee's Cumberland Valley. Travelers often remarked on the breathtaking natural beauty of this landscape. Joe, Cornelius, Enos, and Alex were city boys used to the flatlands around Philadelphia. To them, the winding valleys, rushing waterfalls, and "huge, blue-looking rocks" they saw from the road must have seemed wondrous. The same could not be said of the human settlements they passed. State officials had erected index-finger-shaped mile markers along Tennessee's principal roads in the 1810s, but the "poor, contemptible looking" towns they pointed to seemed hardly worthy of the attention.[25]

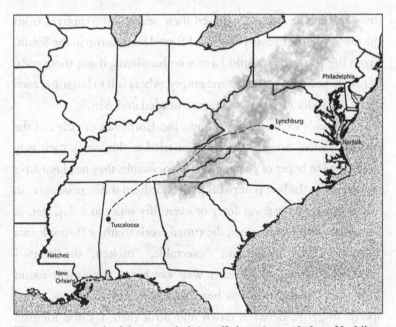

The precise route the Johnsons and their coffled captives took from Norfolk to Tuscaloosa is unknown, but a passage via western Virginia, eastern Tennessee, and northern Alabama is most likely given the habits of other travelers between those points. Digital cartography by Caitlin Burke. (Courtesy of the GIS and Geospatial Services Center, University of Maryland.)

The Johnsons had driven their captives past 220 of these Tennessee mile markers by the time they crossed into Alabama just north of Huntsville. Eight or nine more days snaking their way through hilly pine forests would bring them to Tuscaloosa. From there it was another three weeks' journey to Natchez, Mississippi, the bustling slave-trading town on a bluff overlooking the great river that gave that state its name.[26]

As they walked, summer surrendered to fall and then to winter. The earth beneath Sam's shoeless feet turned from brown to yellow to red—and then, finally, to black. The only constant was the fact of slavery all around them. Traveling eleven hundred miles through four slave states exposed these seven coffle captives from the mid-Atlantic to every species of forced labor camp in the South. From the road, they would have seen hundreds, if not thousands, of rough-hewn slave huts, some empty, others full to bursting, each one a reminder of where they were headed and why.[27]

The roads were terrible. If Sam, Joe, Cornelius, or either of the two Marys had dragged their feet or tried to slow-walk their way southward in hopes of postponing the inevitable, they need not have bothered. On the best post roads in the northern states, passengers in a stagecoach might cover forty or even fifty miles in a day. Yet, as travelers' diaries make clear, the rutted roads south of Pennsylvania were "infernal," "intolerable," "execrable," "broken," the "worst I ever saw." Although this "beaten way" saw heavy, almost year-round traffic, the road conditions heading south and west kept travel speeds sluggish. Between dawn and dusk each day, the Johnson coffle probably managed no more than fifteen miles.[28]

Basil Hall, an English visitor to the Deep South, made several dozen etchings of southern people and places, including this one that emphasizes the natural obstacles to rapid road transport in this frontier region in the 1820s. Basil Hall, "Pine Barren of the Southern States" in Forty Etchings from Sketches made with the Camera Lucida in North America *(London, 1829). (Courtesy of the Library Company of Philadelphia.)*

The weather did not help. The Johnsons wanted to press on no matter what the conditions, but scorching sun in late summer could sometimes force traders to halt at midday, allowing captives like forty-year-old Mary Fisher to "[rest] themselves under the shade of some larger trees which overshadowed the road." Rain brought delays of its own. The water got everywhere, turning trails into quagmires, bogging down the wagon and the gig, water-logging clothes and supplies, and preventing forward progress after dark by making pine torches impossible to light.[29]

On days like those, almost everyone in the convoy had to pitch in. On some of the worst stretches of road, it was too dangerous to ride in the gig or the wagon. Everyone had to walk, taking turns clearing stones, stumps, and fallen limbs from the vehicles' rumbling path and digging out axles when they sank into mud or sand. Each time the wagon overturned or the gig's wheel broke, the Johnsons expected the older, stronger boys to put their shoulders to it to get it moving again. And when the nine of them took their chances on rickety river bridges, or waded their way through waist-deep fords, it might have seemed for a second or two that they were all in this together.[30]

❖

They were not. The Johnsons were outnumbered seven to two so made skillful use of a terrifying blend of physical restraint, corporal cruelty, and psychological coercion to impose their will and protect their own lives. Some legal slave traders prided themselves on their supposed humanity. Not the Johnsons. Rumors had circulated around the mid-Atlantic for years that members of their gang clubbed to death any captive who tried to escape, and neither Ebenezer nor Sally saw anything to gain by dispelling that myth on this particular journey. To prevent escapes and attacks, they chained everyone up at night and punished any sign of disobedience quickly and sharply, usually with the whip that Ebenezer had made from hickory switches he had gathered along the route.[31]

The grinding hardships of this forced migration only amplified the power imbalance between captors and captives. For one thing, the Johnsons knew where they were going and how to get there. Sam, Cornelius, and their fellow prisoners had never ventured so far from home; everything they saw, heard, and felt on this grueling procession was strange and unsettling. And they were exhausted. Decades later, other black people who had made this awful overland passage could still vividly remember how their bare feet had felt at the end of each day when blisters "as large as dollars" had formed, opened, and then re-formed on their soles. The cuffs they wore at night rubbed their wrists raw while they slept, and everyone experienced the daily and cumulative effects of sunburn, frostbite, thirst, and hunger. By the time the Johnson coffle got where it was going, some of the boys were "ragged as colts," flesh and bone "worn down by fatigue and poor living."[32]

The two black women also had to deal with the ever-present threat of sexual assault on the trail. Male slave drivers forced themselves on the women in their custody whenever they thought they could get away with it, sometimes in full view of other captives. A coffle slave named John Brown never forgot having witnessed his driver rape a woman he had yanked onto his wagon at a rest stop, before inviting his hired hands "to treat her in the same manner." Sally Johnson is the only white woman to work as a coffle driver of whom historians are aware, a fact best explained by her recent marriage to Ebenezer. She must have reasoned that by joining her new husband on this hellish honeymoon, she could make sure that he never had the opportunity to stray. The two Marys took no chances anyway. Given what seems to have happened to Mary

Fisher during the slow sail from the Nanticoke to Norfolk in late August, she would have known better than to think that Sally's presence at her husband's side could safeguard her from that sort of harm. To try to avoid drawing Ebenezer's attention, she and her namesake, Mary Neal, would have taken their own precautions by staying quiet, keeping their eyes fixed on the ground, and doing their best to appear unworthy of his notice.[33]

The effects of this ordeal upon the psyches of these women and children must have been extreme. Kidnapped, beaten, and then driven ever farther from families they would likely never see again, the Johnsons' captives each spent months on the road grieving for lives now lost to them and for loved ones left behind. A small boy in a slave coffle that made a similar journey could not stop thinking about his mother as he walked. "It came to me, more and more plainly, that I would never see her again," Louis Hughes later recalled. "Young and lonely as I was, I could not help crying, oftentime for hours together." Effectively orphaned, other coffle children simply turned in on themselves, too depressed to speak or eat. Each coffle prisoner mourned in his or her own way, but their collective dejection was unmistakable. Traveler after traveler described the convoys of black people that shuffled past them on southern roads as looking like nothing so much as funeral processions.[34]

Blunting the worst of this distress required extraordinary strength of mind, and coping strategies varied. Devout Christians found solace in the promise of someday being reunited with parents and friends. Other coffle captives put on the bravest faces they could, singing and whistling to try to wrestle down their dread while they walked. A few affected indifference and kept to themselves each day, apparently numb to what was happening to them. Most forced migrants, however, turned to one another, holding hands, sharing stories, and whispering secrets—anything to bring a shred of comfort to themselves or the person next to them.[35]

The end of each day's march brought little respite. When they pulled off the road each evening, everyone in the Johnson coffle had to work together to make camp, lighting large fires of fallen or cut timber. Supper was usually boiled rice and perhaps bread or "an allowance of corn cakes" or bacon fat. Aching and spent from each day's slog, they ate whatever was put in front of them, grabbing at it, in the words of one witness, in hungry handfuls "as if half-famished."[36]

When it was time to bed down, the Johnsons cuffed them all, even eight-year-old Alex. If the weather cooperated, they would all lie on blankets under the vast field of stars. When it did not, they looked for empty barns, or took shelter under the wagon itself. Everyone slept in their clothes. If they were lucky, fatigue knocked them out right away. Often, coffle children "sobbed and moaned themselves to sleep" as the night fell in on them. Sometimes they barely slept at all. A stinging wound from a whip inflicted earlier in the day, a wave of grief, or the attacks of mosquitoes and fleas conspired to leave many coffle slaves lying awake long after the fire had fizzled, "the silence of night broken by their [own] sighs and sobs." Even when they finally settled, they sometimes woke with a start, roused by the roll calls that traders took "two or three times during the night" to demonstrate just how closely they were watching.[37]

Coffle drivers had good reason to be vigilant. Some of their captives used the cover of night to test each link of their chains, looking for a weak one. Others refused to shut their eyes before they had quietly recited the names of all the rivers they had crossed, desperately trying to commit them to memory for the moment they might try to escape and retrace their steps. And if sleep came, even just for an hour or two, dreams of freedom could flood their unconscious. A coffle slave named Charles Ball later recalled that in one of his own night visions out on the road, his son had come to him to hack desperately—but uselessly—at his chains.[38]

Whatever the night brought, the next morning always came too quickly. Most slave drivers, the Johnsons likely included, woke their prisoners at first light and usually gave them only a few minutes to gobble down a breakfast of cornmeal soup. The coffles had often broken camp and set out by five or six each morning, usually "before the stars had disappeared from the sky."[39]

✛

It was on a broiling mid-October afternoon, almost two months into this forced march, that the Johnsons made their first sale. Low on provisions and funds, they had been looking for the right time to trade at least one of their captives for cash so they could buy more corn and bacon, as well as fodder for the two horses. They had crossed into Alabama a few days earlier. Now they bivouacked just outside Tuscaloosa so Ebenezer could look for a likely buyer.[40]

Tuscaloosa was a new town that had sprouted up at the last navigable point of the Black Warrior River. It served as a commercial hub for the area's burgeoning cotton industry and as a resupply center for migrants and slave traders heading on toward Mobile or Mississippi through what remained of Indian country. The first American settlers had arrived in 1818 in the wake of US victory in a long-running war with the region's Native inhabitants, the Creeks. Tuscaloosa had grown quickly since. By the time the Johnsons and their small, lumbering posse of people for sale arrived there in October 1825, the town already boasted its own federal land office, as well as a post office, a jail, a weekly newspaper, at least three churches, and more than thirty stores and groceries, most of them clustered near the intersection of the two main streets, Market and Broad. Tuscaloosa had just been designated the county seat and would soon be named the state capital.[41]

After asking around, Ebenezer Johnson found his way to a workshop on the south side of Broad Street owned by a man named James Paul. He was a tinner who had come to Tuscaloosa from neighboring Tennessee in 1819. Paul had prospered in Tuscaloosa, making cups, buckets, milk pans, coffeepots, and washbasins for new residents and for all those passing through. He was large and rugged with a prominent nose and dark eyes—local historians said he was handsome—but he was also reclusive, a bachelor with few friends who was as blunt as a kick to the shins. A craftsman of considerable talent who had long resisted using any sort of machine tools, Paul preferred to make everything by his own hand and charged the prices he thought that sort of work deserved. By October 1825, Paul's years of labor had brought him modest wealth. According to one reminiscence of him, "a few thousand dollars probably might have been the uttermost of it."[42]

It was not a fortune, but it was certainly enough to dream with. Three months before he met Ebenezer Johnson, James Paul bought 117 acres of cotton-growing land. He did so with the intention of diversifying his income and reinventing himself as a gentleman cotton planter, replete with a small army of slave laborers at his beck and call. By 1825, enslaved people made up more than 40 percent of the population of Tuscaloosa County, and Paul understood that the purchase of slaves was essential to realizing his aspirations, a means for him to transform himself from a simple artisan into a respectable master of men.[43]

That October, James Paul bought Cornelius Sinclair from Ebenezer Johnson for $300 ($6,600 today) in an all-cash deal. A smart, alert lad of ten, and touted to be the only boy in the coffle who knew how to read, Cornelius was obviously a quick study, a fact that appealed to Paul. So too did the very reasonable price Johnson asked for him. Paul would later deny having known that Cornelius was a kidnapped rider on the Reverse Underground Railroad, and would tell anyone who asked that he had acted in good faith and that Johnson had defrauded him with a fake bill of sale. That was a bald-faced lie. Three hundred dollars was half of what legally traded boys Cornelius's age could fetch, and literacy usually commanded a premium—not a discount.[44]

The low purchase price Paul paid for this boy's life and labor suggests that he knew all too well that he was breaking the law and buying from the black market. Cornelius surely told him just that in hopes of sinking the deal and blowing the whistle on the Johnsons. Paul, however, was not put off. Instead, he dipped into his wallet and handed over the cash. Ebenezer Johnson took the money and shoved the child toward his new owner. Then he turned on his heels, rejoined his wife and the rest of the coffle, and hurried back out to the road.[45]

Chapter 6

THE BODY IN THE WAGON

C ornelius's sale marked a grim milestone in the coffle's progress south. The makeshift black family these seven captives had forged on the South's muddy roads had just lost a son and a brother. Watching Cornelius—a child with whom they had shared so many miles and meals—sold and separated from them must have left the six survivors dreading what was next. It might now be only a matter of days until Ebenezer and Sally Johnson sold another of them away, and then another, and another.[1]

In fact, nothing of the sort happened, at least not for another six weeks. Instead, the Johnsons marched their procession of mourners two days eastward. They halted in Ashville, a tiny sliver of a place tucked inside northeastern Alabama, just sixteen miles south of the Cherokee nation. Ashville sat on land that had been a battleground during the Creek War a dozen years earlier and was too new and thinly settled to appear in many of the first maps of the state.[2]

✣

Ebenezer Johnson had been to Ashville before. Convinced of the village's prospects and strategic location, he had purchased "a log house and some land there" during a previous expedition, and it was toward that rough homestead that he now led his six remaining captives. The log houses in the area were usually very modest, no more than a sandstone chimney and two rooms separated by a breezeway called a dogtrot. Johnson's cabin would have had an earthen floor, a roof made of slabs of bark laid out like shingles, and a handful of small windows covered over for privacy by paper coated with pig lard. Empty for months at a time, the Johnson house probably had no more than a few sticks of furniture and was too tiny to accommodate all eight arrivals. Ebenezer and Sally Johnson likely locked the younger boys, or perhaps the two women, in a shed or some other outbuilding for each of the forty nights they would stay there.[3]

The Johnsons needed those six weeks in Ashville to prepare their merchandise for successful sale. Part of this was just timing. If they hoped to sell their six assets for more than they had made from off-loading Cornelius, they would have to lie low for a while. The coffle had made good time since leaving Norfolk at the end of August; using the little wagon to carry the smaller boys had made all the difference. Still, it did not pay to get to the Cotton Kingdom too early. Yellow fever stalked most of the large and midsize towns that lay ahead of them this time of year, and repeat visitors knew to avoid the fall sickly season.[4]

Besides, it was better business to wait. As the Johnsons knew from experience, the slave-buying season in and around Natchez only really started in earnest after the harvest. It was not until planters sold their cotton crops in November and December that they typically had enough time or cash on hand to think about buying new slaves. The same was true of sugar planters down in New Orleans. There, the six months from November to April accounted for nine out of ten of all legal purchases of slaves from out of state.[5]

Both Ebenezer and Sally Johnson worked hard while they waited. The cabin was not just a warehouse, a place to hold captives in limbo until the time was right to press onward. It was also a workshop, a factory in which these seasoned flesh dealers tried to turn rough commodities into finished goods that would catch a buyer's eye. Flush with cash from the sale of Cornelius, the Johnsons likely doubled food rations right away and raided the woods around the cabin for deer, turkeys, ducks, and wild pigeons, as well as grapes, persimmons, and various other wild autumnal fruits. The goal, a survivor of another slave coffle later reported, was "to make us look fat and hearty, to enable [traders] to obtain better prices for us." The right kind of exercise could help achieve the same effect, and during their weeks in Ashville the Johnsons may have set Enos and Alex, the two scrawny, slim-built boys who had ridden most of the way there, to jumping rope or some similar daily physical humiliation to try to tone their muscles and bulk them up.[6]

Transforming the appearances of their six slaves to maximize their appeal to buyers was a major operation. After weeks on the road, their captives were bedraggled and filthy. The Johnsons now bathed and scrubbed each of them from head to toe, cutting their hair and trimming their nails. Other traders went much further. One Natchez resident remembered noticing that a slave dealer there had taken the time to braid the hair of all the black women and girls that he had put up for sale and had fixed pink ribbons at their necks.[7]

Fitting each person for a new set of clothes to wear during the selling season would also take time. As another coffle survivor explained, captors approaching New Orleans, Natchez, and all the smaller slave markets in the Black Belt each winter, often stopped for "several days for the purpose of arranging our clothes." What garments the Johnsons chose for Mary Neal or Mary Fisher, or for Sam, Joe, Enos, or Alex, goes unrecorded, though we know from Solomon Northup and Charles Ball that high-end trading firms typically spent ten dollars per person (more than two hundred dollars today) decking out boys in smart blue suits and dressing women in white aprons and identical calico frocks. On the one hand, black-market operators like the Johnsons wanted their captives to look like every other slave for sale. On the other hand, they were more cost-conscious and far more likely to put their merchandise in pantaloons, shirts, and simple dresses bought second-hand or stitched from the canvas of the wagon in which they had traveled.[8]

Clipped nails, washed hair, and clean clothes made a good impression. But Ebenezer Johnson, an experienced conductor on the Reverse Underground Railroad, knew that training his kidnapped captives not to give the game away when questioned by prospective buyers was vastly more important—and potentially much more time-consuming. Southerners willing to spend hundreds of dollars on a new slave or two typically spent at least thirty minutes or so prodding, poking, fondling, and interrogating the black men, women, and children in front of them before making up their minds and making an offer. Buyers looked for physical weakness, probed into backgrounds, and tried to assess stamina, fertility, docility, and loyalty by any means possible. They expected to be able to question each slave extensively, and sometimes privately, and anticipated that traders would let their captives answer freely and honestly.[9]

The answers they received could matter a great deal. Buyers knew it was all too easy to be taken in by slick salesmen who might fail to disclose deal-breaking problems relating to an enslaved person's health or history. With so much money at stake and refunds usually out of the question, potential purchasers could not afford to choose poorly. No wonder, then, that even the most reputable legal traders worked hard to ensure that their slaves would say the right things. In the days and weeks before they delivered their slaves to market, they beat them and drilled them over and over to appear, in Northup's words, "smart and lively."[10]

Criminal traffickers had to go to even greater lengths. Ebenezer Johnson knew full well that one wrong word from any of his six captives could be disastrous. It might force him to slash his asking price in half to help a prospective buyer overcome his scruples, or it could scuttle the sale completely. It might even land both him and his new bride behind bars. The majority of planters in the Deep South did not want to be seen publicly doing business with kidnappers like the Johnsons and were wary of buying men, women, and children who had been born free. They regarded such slaves as more trouble than they were worth: more likely to run away, more likely to shirk work, and more likely to stir up trouble among other slaves in the quarters.[11]

It took Sally and Ebenezer Johnson about a month and a half to train the two Marys and the four remaining boys to act like docile, desirable, legally traded slaves. They flogged and intimidated them over and over until Sam and the others would recite "any story," and likely gave them new identities and biographies to memorize. This was standard operating procedure among professional traffickers on the Reverse Underground Railroad. As an exposé of these practices in an antislavery newspaper later explained, "This discipline is continued at intervals until they become completely drilled, that a stranger, whether the professed owner is present or not, can scarcely obtain from them, by any means whatever, any other account than the false one which has been prepared for them."[12]

Finally satisfied that they had done all they could to limit their exposure, the Johnsons ushered their captives out of Ashville in early December. The gig and the small one-horse wagon in which Enos and Alex had ridden were nowhere to be seen; Ebenezer had traded them for a larger and sturdier four-horse wagon better suited to the roads ahead and had bought two extra horses to fill out the team. He and Sally would ride in this new wagon; everyone else would walk. They were headed, once again, in the general direction of Natchez, though, Ebenezer, having been down here before, knew that their best hopes of selling their human cargo would be in ones and twos in furtive cash deals struck en route.[13]

❖

There was still a lot that could go wrong, and the farther south they ventured, the more tense and bad-tempered the Johnsons became. As they crossed Alabama in the direction of Mississippi, the distance between settlements grew, leaving their convoy isolated for long stretches and exposing them to raids by bandits and horse thieves. Winter was coming on too. Most coffle drivers arrived in Natchez with heavy colds and complaining of rheumatism, and the Johnsons feared the effects of frostbite on everyone's feet and hands.[14]

Most of all, Sally and Ebenezer worried for themselves. They lived in daily dread of being murdered by the children and women they had taken as their prisoners. They were right to worry. As one antislavery writer put it, "It would be surprising indeed if men and women, frenzied with the loss of their relatives, goaded to desperation by the lash of the driver, and knowing the frightful oppressions to which they were tending on the plantations of the South, would not rise, even in their chains, and crush their merciless tyrants." Coffle slaves often slipped their fetters and tried to escape, and a few of them did manage to overpower their captors. A band of slaves originally from Maryland once succeeded in cutting the throats of the two Georgia men transporting them south, cleaving open the head of one man with his own ax and then relieving the two butchered bodies of $3,000 in cash before disappearing into the night.[15]

The Johnsons were more vulnerable than most. Traders operating within the law tended to look out for one another on the road. They often camped together at night, taking turns keeping watch while the others drank, cursed, and boasted till they blacked out. There was strength and security in that sort of camaraderie. By contrast, Ebenezer and Sally Johnson were pariahs. Legal traders out on the roads knew they were toxic and so intuitively avoided them, knowing it would be bad for their own business to be seen keeping company with kidnappers. Their own respectability was already in steep decline. By the 1820s, legal traders were the regular targets of antislavery attacks in the press and were dogged by the public's growing realization that their pursuit of profit ripped families apart. Calling someone a "slave trader" was fast becoming an insult across the southern states as well as in the North.[16]

So the Johnsons were on their own. Shunned by drivers of legal slave coffles who did not want to be mistaken for criminals, they knew they could rely on no one but themselves. For that reason, they reached for the tools of terror at any sign of insubordination. They drilled it into their prisoners that they were not to talk to any white people unsupervised and promised them each a savage flogging, one of their captives later recalled, if they ever whispered a word about being free. They seem to have spared Mary Fisher and Mary Neal from the hickory whip, but the boys felt its lick anytime they carped, dawdled, or "complained of sore feet and being unable to travel." Sam, fifteen years old, bore the worst of it and once "received more than fifty lashes" before Ebenezer Johnson's arm gave out.[17]

There were limits, of course. Eager to dispel any suspicion that she was a soft touch, Sally Johnson once told Sam "that it did her good" to see her husband beat him and the three boys, a calculated boast to show that she too had ice in her veins. Still, she understood that if her husband used the whip too much, he risked leaving the sorts of scars and wounds that could jeopardize a sale. Reaching for the paddle or the flat side of a saw too readily also risked stirring the sort of rebellion they were so determined to suppress. The Johnsons grasped this well enough, and so used both carrot and stick. They knew what the offer of a slug of whiskey could do on a rainy day "when the Negroes were wet and almost ready to give out." They knew when it made sense to let their captives sing sad songs together for a mile or two, and when it was wise to let the slowest, weakest walkers like Alex and Enos climb into the wagon to rest for a spell. One wonders too whether either of them ever tried to convince the youngest boys that the life awaiting them in the Deep South was not nearly as bad as they had heard.[18]

Whatever they tried, the Johnsons never felt truly safe. They spent every day and night on edge, unable to drop their guard. They had sold Cornelius away at the first opportunity because he had seemed dangerously intelligent and more than capable of conspiracy, but that still left the others. Back in Philadelphia, Alex had earned a reputation for being uncommonly smart and difficult to control. Out on the road, he, Enos, and the two Marys had been conspicuously quiet. Who was to say what they were thinking or what they might be planning?[19]

The other two boys presented the Johnsons with different problems. Joe, the second-oldest child in the coffle, had been a thorn in their sides every step of the way. Some young kidnapping

victims developed feelings of love and trust for their captors—
behavior reminiscent of the symptoms associated with Stockholm
syndrome. Not Joe. A boy with an appetite for argument, his complaints about "the vile durance in which he was bound" had become a part of daily life. Yet it was Sam the Johnsons worried
about most. He seemed furtive, watchful. On the sloop from the
Nanticoke River to Norfolk back in August, they had surely seen
him staring at the crew as they worked, as if trying to figure out
how to control the ship. All the floggings they had given Sam since
were supposed to sap his spirit. Yet they seemed to have had the
opposite effect. Whether the Johnsons knew it or not, Sam had run
away from one master back in New Jersey already. He was on the
lookout for the first opportunity to do it again.[20]

But where to go? If Sam had managed to escape in Delaware,
or even Virginia, he might have been able to make it back to Philadelphia. Every creak and turn of the wagon's wheels since then
made that less likely. Even if he did run away down here in Alabama, which way would he go? What would he do for food? Fish-
ing was one thing, but did he really have the stomach and
wherewithal to bait a deer, trap a raccoon, or skin a rattlesnake for
meat? Could he sleep in undrained swamps during the day and
run safely and swiftly through the woods at night? Could he stay
off the roads and still somehow know where he was going?

If Sam ran, he would never be sure whom to trust or from
whom to seek help, a simple fact on which every slave trader, especially conductors on the Reverse Underground Railroad, relied.
As one British traveler noted a few years later, "In the Southern
Slave-States all men have an interest in protecting this infernal
trade of slave-driving." The prospect of large fines was usually
enough to dissuade riverboat captains from turning a blind eye to
black stowaways who sneaked aboard their vessels. Even poor

whites who did not own slaves knew they could earn cash bounties if they captured likely fugitives and dragged them back to their captors.[21]

Runaways from coffles like Sam's seldom made it far, and the boy surely knew that if he was captured and returned, the Johnsons would not hesitate to make an example of him. "I never flog," a coffle driver informed Charles Ball as he described how he handled repeat runaways. "My practice is to cat-haul." By that he meant dragging the nearest farm cat across the backs of his victims so its claws shredded their skin and tore at their muscle tissue. "If you run away, and I catch you again—as I surely shall do—and give you one cat-hauling, you will never run away again, nor attempt it." Knowing their odds and the likely fate that awaited them if they failed, captives despairing of their chances of ever finding safety so far from home sometimes cut their own throats.[22]

❖

Undaunted by the odds against him, Sam made the decision to run—and then he ran. No one recorded exactly when he fled or how he got away, but a later account makes clear that he made his move as the convoy shambled through the Choctaw territory, a massive tract of oak, chestnut, and hickory forest that straddled western Alabama and eastern Mississippi. He had seen a growing number of Native faces along the road since leaving Ashville. Some of them belonged to the owners of the ferries and toll bridges. A great many more belonged to the staff of the roadside stores at which the Johnsons paused every few days to buy fresh supplies.[23]

Sam could see plainly enough that passing through Indian country made the Johnsons uneasy. White travelers typically hurried through western Alabama and eastern Mississippi as quickly as they could for fear that Native horse thieves might strike or that the highwaymen widely believed to take refuge among the southern Indians would leap out to rob them. These sorts of hijacks were actually very rare by the 1820s, but the sense of being in hostile territory lingered. Sam surely reckoned that by making his break for it here, the Johnsons might think twice before coming after him.[24]

Sam was one of hundreds, if not thousands, of coffled people to make this sort of frantic calculation in the decades after the American Revolution. Sometimes their gambles paid off. Over the years, many fugitives—including Josiah Henson, the inspiration for the title character in Harriet Beecher Stowe's *Uncle Tom's Cabin* (1852)—had received timely, invaluable aid from southern Indians. Cherokees, Chickasaws, Creeks, and Seminoles, along with many members of the Choctaw nation toward which Sam now fled, had all taken in black runaways from time to time, feeding and sheltering them, hiding them in caves, ferrying them across wide rivers, giving them directions, or providing them escorts and onward transportation.[25]

Yet by the 1820s, that sort of help was getting harder to find. Fugitives now often found that they had overestimated the warmth of the welcome they would receive in Indian country. In the Choctaw territory the reason for that shift was political. Despite demonstrating loyalty to the United States during the War of 1812, the eighteen thousand members of the Choctaw nation spent most of the 1810s and 1820s under siege, the targets of ever more frequent encroachments onto their hunting grounds by American farmers who built houses, cleared land, and then declared ownership rights as squatters.[26]

After an 1820 land treaty failed to stem these invasions, the Choctaws had turned to appeasement, embracing a program of reforms designed to show their white neighbors that peaceful coexistence was possible and that removing them from this land by force would be unnecessary. To do so, the Choctaws had welcomed Christian missionaries into their towns to teach them English, spelling, and arithmetic, as well as the Gospel. The Choctaws also reorganized their tribal government to rein in the power of unpredictable local chiefs and abandoned hunting in favor of cash-crop agriculture. The wealthiest of these Natives had even purchased several hundred black slaves from passing traders to pick cotton for them on these plantations, a miserable yet unmistakable attempt to demonstrate to regional state governments that tribal lands were already under profitable management.[27]

Sam knew none of this. He was equally oblivious to the fact that several Choctaws now made their way in the world as slave catchers and bounty hunters. This sort of work burnished Natives' credentials as good neighbors to white farmers, and it paid well too. Seasoned slaves on nearby plantations had gotten wind of this, and by 1825, they generally knew better than to route their own escapes through the Choctaw territory. Sam, of course, did not. Like the three other boys he left behind as he fled the Johnsons, Sam was illiterate. He could not have read the large signs that they had passed every mile or two for the last few days. "Take Notice," those signs warned. Be advised that members of the Choctaw nation would arrest and return any "runaway negroes effect[ing] their escape through the Indian countries."[28]

Later newspaper accounts say that Sam "attempted to escape while in the Choctaw nation, but was caught by an Indian." Exactly what happened in those woods is anybody's guess, though it seems he did not make it very far. Most likely, a Choctaw man heard him crashing through thickets somewhere in the forest and bolted out to grab him as Sam approached. (This is precisely what happened to John Marrant, another fifteen-year-old black fugitive, when he tried to make his own escape through the nearby Cherokee territory.) The man who seized Sam then marched the boy out to the road and back toward the Johnsons to try to collect a reward. The going rate for the safe return of a runaway was about fifty dollars, money that Ebenezer now forked over readily, using some of the cash that James Paul had given him in Tuscaloosa.[29]

As soon as the Choctaw man had gone, Ebenezer Johnson flew at Sam. He stripped him to the waist and tied him to the side of the wagon, tight enough that Sam could not move. Using the broad side of a carpenter's saw that he had brought from Norfolk and his familiar hickory-switch whip, he then flogged the boy as hard as he could. Over and over again Johnson battered Sam with his metal paddle and his homemade lash, first raising welts, then blister upon blister on the boy's upper body and the side of his head. By the time Johnson's arm fell to his side, Sam was screaming in agony, his back scarlet. If Sam's wounds ever healed, the scars they left would be with him as long as he lived.[30]

❖

On they walked, driven like a parcel of hogs. Natchez now lay just two or three weeks ahead of them, and the Johnsons still hoped to sell all their remaining captives—even poor Sam—on the road between here and there. That road was the Natchez Trace, a 450-mile trail through the dark, heavy forests of western Alabama and central Mississippi. The Trace had been a bustling thoroughfare for military, settler, and slave-trading traffic in the 1810s. It was now a bit of a backwater, rendered largely obsolete when Andrew Jackson's Military Road opened in 1820. By mid-December 1825, the Trace's deeply rutted, tree-canopied route was overgrown and difficult to pass in many places.[31]

Since leaving Ashville three weeks earlier, the two captive women and the four captive boys had begun to feel the cold. Joe, the slight-framed chimney sweep, struggled particularly hard to stay warm. Several times he complained to Sally Johnson or to her husband that his bare feet were half-frozen and that he could not feel his fingers. On days when the conditions on the Trace made it impossible to stash him in the wagon, Joe would soon fall behind. He fell frequently, his lame limbs and frostbitten toes making it hard for him to keep up. Ebenezer Johnson thought Joe was malingering, trying to slow up the coffle and delay their inevitable division and sale. He was also still fuming about Sam's recent escape. So each time he caught Joe lagging, Johnson beat him cruelly, though each blow only left the boy weaker still.[32]

On December 21, 1825, three weeks after they had left Ashville, something snapped in Johnson, and he lashed out at Joe more savagely than ever before. Joe had a habit of getting smart and talking back, but exactly what he had done that day to bring down Johnson's wrath went unrecorded. Both Sam and Enos witnessed what happened next. Johnson grabbed the wan, weak-looking youth and "severely flogged [him] with a cart whip," delivering an "inhuman beating." He then "knocked him down with the but[t] end of his wagon whip, stamped him and coshed his head against the wagon tire." Johnson then heaved the boy into the wagon as if he were a broken marionette. Joe had lost consciousness, so Ebenezer told his wife to climb in too and to let him know when Joe woke up. He never did. Two hours later, with Sally Johnson still looming over him, Joe died of his injuries, the blow to his head against one of the cart's massive iron wheels the most likely cause of his death.[33]

Images of the physical cruelty inflicted by coffle drivers on the men, women, and children they trafficked southward became staples of the antislavery campaign in the 1830s. George Bourne, Picture of Slavery in the United States *(Middletown, CT, 1835). (Courtesy of the American Antiquarian Society.)*

Ebenezer Johnson had not meant to kill the boy. The murder of unruly property by slave dealers out on the trail was almost unheard of. Youths Joe's age could fetch a good price in the Cotton Kingdom, and Johnson would not have brought him this far if he had not meant to sell him for several hundred dollars. Joe's death upset those plans. Now, Johnson had a "mangled" body to bury and five extremely distressed and restless prisoners to manage. The sooner he was rid of all of them the better.[34]

Johnson led his wife and what had now become a bona fide
funeral procession a few miles farther down the Trace toward the
next town, Rocky Springs, Mississippi. It was another of the hundreds of settler communities that had sprung up across the Deep
South since the end of the last century. The town sat eighteen miles
shy of Port Gibson, the capital of Claiborne County and the site of
the nearest courthouse and jail, which in turn sat another forty-five
miles short of Natchez, the hub of the region's cotton market. Apart
from the springs themselves, which had once been a watering hole
for Choctaw and Chickasaw horses, Rocky Springs was little more
than a way station. Really, it was just a few log cabins and a brightly
painted tavern, dubbed the Red House by unimaginative visitors.[35]

The town's true center was its periphery. Rocky Springs was
ringed by a necklace of new cotton plantations owned and occupied by transplants from points north. Word had gotten around

*Basil Hall etched this view of a southern village similar in size and stature to
Rocky Springs, Mississippi. Basil Hall, "Embryo Town of Columbus [GA] on
the Chatahootchie," in* Forty Etchings from Sketches made with the Camera
Lucida in North America *(London, 1829). (Courtesy of the Library Company
of Philadelphia.)*

that the rich, sandy soil of west-central Mississippi, and of this part of Claiborne County in particular, was perfect for cotton, and settlers soon showed up. Despite relentlessly hilly and thickly forested terrain, by December 1825 Claiborne was the fourth most populous county in this new frontier state. A great many of the residents were black and enslaved, most of them supplied by the several legal slave traders who stopped at these fledgling labor camps on their way through to Natchez.[36]

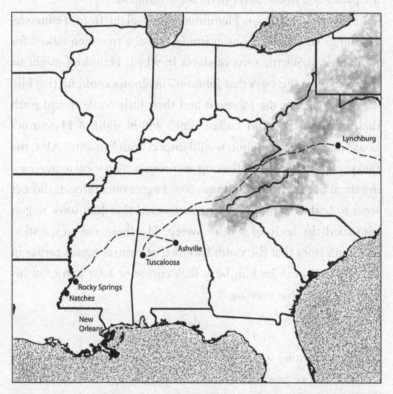

After six weeks in Ashville, where Ebenezer Johnson owned a small log house, he and his wife, Sally, drove their depleted coffle onward, resuming their southern and westward route, passing through the Choctaw territory and then reaching Rocky Springs, Mississippi, in late December 1825. Digital cartography by Caitlin Burke. (Courtesy of the GIS and Geospatial Services Center, University of Maryland.)

Wobbling its way along the Natchez Trace, the Johnsons' wagon and its walking wounded came to one of these new plantations before ever reaching Rocky Springs itself. Evidently a start-up operation with lots of land still to clear and plant, the place smelled to Ebenezer Johnson like the sort of spot where he could make a sale or two—or perhaps even off-load everyone. Leaving Joe's battered body in the back of the cart, and giving custody of everyone else to his wife, Johnson strutted off in the direction of the plantation house to try to do some business.[37]

His mark was John Hamilton, a transplant from Tennessee. Hamilton welcomed Johnson inside, and the two men talked for some time about the sorts of slaves in which Hamilton might be interested and the ways that Johnson's inventory could fill that bill. They agreed that the Johnsons and their little coffle would pitch their camp at the "Old Indian Line" within sight of Hamilton's house that night. Hamilton would inspect both Enos and Alex, the two youngest boys, the following morning, with a view to purchasing them both if he and Johnson could agree on a price. It did not seem to bother Hamilton when he learned that Johnson's wagon contained the body of a dead sweep. He chose not to question Johnson's story that the youth had died of natural causes earlier in the day, and even let him bury Joe's corpse in a far corner of his property later that evening.[38]

✢

The next morning was clear and cold—just thirty-three degrees in the hour before dawn. Still, it must have been a fevered night. The five black people camped out on the edge of this plantation owner's estate surely understood that a sale was in the offing. It is difficult to believe that any of them slept.[39]

The Johnsons rose early. They had planned to spend the breakfast hour smartening up both women and each of the three children in hopes that Hamilton would buy them all. But Sam was gone. He had vanished. If he had told Enos or Alex or either of the Marys where he was going, the Johnsons could not get it out of them. Had he run back the way they had come, back in the direction of Indian country to try his luck again? Or had he pressed on ahead, in the direction of Natchez and the mighty Mississippi River, in hopes of finding the captain of a flatboat or steamship who would listen to him and liberate them all?[40]

As it turned out, he had not gone nearly so far. Sometime before ten that morning, John Hamilton found the gaunt-eyed child hiding "somewhere on the premises." Sam was scared stiff, and "the poor creature manifested . . . extreme unwillingness to return to Mr. Johnston [*sic*]." Hamilton pressed Sam to explain himself. Now the whole story spilled out of him—that "he and the other boys were stolen from Philadelphia in the latter part of the summer," and that Enos and Alex and Mary Fisher were each legally free, despite the bogus bills of sale the Johnsons carried around that said otherwise.[41]

Sam told Hamilton that Ebenezer Johnson was a monster, that he had whipped him so often that he was "scarcely able to walk." Then he lifted his shirt to show this stranger his scars. He told him too that the boy they had buried twelve hours earlier had not died of natural causes but had been "cut to pieces" by Johnson's lash.[42]

Rushing his words, his heart beating against his chest like a bird against a door, Sam threw himself on this slave owner's mercy and "begged of Mr. Hamilton to protect him."[43]

Chapter 7

THE HALFWAY HOUSE

J OHN HAMILTON STARED at Sam's wounds and listened to his story. Then he called Ebenezer Johnson to his house to get to the bottom of it. Face to face, the two men argued—loudly and for a long time. Johnson said Sam and the four other captives were his to sell as he pleased. He waved around several forged bills of sale by way of evidence, and claimed to have "been deceived if the blacks were free." But Hamilton was unconvinced by Johnson's "inconsistent and incredible conversations"—and said so. Rattled, Johnson changed tack, and instead tried to sell everyone to Hamilton at a knock-down price, no more questions asked. All the while, Sam kept badgering Hamilton, pleading with him to do the right thing: not to buy him, but to liberate him and the others then and there.[1]

As far as Sam could see, Hamilton proceeded to do just that. He sent a runner to some neighbors' houses, who came back with William Miner and Jack Gee, two justices of the peace. By then, Hamilton had shooed Sam, Enos, Alex, and Mary Fisher into another room of his large, wood-framed house, separating them from the Johnsons and Mary Neal, who "acknowledge[d] herself a slave" and "believe[d] she was fairly purchased." When the two justices of the peace arrived, Hamilton told them that he was taking temporary custody of Mary Fisher and the three boys. It was for their own good, he said, because, as best as he could tell, "Johnson had not come fairly by the negroes."[2]

Hamilton asked the two lawmen to draw up a contract to legalize this confiscation. He then browbeat Johnson to sign it, promising him that if he could ever prove he had bought Sam and the others fair and square, he could have them back with apologies. Johnson hedged, still hoping to talk his way out of the hole that Sam had dug for him. Hamilton grew angry, threatening Johnson that "if he did not do it," the two justices of the peace would charge him with murdering Joe, the boy whose body lay in a shallow grave nearby, and arrest him on the spot.[3]

This was bluster, of course. Black testimony was usually inadmissible in Mississippi's courts, and Sally Johnson was the only white witness to have seen her husband batter Joe to death. Ebenezer Johnson, who "perhaps did not know the law," took the bait anyway. He grew "very much alarmed" by Hamilton's talk of murder charges and finally signed the transfer agreement. Johnson left the house spitting and cursing, vowing to sue Hamilton for coercion and theft, and promising to return to reclaim his property and clear his good name.[4]

The last that Sam, Enos, Alex, and Mary Fisher saw of the Johnsons, Ebenezer and Sally were heading north, back the way they had come, dragging poor Mary Neal with them. They stopped the next morning in Vicksburg, on the banks of the Mississippi River, to sell their wagon and horses and to hire Robert Garland, a lawyer, to file their suit. They paid Garland's fees in advance and authorized him to act as their agent in their absence. Then the Johnsons hauled Mary Neal on board a southbound packet boat that delivered them to New Orleans a day later. There, they likely sold Mary Neal to the first buyer they could find. When they left New Orleans just after Christmas, aboard a ship bound for New York, she was not with them.[5]

❖

The Reverse Underground Railroad was not supposed to work like this. Victims of kidnapping and human trafficking were supposed to be seen and not heard, brutalized into silence by the time they came up for sale. Over the past four months on the road, Ebenezer Johnson had delivered that message time and again. He had made it crystal clear that telling tales would bring down his wrath. He had reached for his hickory whip dozens of times and battered a boy to death for nothing more than idling.

By speaking up, Sam had taken his life in his hands, but he was still far from safe. His decision to confide in a slave-owning stranger like John Hamilton was as dangerous as it was desperate. Back in October, Sam had witnessed James Paul buy Cornelius Sinclair and had observed the man's obvious indifference to the boy's true legal status. Sam had no cause to think that any other slave-hungry planter would respond any differently. On the contrary, abductees brave or naive enough to plead their cases to prospective slave buyers usually regretted it straightaway. When Jane Loguen, a woman abducted from Ohio around this time, told her story to a pair of purchasers, one grabbed a whip and lashed her till she promised that "she would never again repeat the offensive fact of her freedom." Then her new owners paid off Jane's traffickers and entered her name as "Cherry" on the bill of sale to disguise what they had done.[6]

So what possessed John Hamilton to respond so differently? Confronting an armed stranger who arrived with the mangled body of a dead boy in the back of his wagon was a reckless, surprising thing to do. In a similar situation, another slave dealer had drawn pistols upon a "gentleman of respectable character" who had dared to question the origins of the coffle slaves in his care. Yet Hamilton had good reason to interfere. He was deeply in debt, his plantation was in trouble, and his only hope of making money at the next harvest lay in clearing as much land and planting as much cotton as possible in the new year. Hamilton was also a gambler and knew an opportunity when he saw it. Four new cotton pickers could make him an extra $800 to $1,000 a year. The promise of temporarily growing his workforce and his income under the guise of Christian benevolence surely preoccupied him as he drew up the contract to take custody of Mary Fisher and the three surviving boys.[7]

In the end, it took Hamilton a full nine days after the Johnsons left to acknowledge the monstrosity of his fantasy, reluctantly concluding that it would be impossible to keep the true origins of four new plantation slaves secret from his fellow Rocky Springs residents. Two justices of the peace had heard Sam and the others declare that they were victims of kidnapping, after all. It would be only a matter of time before that news got around. The last thing he needed was a neighbor accusing him of some form of slave stealing or of augmenting his own black labor force by underhanded means.[8]

By New Year's Day 1826, Hamilton was leaning toward sending Sam and the others home. This too was a gamble, a wager that his neighbors would not tag him as a secret abolitionist in league with northern radicals if he sent Mary Fisher and the boys back to Pennsylvania and Delaware. Hamilton hoped doing so might actually raise his stock locally. He told himself that if he played his cards right, his fellow planters might even applaud him as a "bold and manly" champion of liberty, a gentleman of conscience who had "nobly stepped forward in staying the hand of the oppressor, even before he had positive proof of their guilt."[9]

That afternoon, January 1, John Hamilton rode out in search of a local lawyer named John Henderson. Hamilton told him what had happened and asked for his help. Henderson knew the law and his advice was clear and sobering. It would be criminal, the lawyer said, to detain these four free people a moment longer than strictly necessary. They should be sent home right away. The pair then rode back to Hamilton's estate, where Henderson set about interviewing each of the former captives at length. They all "asserted the fact of their having been kidnapped" and tormented by the Johnsons, each telling the lawyer "a simple and unaffected story of their wrongs." Sam, Enos, and Alex also hiked up their shirts to show him that "the truth of what they said" was still indelibly inscribed upon their bodies, in wounds "not yet completely cicatrised."[10]

The next morning, John Henderson wrote a 1,300-word memo describing all that he had seen and heard at John Hamilton's house. He addressed it to the mayor of Philadelphia, among whose official records it still resides. Henderson did not know much about the man to whom he was writing and apologized that "not having an opertunity to learn your name, I am compeled to address you by your title." He began by describing how Sam, Enos, Alex, and Mary Fisher had been kidnapped in Philadelphia and Delaware and trafficked halfway across the country. He then relayed deliberately meticulous physical descriptions of each of them, noting heights, builds, and ages. He copied down their oral histories too, rendering precise cross-street addresses for each of the places they said they had lived and worked and transcribing the names of their family members with lawyerly care. Henderson did the same for Joe, the dead sweep buried on Hamilton's property, and for Cornelius, the ten-year-old child whom Johnson had sold to James Paul back in Tuscaloosa.[11]

Exhibiting a concern for black people that, on the face of it, seems highly unusual for a white southerner in this period, John Henderson then told the mayor of Philadelphia what to do with this cache of information. "With the aid of the Officers under your control and the benevolent Individuals of your City I trust you will be able to find the parents and masters of these children." The first objective, the southern lawyer told the northern mayor, should be to verify their stories, and then dispatch some "proper authority" to Mississippi to claim these four souls and return them to the bosom of their families. The second objective should be to get news of the Johnsons' activities into the pages of local newspapers as quickly as possible, so "that the coloured people of your City and other places may be guarded against similar outrages." The mayor's third objective, Henderson insisted, should be to hunt down any of the gang members still lurking in or around Philadelphia "and have them arrested."[12]

On the afternoon of January 2, 1826, Henderson rode his letter to the post office in Port Gibson, some fifteen miles away. More than ten weeks would pass before he received a reply.

❖

In the meantime, this lawyer called in a doctor. Ebenezer Johnson's hickories and handsaw had left the boys' backs, necks, and heads covered with welts and scars. The soles of their feet were torn up from trudging so many miles without shoes. Frostbite mangled their toes. So John Henderson paid for someone to come evaluate them, most likely one of the dozen or so specialists down in Natchez with surgical experience.[13]

Gestures like this helped Henderson quickly gain the trust of

Mary Fisher and the three boys. When he had taken down their testimonies, they had discovered that he had been born in southern New Jersey like Sam, and that he knew Philadelphia almost as well as Enos and Alex did. And he was obviously sympathetic. As a youth, Henderson had worked as a flatboat man on the Mississippi River and so had seen firsthand the ravages of the legal slave trade upon black families. Now those boyhood memories came flooding back.[14]

Henderson also knew from personal experience what it was like to be ripped away from loved ones. His wife had died in childbirth in 1822. Soon after, Henderson had come to Mississippi with his infant son, John Jr., to try to outrun his grief and start over. Trained as a lawyer, the young widower set up a legal practice in a village outside Natchez. There he married Louisa Post, a widow whose daughter he agreed to adopt. Their blended, bandaged family then moved to Rocky Springs in 1824, giving Henderson access to many litigious new clients. He handled his share of wills and probates, but he soon began to specialize in real estate disputes, a lucrative line of work given the ongoing land rush. A man of ramrod bearing, with a strong aquiline nose, a high forehead, and a bouffant brush of black hair, Henderson earned the reputation of having a quick and sharp legal mind. Throughout his career at law, his clients and colleagues praised his doggedness, his integrity, and the unexpected depth of his tenderness toward those he saw suffering.[15]

Still, no one in Rocky Springs ever mistook John Henderson for an antislavery activist. He did not own any enslaved people himself—at least not yet. Even so, his livelihood depended on representing men who measured their wealth and status not only in acres and bales but also in hands, bodies, and wombs. He was not yet thirty years old at the time his slave-owning neighbor John Hamilton called on him for help. By then, Henderson had emerged as

Before entering politics and rising to the rank of US senator, John Henderson was a Mississippi lawyer specializing in family and real estate law. Henderson posed for the silhouette at left in Washington, DC, on February 17, 1841. (Left: Courtesy of the US Senate Historical Office, Washington, DC. Right: Courtesy of the National Portrait Gallery, Washington, DC.)

one of the most respected lawyers and civic leaders in this new slave-dependent society. He was among the organizers of the Fourth of July celebrations in Rocky Springs that year and had begun lining up local support to launch a political career.[16]

John Hamilton envied John Henderson's position as a pillar of the local community. Hamilton was eager to earn respect and status in Rocky Springs, but in 1825 he had more debts than friends. He had arrived in Natchez from Tennessee on the eve of the War of 1812, dragging a young family and half a dozen slaves with him. He had come to try his luck at planting, a livelihood widely regarded as "far and away the most prestigious occupation in the South." Every aspiring planter needed between $25,000 and $50,000 to get on his feet, so

Hamilton had likely cashed out any inheritance, liquidated any capital his wife had brought into their marriage, and loaded up on loans from banks back home in Tennessee in order to make this move.[17]

But John Hamilton's path to prosperity and gentility as a Mississippi cotton planter proved rocky, and by 1825 he had already stumbled repeatedly. He lost some money by lending it to strangers he met in Natchez who did not pay him back. Then, when he moved his family to Amite County, just south of that city, sometime before 1820, the land on which they tried to settle almost got the better of them. The Hamiltons, their several children, and their half-dozen slaves slept those first few months in dank, dirty, and dim tents that crawled with spiders and insects. Tasked with preparing food over an open fire, grinding corn into meal by hand, and making clothes from homespun fiber, his wife and three young daughters surely found the conditions particularly primitive and depressing. Other disappointments quickly piled on. The Mississippi sun broiled them in summer, and Amite County's contaminated water soon made them sick.[18]

After mosquitoes carrying yellow fever bit Hamilton and his son in July 1822, they both fell seriously ill, confined to bed by headaches, back pain, jaundice, nausea, chills, and high fevers. Known then as the "stranger's disease" because of the deadly toll it took upon newcomers to the Gulf South, yellow fever attacks the kidneys, causing renal failure, delirium, and convulsions, and often sends its victims into comas. The Hamilton men got so sick they had to stay with a friend in Adams County, a rural retreat far from the pestilence in Amite and Natchez. They hired Samuel Monett, an expensive Natchez doctor, to treat them, but there was little he could do beyond keeping them hydrated, comfortable, and cool.[19]

It was not enough. John Hamilton eventually recovered, acquiring lifelong immunity by virtue of surviving, but his son died, leaving behind a distended corpse "swollen and stained with blood and black vomit." Then, as Hamilton convalesced, Monett's medical bill arrived, demanding more than $100 ($2,200 today) for the care he had given and as compensation for the risk of infection to which he had been exposed. The bill put extra pressure on the family's already strained finances, and Hamilton quickly fell behind on his payments. In November 1822, Dr. Monett dragged him into court to settle that debt. Another suit for unpaid bills followed fifteen months later, this time from creditors in Tennessee who said he owed them more than $1,000.[20]

Unwilling to place what remained of his family in the path of another yellow fever outbreak in Amite County, Hamilton moved farther away from Natchez. This time he took more care to look for fertile, lightly settled land that was not only close to river transport but also far enough away from the places most prone to fevers or sickness. In October 1824, just over a year before he met Ebenezer and Sally Johnson, John Hamilton purchased 404 acres of former Choctaw land, just east of Rocky Springs. He also bought cattle and plows and several more enslaved laborers, most likely using the long-hoped-for promise of future cotton profits as collateral to secure these several new mortgages.[21]

If Hamilton imagined that great wealth was just around the corner, he was to be disappointed. It usually took three years before the first substantial harvests came in and a new plantation finally began to make money. In the meantime, John Hamilton's debts mounted. When he took custody of Sam, Enos, Alex, and Mary Fisher in December 1825, Hamilton had owned his new plot for less than eighteen months. In that time, his small crew of slaves had built him "a large Frame Dwelling-House" that visitors said had the look of a tavern, though they had managed to clear only the first few acres of land for cotton.[22]

No wonder, then, that the man upon whom Mary Fisher and

these three children now depended seemed so stressed and insecure. Thoroughly preoccupied by a recent slump in the price of
cotton, Hamilton was still weak from yellow fever and grieving
the loss of his son. He worried a great deal about money and about
his status and reputation in the Rocky Springs community. To that
end, he had recently taken to insisting that neighbors call him
"Colonel," an honorific usually reserved for veterans of the War of
1812—a conflict in which Hamilton seems not to have served.[23]

❖

Concerned about his mounting debts, John Hamilton could not afford to house, clothe, and feed Sam, Enos, Alex, and Mary Fisher for
more than a few days without getting something in return. So while
he and Henderson waited for a reply from the mayor of Philadelphia, he put his four new charges to work alongside his slaves. Mary
Fisher probably took on cooking and washing responsibilities. Using
a large open fireplace inside one of the low-slung wooden huts, she
would have heated water, scrubbed clothes, and made meals. Her
labor would have helped to provide for herself and the three boys, as
well as the plantations' small enslaved workforce.[24]

Hamilton likely tasked Sam, Enos, and Alex with clearing and
leveling the ground to ready enough of it to sow a cotton crop. This
was hard, manual work that would have involved chopping trees, rolling logs, digging up stumps, grubbing out roots, and burning under-
brush debris. These were all jobs the boys had never done before and
that usually went to enslaved men who were stronger and a decade or
so older. Hamilton might also have set them to construction work,
raising more cabins and outbuildings, digging wells, and putting up
fences. Sam, Enos, Alex, and Mary Fisher would have been laboring
like this for almost two months by the time Ebenezer Johnson's law-
suit against John Hamilton finally got a hearing.[25]

On February 3, 1826, Robert Garland, the Vicksburg lawyer hired by Ebenezer and Sally Johnson, filed a writ in the Claiborne County court. Ten days later, on February 13, John Hamilton took his four black dependents by carriage to Port Gibson to answer the Johnsons' accusations that he had stolen their slaves. Garland told the assembled three-judge panel that Hamilton had hoodwinked his clients, detaining their legally purchased property "by force, fraud and stratagem . . . without any process of law, and without even the color of claim or right." But he could not produce the disputed bills of sale and seemed shaky as to the details of the case, as if the Johnsons had briefed him too hastily. He referred to Mary Fisher throughout as "Sarah."[26]

To rebut Garland's accusations, Hamilton had hired John Maury, a Port Gibson lawyer. Maury put into evidence the contract that Ebenezer Johnson had signed. Then he put his client, John Hamilton, on the stand, who swore under oath that he had acted in good faith. Next, the clerk read affidavits sworn by William Miner and Jack Gee, the two justices of the peace. They both acknowledged the coercive tactics Hamilton had used to make Johnson sign the paperwork, but confirmed his basic version of events.[27]

The next day was Valentine's Day. Having spent the night at Port Gibson's only inn, John Hamilton, Mary Fisher, and the three boys returned to the log-built courtroom at ten in the morning. A few minutes later, the presiding judge, Peter Van Dorn, dismissed the Johnsons' suit and cast serious doubt on their claims to have purchased the four of them legally. Van Dorn ruled that the contract Hamilton and Ebenezer Johnson had signed in December remained binding, and that "the property of negroes heretofore referred to must remain in the possession of the defendant."[28]

After the excitement of that trip to the courthouse, the workday routines that Sam, Enos, Alex, and Mary Fisher resumed back on Hamilton's plantation must have seemed particularly dull and repetitive. Still, in the months following their return from Port Gibson, the four of them tried to make the best of their lives in limbo. They tried to recover their strength, resting when possible and eating as much as they could. No longer bound to silence, they spoke openly about their past lives to one another and to their new friend John Henderson, who had written to the mayor of Philadelphia back in January, instructing him to make direct contact with John Hamilton, in whose custody they were now kept. In the meantime, they searched their memories for the names and addresses of white Philadelphians who could vouch for them, information they would share with the city's mayor if, indeed, he ever wrote back.

Eager for news, they badgered John Hamilton as much as they dared. They flattered him for his selflessness and fawned over him as their savior, all in hopes of getting him to ride out to the post office as often as possible to check for mail from out of state. There was, however, only so much they could do. They were dependent on this slave-owning stranger for everything, and found it hard to take the measure of the man in whose hands their fates now rested. They could never be sure if Hamilton was their protector or if they were his prisoners. All they could do was wait and see. That must have been excruciating. As with refugees stranded in modern transit camps, their distress was compounded by the daily dislocation, alienation, and uncertainty of life under Hamilton's care. Sam, Enos, Alex, and Mary Fisher were not his slaves, though neither were they free to leave.[29]

❖

John Henderson's letter to the mayor of Philadelphia—Joseph Watson, a forty-one-year-old Quaker—had arrived on January 30. Watson received dozens of letters at his first-floor office at city hall every day, usually from job seekers or constituents with complaints. This one, though, was not like the others. The Mississippi return address was unfamiliar and unusual, and Watson slit open Henderson's letter without quite knowing what to expect inside. What he read unsettled him, and he replied the same day—a rare thing then as now. In that short, scribbled note, Watson promised to use every means at his disposal to establish whether Sam, Enos, Alex, and Mary Fisher were telling the truth. If their claims held up, he pledged to do whatever it might take to rescue them and hunt down their kidnappers.[30]

Watson wasted no time turning his office into a detective agency. The mayor ordered his subordinates to set aside their other duties and sent out a squad of justices of the peace to conduct interviews and gather evidence. Their first task was to find the families and former employers of the four city boys Henderson had described and to determine if a woman named Mary Fisher had disappeared from Delaware the previous summer. In early February, his magistrates went to work, locating the "parents, relatives, and friends" of Cornelius, Enos, and Alex, as well as poor Joe— and then knocking on their doors.[31]

What must those visits have been like? Since last August, these boys' parents had lived in their own private purgatory, not knowing whether their sons were alive or dead. They had come home from their day's labors one evening five months previously to find their children gone without a trace. If their reactions bore any resemblance to those of Stephen Dredden and his wife, who lost two children to kidnappers in Philadelphia in 1817, the "sorrow and anguish of soul" they felt that first day would have been indescribable. The Dreddens had wailed so loudly and uncontrollably that even their white neighbors had come running, only to "burst forth" into tears themselves when they learned what had happened. "They were parents and had children," Stephen Dredden later wrote. "They saw that we, though black, were parents too, and felt as such."[32]

Sam's parents remained term slaves in West Jersey. They missed their son, but were wholly unaware that he had been kidnapped soon after he had fled his new master's farm in Amwell. For the Philadelphia families of the other boys—the Sinclairs, the Tilghmans, the Johnsons (Joe's parents), and Amy Douglass and John Raymon (Alex's mother and stepfather)—it was a different story. They had searched everywhere that first August evening, racing to each child's work site and favorite afternoon haunts. They interviewed their children's friends, interrogated their employers, and likely even waylaid strangers to see if anyone had heard something or seen anything. There was a fierce, frantic urgency to their efforts, because black parents knew all too well what it could mean when a child did not come home. For a day or two, they could cling to rumors that their son had simply run away to Baltimore or New York and would send word when he got there. However, as news spread that five boys had vanished on the same day, and that not all of them knew one another, it became harder to deny the truth of what had really befallen them.[33]

Since that terrible evening, 180 days and nights had passed. Parents, siblings, and friends had searched in vain. The missing-persons notice the Sinclairs had paid for had turned up nothing. The families had reported the missing children to local constables, but their attempts to lobby law enforcement to investigate that August had been fruitless. With no firm leads as to who had done this or where the boys were, the constables had blocked these black families from securing an audience with the mayor. At the time, Watson himself had been only dimly aware of what had happened. "A whisper of the kidnapping was circulated at the time it took place, when the boys suddenly disappeared," the mayor later recalled, "but was buried in mystery, and utterly lost sight of until revived by the letter of Mr. Henderson."[34]

Never once did the boys' families lose sight of them, of course.

By the time Watson's deputies knocked on their doors in early February 1826, the burden of accumulated loss must have been almost unbearable. In 1817, Stephen Dredden had confessed that the abduction of his children soon "broke down my spirit with grief" and "pierced it thro' with sorrow." So it was unsurprising, though no less tragic, that when one of Watson's agents tracked down Joe's family, the boy's brother told him that Joe's mother had just died. A widow who had long suffered ill health, she had gone to her grave in "grief for the loss of her son."[35]

Joe's mother's death was the most extreme symptom of the heartache that these parents had grown used to carrying with them. Accounts of other black people whose families were forcibly separated in this period make clear that mothers and fathers often struggled to find the will to get up each day. It was easier to retreat from the world or to pretend that nothing had changed. Describing how a woman named Eliza had caved in on herself after traders snatched her son Randall and her daughter Emily, Solomon Northup recalled that she went on "talking of them—often *to* them, as if they were actually present." Another mother consumed by the same sorrow continued to "make clothes and knit" for her own departed children.[36]

The news these deputies delivered to the families of Joe, Cornelius, Enos, and Alex that first week of February carried with it a weight and burden of its own. After Michael Freytag went to Hester Tilghman's house to tell her that her son Enos was still alive but sequestered somewhere in Mississippi, the woman collapsed and took to her bed. When Freytag's colleague Joshua Raybold visited the house three days later, Mrs. Tilghman was still so distraught and distracted that she could not even tell him what Enos looked like.[37]

Both Freytag and Raybold were under instructions to persist, and after the initial shock, the lost boys' relatives and friends rushed to cooperate with investigators. Sometimes in pairs, sometimes arriving alone, they came to city hall to stand before the mayor in his grand chambers to share what they knew and to see what else they could do. Usually wary of talking to law enforcement, members of Philadelphia's black community poured into the building throughout February. On February 4, for instance, Mayor Watson interviewed John Raymon, Alex's stepfather, and Caleb Carpenter, his former master in the mat-making workshop. A few days later, he heard testimony from Joseph Sinclair, Cornelius's father.[38]

Mayor Watson kept an annotated list of the interviews and depositions he and his officers conducted. This detail from that document briefly summarizes the testimony given to him by Enos Tilghman's mother, Hester. "A List of Documents and Depositions Sent to Rocky Springs, Mississippi," March 13, 1826, item 274, Joseph Watson Papers. (Courtesy of the Historical Society of Pennsylvania.)

Watson chased down all the leads they gave him, and soon began interviewing the few white residents the boys had known. The mayor himself took down the deposition of Caleb Kimber, Alex's former teacher, and James McCann, the official who had administered the child-support payments made to Alex's mother by his father, Solomon Manlove. Watson's deputy also copied out a statement from Joseph Middleton, a white man who knew both Alex and his stepfather. The mayor heard testimony too from Thomas Earle, an attorney who had met Alex at the Philadelphia almshouse, and William Warwick, a city constable who had arrested Enos the previous year "on some trivial charge." After two weeks' work, Watson had heard enough. He was now certain that everything Alex and Enos had told John Henderson back in Rocky Springs in December was the truth.[39]

That still left the claims made by Sam Scomp and Mary Fisher. Those too had to be verified, though neither of them had ties to Philadelphia or its black community. So Watson called in favors from friends and colleagues in New Jersey and Delaware. He quickly saw results. On February 17, David Hill, Sam's former owner, and Hill's father-in-law traveled from Amwell to Trenton to meet with Charles Ewing, the chief justice of the Supreme Court of New Jersey. Both men gave depositions under oath confirming Sam's identity and status as a fugitive from slavery. Watson also reached out to contacts in Kent County, Delaware, and soon received written testimony from two white people who had known Mary Fisher there, and who could still describe her appearance lucidly and at length.[40]

By then, Mayor Watson was busy sifting through tips from the general public. In early February, he had sent a press release to several city and local newspapers asking readers with "knowledge of any of the parties in question" to step forward. Members of the city's abolition group, the Pennsylvania Abolition Society, certainly read the subsequent press coverage, as did James Rogers, the attorney general of Delaware, who wrote to Watson right away to tell him all he knew about Ebenezer Johnson and his brother, Joseph. He told the mayor about the Johnson family's long history in the trafficking business and their talent for evading arrest. He also told Watson where on the Delmarva peninsula the brothers lived and offered to help in any way he could to "bring both these persons, particularly Joseph, to the bar of justice."[41]

Three more letters like this arrived in the mayor's office between February 15 and 20. The first came from two men who were the Johnsons' Nanticoke neighbors. Summoning their courage to inform on the gang, they swore that they had seen some black boys at Joseph Johnson's house back in August, and that Ebenezer had recently "returned home about the 4th of February from New Orleans by the way of New York with his wife." The second letter, this one from James Gaskins, a resident of Maryland's Eastern Shore, said much the same. Gaskins informed Watson that Ebenezer and Sally Johnson had "passed through this place" ten days earlier following a visit to Mississippi. The third, written by a resident of Sussex County, Delaware, also confirmed that Ebenezer Johnson lived locally and "has lately Returned." Fearing both brothers' wrath, the author of this last letter asked that his name be kept out of the papers.[42]

Chapter 8

THE LIFEBOAT

O N FEBRUARY 17, 1826, Joseph Watson filed criminal charges of kidnapping and conspiracy to kidnap in the Philadelphia courts. Armed with the trove of evidence he had collected, the mayor signed warrants for the arrest of Ebenezer and Joseph Johnson, as well as for John Purnell, the confidence man who had lured the children away, and Thomas Collins, the sailor on the *Little John* from whom Ebenezer had claimed to have bought Mary Fisher and the five boys. On March 6, the seventeen members of the Philadelphia grand jury assembled to review the cases that Watson had built against each of these men, and quickly handed down "true bills" that endorsed the charges. Next, the mayor wrote to the governor of Pennsylvania, John Schulze, requesting him to initiate interstate rendition proceedings to arrest these four suspects wherever they might be and deliver them to Philadelphia to stand trial.[1]

Interstate rendition requests took time to process. While Watson waited for a response from Harrisburg, he turned his attention to making "some speedy arrangement for the return of these Children to their parents and masters." He was under great pressure from many of the city's black residents to get this done. Watson also had other reasons for haste: he needed the boys back in Phila-delphia so they could testify against "any of the kidnappers that I may hereafter succeed in taking." For them to do that, however, Watson would first have to convince John Hamilton that putting Mary Fisher and the boys on a ship bound for home (and thereby breaking the custodial contract he had made with Ebenezer John-son) would not expose him to any legal jeopardy.[2]

On March 13, Mayor Watson mailed "a mass of depositions and documents" to Rocky Springs. The dossier itself has not sur-vived, but Watson kept a list of its contents. It ran to more than thirty files, including seventeen depositions as well as arrest war-rants, grand jury bills, records of the Johnson brothers' prior in-dictments and convictions in Delaware, copies of some of the boys' apprenticeship indentures, a missing-person's notice, and even a child-support agreement. Not knowing whom else to contact, Mayor Watson also sent a second, smaller packet of depositions documenting Cornelius Sinclair's legal freedom to the editor of Tuscaloosa's only newspaper, and he may also have mailed copies to another Tuscaloosa resident, Constantine Perkins, Alabama's at-torney general.[3]

The package Watson mailed to Mississippi was big and bulky, and the postage cost more than eight dollars—a hefty sum equiva-lent to the wages a laborer might earn in a week. The postal system was not always reliable, and in a cover letter written to both John Hamilton and his lawyer-neighbor John Henderson, Watson wor-ried about whether the packet would reach them intact. "If unfor-tunately lost by mail," he fretted, "the loss of these documents would indeed be serious as well on account of the difficulty of pro-curing other copies, as of the great labour attending it."[4]

✠

Watson was plainly proud of the "great labour" he had already devoted to investigating this case and assembling this doorstop-size dossier, though it is not immediately obvious why all this mattered so much to him. The Reverse Underground Railroad ensnared thousands of free black people in the early nineteenth century, and they went missing from towns and cities across the region all too often. Very few elected white officials ever paid more than lip service to the threat that kidnappers like John Purnell, Joseph Johnson, and Patty Cannon posed to black residents.[5]

Why was Watson any different? Why was he willing to invest so much of his own time, energy, and effort—and a good deal of government resources—to pursue a case that he could have just as easily ignored?

The answers lie in the alchemy among Watson's character, his faith, and the circumstances of his work as mayor. The two hundred or so letters of his that survive are all variations on the theme of earnestness; they conjure a spirit garrulous and friendly but also serious and sensitive. Colleagues and contemporaries confirm that the mayor's defining traits were his "integrity of character and amiable disposition." A half-length portrait of Watson commissioned during his administration captures something of the man's affable sincerity—though by drawing attention to his small mouth and rosy cheeks, the artist also makes the mayor look a little like an overgrown schoolboy dressed up in his father's clothes.[6]

As a public servant, Watson appears to have been driven by a need to be useful. Having made his money as a lumber merchant, he won election to Philadelphia's common council as an alderman in April 1822. After the incumbent mayor resigned due to age and ill health, Watson agreed to run as a caretaker. He assumed that office in April 1824, the year he turned forty, becoming the city's fifty-seventh chief executive.[7]

Joseph Watson served four terms as mayor between 1824 and 1828. This undated oil on wood portrait by an unidentified artist likely depicts Watson during his final one-year term. (Courtesy of the Pennsylvania Academy of the Fine Arts, Philadelphia. Gift of Mrs. John Frederick Lewis [the John Frederick Lewis Memorial Collection].)

As mayor, he buried himself in constituent services. He answered a flood of mail from inmates pleading for pardons and heard near-daily complaints about noisy neighbors, rowdy kids on the corner, and watchmen and constables on his payroll who were far too free with their nightsticks. No wonder that Watson's official portrait, likely completed during his fourth and final year in the job, shows him having grown slump-shouldered by spending too much time at his desk.[8]

Watson seems to have taken particular interest in the dozens of letters he received from city residents duped by gangs of counterfeiters passing forged bills. Raised in Quaker meeting-houses and merchant offices, Watson loathed these con men who made their living bearing false witness. As administrator of the mayor's court, Philadelphia's central criminal tribunal, he launched a crusade to bring them to justice. He collected tips assiduously and was positively gleeful when his high constable was able to confiscate a set of counterfeit engraving plates and a wad of fake banknotes with a street value north of $14,000.[9]

The same loathing for liars and charlatans seems to have stirred his first forays into defending black liberty. In September 1824, when Watson was barely six months into his first term, Isaiah Sadler barreled into his office. Sadler was the seventeen-year-old free black boy who had been kidnapped from the city and carried off to Delaware by Tilly James, one of Joseph Johnson's regular accomplices. Sadler had since escaped and returned, and came to the mayor's office to tell his story. This was the first Watson had heard of Joseph Johnson and the counterfeit kin he paid to lure away street children. The mayor listened to Sadler attentively and took page after page of notes, absorbing the horror of what he was hearing one sentence at a time.[10]

With each passing month in the job, Watson learned more about the elemental dangers black people faced in his city. In the weeks before he received John Henderson's letter from Rocky Springs, he heard testimony from those who had witnessed or survived kidnapping several times. One day, Watson interviewed a captain whose ship was boarded by men who carried away a black sailor they claimed was a runaway slave. A few hours later he listened as a free black woman told him how two men grabbed her son, a physician's apprentice with a pronounced stammer, and dragged him off to Delaware, alleging that he too was a runaway.[11]

Watson's growing awareness of racial injustice was plainly

the result of all that he was exposed to as Philadelphia's chief magistrate. Beyond that, the mayor was also the product of a Quaker upbringing, a faith that rested on a commitment to non-violence and an enduring belief that the light of God shone in every human heart. Kidnapping and enslaving free people of color was anathema to that Quaker credo, and while Watson seems to have drifted away from weekly worship after his marriage, the Society of Friends formed his political base and his social network throughout his public life, coloring his convictions and inflecting his agenda.[12]

Still, his racial sensitivity had obvious limits. While he counted among his friends the outspoken Quaker abolitionist Enoch Lewis, Watson's name does not appear on any surviving list of members of the Pennsylvania Abolition Society, the most visible marker of antislavery activity in the city at this time. Watson's own charitable efforts were focused not upon antislavery work but instead upon the particular struggles of children, both white and black. This work evidently meant a great deal to him personally, and might even have been a subconscious response to his and his wife Sarah's childlessness.[13]

Soon after winning election as mayor, Watson had joined with some Quaker friends to establish an "Asylum for Lost Children" in an alley behind his office. Conceived as a meeting point for city kids who had lost their bearings and the parents who had set out to look for them, the asylum employed a full-time matron and a superintendent, and was covered with garish signage announcing its presence and purpose. It quickly became the scene of dozens of tearful reunions, some of which Watson witnessed personally. In its first full-year report, published early in 1826 as Sam, Enos, and Alex languished in Rocky Springs, Watson and the asylum's other directors congratulated themselves for having "removed the anguish of many distressed parents, by restoring to their families during the past year about one hundred lost children."[14]

Clearly, Watson's concern for lost children and his empathy for their distressed parents preceded John Henderson's letter. Because of his time on the asylum's board and as mayor of this treacherous metropolis, Watson was used to imagining the anguish of children and parents divided by distance, and he knew from experience how it felt to be moved enough to act. So when that unexpected envelope from Rocky Springs arrived on his desk at the end of January 1826, he did just that.

Soon there was no turning back. Once the lost boys' parents and relatives learned that their children were alive and well in Alabama and Mississippi, they began "continually inquiring after them," putting Mayor Watson under extraordinary and escalating pressure. Joseph Sinclair, Hester Tilghman, Amy Douglass, and their spouses set aside their bone-deep suspicions of white officials, especially those with the power to arrest or imprison them, and pressed Watson relentlessly for more answers and more action, insisting that he do everything in his power to bring their sons home immediately.[15]

❖

Watson did his best. As he told Hamilton and Henderson in the dossier's March 13 cover letter, the best way to get Sam, Enos, Alex, and Mary Fisher out would be to get them aboard a brig or schooner departing from the closest deep-water terminal. "If New Orleans is your nearest Seaport," Watson wrote, the two Mississippi men could deliver "these unfortunate blacks" to the care of either Benjamin Morgan or Joseph Bennet Eves, two Crescent City merchants whom he knew and trusted. "They will I know procure them the means of a passage to Philadelphia, and restore them to their distressed parents and relatives."[16]

Watson made the arrangements without waiting for a response from Rocky Springs. On March 20, he wrote to Morgan and Eves, two "worthy townsmen" who had each grown up in Philadelphia before migrating to the Deep South. He sought their help by couching it as service to "the cause of humanity" and promised it would not be burdensome. All Morgan or Eves had to do was meet a riverboat inbound from Natchez and then deliver the four refugees aboard onto a brig bound for Philadelphia. "A few humane persons here, whose feelings have been deeply interested by the atrocious conduct of this gang of miscreants," would, Watson said, promptly reimburse all expenses. Evidently unmoved, Eves did not respond to the mayor's letter. Morgan, however, wrote back immediately, willing to do a favor for an old friend.[17]

When John Henderson learned of Watson's plan, he was no less keen to cooperate. In his legal judgment, the verdict of the Port Gibson circuit court in February voiding Ebenezer Johnson's claims on Mary Fisher and the boys had cleared the way for them to leave his neighbor's custody and return home right away. Henderson wrote to Mayor Watson to tell him to hurry. "It would be well for their friends to contrive some means of getting them home before the sickly season commences here. Strangers to this climate frequently suffer very much the first season."[18]

John Hamilton, the cotton planter who had seen off Ebenezer Johnson, was the real roadblock. Even after digesting the dossier (which arrived intact on April 17), Hamilton stalled, refusing to divest himself of his four new workers, ostensibly on the grounds that Johnson might return at any time clutching proof "of their being slaves for life." His neighbor John Henderson kept badgering him, nonetheless, calling on Hamilton at home several times "to know his determination respecting these people." Weeks went by. Twice Henderson arranged a meeting to discuss the case. Twice Hamilton stood him up.[19]

By May, Henderson had had enough of Hamilton's evasions. "To leave Mr. Hamilton without excuse I offered him an indemnifying bond to warrant against any possible loss he might sustain" if Ebenezer Johnson miraculously appeared with authentic bills of sale in hand. Even that did not work. "Strange to say he still refuses to give them up," Henderson told Mayor Watson. Abandoning honey for vinegar, Henderson tried threats. He promised Hamilton that if he dissembled or delayed much longer, he would leak the story to the local paper in "hope that a respect for public opinion" would force his former friend to do the right thing.[20]

The prospect of being shamed in the press before his neighbors panicked Hamilton, finally stirring him to action. On May 3, he rode over to Natchez to get the blessing of Richard Stockton Jr., the attorney general of Mississippi, to break his custody contract with Ebenezer Johnson and release Mary Fisher and the three boys to Mayor Watson's agents. Stockton knew the law better than anyone else in the state. The scion of a storied family of New Jersey lawyers and magistrates, he had been educated at Princeton. Stockton had migrated to Mississippi in the early 1820s and, before accepting the job of attorney general in 1825, had also been a circuit court judge. In fact, John Hamilton had once appeared in Stockton's court, called there in November 1822 for having failed to pay his doctor's bill in full after his near-death experience battling yellow fever.[21]

Hamilton explained his concerns and showed Stockton the contract he had signed with Johnson as well as the dossier that Mayor Watson had sent him. Stockton, a man with national political ambitions who had his own reasons to take an interest in this case, pored through everything, paying particular attention to the depositions attesting to the prior liberty of the four black people now in Hamilton's household. He told his visitor that he should release everyone to Mayor Watson's care immediately, and that Ebenezer Johnson had no good leg to stand on. After Hamilton left his office, the attorney general wrote to the mayor of Philadelphia himself, promising to throw the book at "those infamous miscreants who thus deal in human suffering" if any member of the Johnson family ever came back to Mississippi.[22]

When John Hamilton returned to Rocky Springs a day or two later, he summoned Sam, Enos, Alex, and Mary Fisher. He informed them that he had "come to the conclusion to give them up" and would ship them home just as soon as arrangements could be made. The boys buried him in thanks. Oddly, Mary Fisher hung back, telling Hamilton that the thought of a long sea voyage filled her with dread and that she "preferred to remain behind" in Rocky Springs.[23]

Mary's decision seems baffling; she had a husband and children waiting for her back in Delaware, after all. To everyone's surprise, she refused to say any more about it, a telling silence that suggests she had experienced something deeply painful and private on the weeklong voyage to Norfolk she had endured back in September— the only time she had ever been at sea. The possibility that a second, much longer sea journey from New Orleans to Philadelphia could expose her to the sexual appetites of another crew of sailors seems to have pushed aside all other thoughts and feelings. She told Hamilton she would stay on with him a little longer "in the acknowledged character of a free person," though only until he could devise some alternative means to get her home overland. Fisher was firm, and Hamilton did not argue. He was happy to have her labor.[24]

❖

On May 18, John Hamilton set out for Natchez again, taking Sam, Enos, and Alex with him in his wagon on the two-day, sixty-mile journey. It was the first time they had left Hamilton's fledgling plantation since their overnight visit to the Port Gibson courthouse back in February. The trace that now took them south and west was the same interstate artery they had traveled with the Johnsons fully six months earlier. The grassy banks along the roadside surely reminded them of the spot just north of Rocky Springs where Ebenezer had beaten their friend Joe to death. What must they have thought and felt as their cart rattled slowly toward Natchez, and the turkey vultures that usually circled above the town came into view?[25]

Natchez was a sight. The homes in and around Rocky Springs were all small and dark, timbered from the trees whose stumps pocked the acres around them. In contrast, the houses in Natchez were handsome, spacious, and brick built, vaguely reminiscent of the homes of merchants and lawyers in Philadelphia, the city where many of the Gulf Coast's better-off residents had been raised or educated. Natchez took on the profile of a port only down by the Mississippi River. There, at the foot of the massive bluffs on which Natchez sat, the town's true character presented itself, unadorned and unashamed. Steamboats and flatboats from Pittsburgh, Cincinnati, Louisville, St. Louis, Nashville, Memphis, Vicksburg, and New Orleans jostled the dockside like animals around a trough. Some were loading raw cotton, piling sacks of it into every corner of available cargo space. Other vessels spewed out enslaved people all dressed in Sunday best. Some would be sold right then and there, the rest from jail cells or showrooms in town, or at auction in nearby "Niggerville."[26]

John Hamilton stopped the wagon by the gangway of a waiting packet boat, the 407-ton *Feliciana*, built in Philadelphia in 1820. He prodded Sam, Enos, and Alex aboard and promised its captain that a man would meet the ship in New Orleans the next morning and pay the boys' fares. Into Sam's hands Hamilton now pressed Watson's dossier, minus a fistful of depositions that he held on to in case the

Johnsons did ever return. Then Hamilton scrambled back to shore before the *Feliciana*'s giant paddles cranked to life and the massive steamer muscled its way out into the center of the great river.[27]

Apart from a few crewmembers, Sam, Enos, and Alex were likely the only black people aboard the *Feliciana* who were free. These riverboats were slave ships, after all. Their freight compartments were often crammed with enslaved children and adults, and traders frequently stashed some of them on the main deck, handcuffing them to chains that ran down its central aisle. As these boats plowed through the night, paying passengers tucked snugly in their cabins could sometimes hear a few soul-sick people up on the main decks rattling their chains, looking for weak links that might give them the chance to run to the railings and jump overboard.[28]

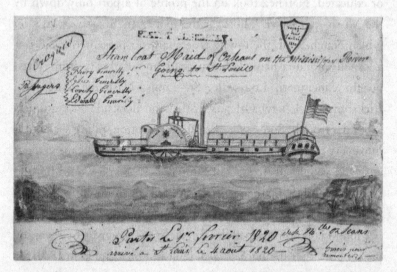

Like the Feliciana, *the* Maid of Orleans *was built in Philadelphia, equipped with a low-pressure engine, and active on the New Orleans to Natchez route in the mid-1820s. The Franco-American artist Fleury Generelly created this watercolor and ink on paper in 1820. (Courtesy of the Louisiana Image Collection, Louisiana Research Collection, Tulane University.)*

Sam, Enos, and Alex were anxious to get home, and so the *Feliciana*'s journey down the Mississippi must have felt painfully slow. Finally, after two hundred miles of switchbacks on the river, the *Feliciana* nosed around one last bend. Ahead stood New Orleans. Warehouses as massive as anything the boys might have seen in Philadelphia crowded its docks, some built to store sugar and cotton, the rest to hold human beings. The whole place seemed to be full to bursting. Home to just eight thousand people in 1803, the city had quadrupled in size by 1826 to become the fifth largest in the United States. A third of its residents were enslaved and worked as deliverymen, peddlers, and washerwomen. Many more were Creoles and other free people of color, but the city was dominated by white migrants from beyond Louisiana, most of whom had come to buy, trade, or otherwise exploit the labor of slaves.[29]

The old man who met the *Feliciana* on the docks that morning had come to New Orleans two decades earlier for just that reason. Benjamin Morgan, Mayor Watson's old friend, had arrived in 1800, in the vanguard of a small army of migrants from Pennsylvania and New Jersey who swarmed the Deep South in the first quarter of the nineteenth century. Since then, Morgan had built a shipping business from scratch by hauling slave products like sugar, molasses, and cotton back to partners in Philadelphia for distribution and sale. Along the way, he had served in both chambers of the Louisiana legislature and on the New Orleans City Council. Apparently modeling himself on his namesake Benjamin Franklin, Morgan also set up the Crescent City's first fire company, library, and Episcopal church, and led a project to pave its busiest commercial streets.[30]

Morgan pressed six dollars into the hands of the *Feliciana*'s skipper, pausing only long enough for the man to write out a receipt. To Sam, Enos, and Alex—none of whom could read—the exchange might have brought to mind a slave sale, an unnerving

Benjamin Latrobe, the British-born architect most famous for designing the US Capitol, went up to the roof of a hotel during a visit to New Orleans in 1820. From that vantage, the hustle and bustle of the city's waterfront was plainly visible. Benjamin Henry Boneval Latrobe, "View from the Window of My Chamber at Tremoulet's Hotel, New Orleans . . ." (Courtesy of the Maryland Historical Society.)

reminder that they were entirely at the mercy of these white men. Morgan certainly seemed in haste. He shepherded them along the bustling waterfront, past one oceangoing rig after another, as if there was no time to lose. The *Catharine*, one of the brigs Morgan sometimes used to ferry freight to points north, had been sitting at the dock for the past three weeks as enslaved longshoremen loaded cotton bales. It had finally reached capacity that morning and was about to depart for Philadelphia.[31]

Morgan rushed the boys aboard. He scrawled out a hasty note for them to give to Mayor Watson, along with the packet-boat receipt and the thick dossier of documents that Sam was clutching. Morgan pulled aside the *Catharine*'s captain, Caleb Adams, to explain the boys' situation. He vouched that they were not runaway slaves. Rather, they were free people with their papers in hand and a powerful friend in Philadelphia—they should not be harassed. Morgan then bid the three of them a safe journey, scuttled off the ship, and disappeared into the crowd.[32]

⁕

Benjamin Morgan was one of four white southerners who helped Sam, Alex, and Enos find their way back toward freedom. John Hamilton, a slave-owning planter, was the first to take their claims seriously and acted decisively to separate them from their traffickers. John Henderson, a local lawyer with political aspirations, then befriended them, sharing their testimony with Mayor Watson in Philadelphia and pushing Hamilton to dispatch the boys there as quickly as possible. Richard Stockton, the attorney general of Mississippi, endorsed their emancipation and exfiltration and promised to put state police on the Johnsons' trail. And now, Benjamin Morgan, a shipper and civic leader from New Orleans, shuttled Sam, Alex, and Enos to the safety of a brig bound for home.

Their actions defied expectations. These men were stakeholders in a slave society, after all. Their livelihoods depended—directly or indirectly—on the enslavement of black people, including children. Free boys and girls were kidnapped, trafficked, and sold into slavery in the Cotton Kingdom all the time. Planters and would-be planters—including James Paul, the tinner who had paid $300 for Cornelius in Tuscaloosa—knowingly bought dozens of captive black children from conductors on the Reverse Underground Railroad every year. It was big business and a major economic driver. If the Deep South had relied solely on enslaved labor supplied by legal traders, fewer crops could have been planted, harvested, and sold, and the region's economy might not have taken off as quickly.

So why then did these four white southern men wade in to help Sam and the others when they asked? Their origins may have played a part. Three of them—Henderson, Stockton, and Morgan—were originally from Philadelphia or its southern New Jersey hinterlands. Each of them kept up close ties to their families or business partners there and likely knew several of the city's antislavery activists from school days or by reputation. Despite years away, they each held Philadelphia and its people in special regard and could surely still bring to mind the streets and alleys that Enos, Alex, and even Sam had once called home.[33]

Still, these men were hardly sleeper agents for the Pennsylvania Abolition Society. Newcomers who openly espoused antislavery views in the Deep South found it difficult to get ahead. So, like most other northern migrants, Henderson, Stockton, and Morgan had embraced acquiescence to slaveholding and slave trading as the price of their own success. "Whoever knew a Yankee, after coming South, to hesitate about owning slaves, if he found them a profitable investment," one Mississippi newspaper columnist later wondered aloud.[34]

In truth, it was self-interest and self-image that motivated these men to help Mary Fisher and the boys. While every community—even one in which race-based slavery is the foundation—sets and polices its own moral boundaries, these four men's decisions were not expressions of their innate instincts to do good. On the contrary, in John Hamilton's case, his choices betray his opportunism and the power of his personal and professional insecurities. Henderson, Stockton, and Morgan had their own self-serving motives. Each of them was politically ambitious; each of them was deeply invested in raising the region's reputation; and each of them understood that taking high-profile action against human traffickers like Ebenezer and Sally Johnson could provide desperately needed positive publicity.

Henderson, Stockton, and Morgan each understood intuitively that the North and the South were deeply intertwined and that the continued prosperity of the Deep South depended on attracting a continuing stream of migrants and money from Philadelphia and places like it. Yet by the mid-1820s, northerners had grown troubled by the tumbling price of cotton and by unflattering newspaper accounts and letters home from prior transplants and were beginning to get cold feet about moving to the Deep South or investing further in it. Such reporting punctured the utopian mythology that had grown up around the Gulf South, instead depicting places like Rocky Springs, Natchez, and New Orleans as lawless, undomesticated hunting grounds where horse thieves and highwaymen, slave stealers and speculators, counterfeiters and card sharps ran amok.[35]

For years, civic leaders like Benjamin Morgan and Attorney General Richard Stockton (who was also the sometime editor of a Mississippi newspaper) had tried to suppress—or better yet, transcend—such bad press. They worked hard to establish the Gulf Coast as a safe place for respectable white people to invest, do business, and raise families. They spilled barrels of ink downplaying the deadliness of yellow fever, decrying crude northern stereotypes of southern people, and depicting the local population as principled and law abiding, not litigious or light fingered. Stockton himself assured correspondents in northern states that the legal systems of the Deep South were uncompromised and uncompromising, and that the region as a whole was well governed and regulated.[36]

In the context of this larger campaign, it was strategic for respectable southerners to be seen lending a hand to their colleagues in northern law enforcement and to be heard cursing kidnappers and enslavers as outcast scum. By doing so, Hamilton, Henderson, Stockton, and Morgan did their parts to disprove northern claims that all migrants to the Deep South were greedy, self-indulgent speculators, hungry for profit regardless of the human cost. "The state of Mississippi, is a slave holding state," Richard Stockton told Mayor Watson in a May 1826 letter. "But be assured, Sir, there is no community that holds in greater abhorrence, the infamous traffic carried on by negro stealers, and none that by public sentiment and by legislative enactment, give greater facilities, for those unjustly detained, to obtain their emancipation."[37]

This calculated antipathy for criminal child snatchers like the Johnsons also had the great benefit of deflecting the attention of antislavery activists in the North away from the far larger legal slave trade between the Upper South and the Cotton Kingdom. By 1826, agitators like Philadelphia's Jesse Torrey and Baltimore's Benjamin Lundy were investigating the everyday atrocities of this legal domestic slave trade—its brutal separation of enslaved black families in particular. Their repeated exposés were finding wide readerships, and had begun to persuade more and more northern citizens that all buyers of slaves were mendacious and undiscriminating and that even the most reputable legal slave traders might be crooked.[38]

To pursue and prosecute the agents of the Reverse Underground Railroad and to liberate their victims was thus to join a broader public-relations strategy to promote the South as a place where individual liberty was respected and private property was protected. Every southern stakeholder was implicated and involved in this broad and long-running campaign. Their efforts also included publicizing southern attempts to stamp out slave smuggling from Cuba and Mexico, and passing legislation to regulate the quality and variety of legally purchased enslaved people arriving in individual states.[39]

Such initiatives were largely for the benefit of northern observers. All of them worked to blunt the worst criticism and impede the federal regulation of the interstate slave trade, a commercial artery that by 1826 had become—quite literally—the lifeblood of the southern economy. The liberation of Sam, Enos, and Alex, then, was the surprising side effect of southerners' ongoing fight to protect their interests, ensure the survival and long-term success of a new slave society in the Deep South, and to defend the legal domestic slave trade from external interference.[40]

❖

A pilot maneuvered the *Catharine* out into the Mississippi River sometime before dusk on May 29. When the brig reached the river's mouth the next morning, the pilot disembarked, leaving Captain Adams and his crew to sail their ship along the Gulf Coast, down and around the Florida peninsula, through the gauntlet of the Bahamas, and up the eastern seaboard toward Philadelphia.[41]

The *Catharine* was supposed to be swift. Its three masts, copper bottom, and squared stern lent it uncommon speed when conditions cooperated, and newspaper ads bragged about its "fine fast sailing." Yet the wind on this particular voyage was lackluster, and a journey that might have taken twenty days ended up taking thirty-one. This left Sam, Enos, and Alex with all too much time to reflect on what had happened and what might happen next.[42]

It was too early to feel relief, especially for Sam, whose New Jersey owner might well be waiting for him when he arrived. Still, each of the boys understood their good fortune. Since her maiden voyage in 1824, the *Catharine* had likely hauled her share of enslaved human cargo southward from the mid-Atlantic toward the Cotton Kingdom. As she sailed northward this time, she would certainly have passed several sister ships sailing in the other direction, delivering more poor souls from ports like Norfolk to be sold and swallowed up in New Orleans.

Sam, Enos, and Alex were not in the Crescent City long enough to have set eyes on its infamous slave showrooms and auction houses. But they had probably heard plenty about them from the people they had bunked with at Hamilton's half-cleared labor camp, and surely counted it as a blessing that they had never seen the insides of those evil emporiums for themselves. Now, with every hour they spent aboard the *Catharine*, their improbable lifeboat, the boys put more distance between themselves and that world that might have been.

Chapter 9

A LIVING WITNESS

O N APRIL 24, 1826—five weeks before Sam, Enos, and Alex boarded the *Catharine* in New Orleans—Cornelius Sinclair signed his name to a piece of paper that he hoped would set him free. He was the only one of the boys with any degree of literacy to speak of. He had learned to read and write in Caleb Kimber's classroom at the Adelphi School back in Philadelphia, but had studiously kept that fact from James Paul, the Tuscaloosa tinner in whose work-shop Cornelius had labored for the past six months.[1]

Free people kidnapped into slavery often kept skills like these a secret. Solomon Northup hid his own literacy from overseers and owners for years, waiting until midnight to scribble Mayday messages that sympathetic white travelers might then smuggle out of state. This was also how Levina, a slave in Georgia, managed to get a letter to her father-in-law back on the Eastern Shore of Maryland in 1824. In it, she told him that the Johnson brothers had abducted her and her two young children. They had marched the family from Maryland to Augusta and sold them to a man named Filpot. The enslaved woman hoped this information would spur some sort of rescue mission, but she knew that the prospects for reunion were grim. "If I should not see you all in this world," she wrote, "I hope to meet you all in Heaven there to part no more."[2]

Just ten years old, Cornelius was probably too young to scratch out a letter to his father or even to know how to address it. So he had pinned his hopes on finding a kindhearted stranger in whom he could confide. Victims of kidnapping often buttonholed traveling merchants, ship captains, and even the occasional black sailor to beg them to contact officials or activists back home.[3]

Cornelius spent months looking for the right person to take into his confidence. Tuscaloosa had a postmaster, a bookseller, a ferryman, and several teachers, doctors, and lawyers. Cornelius surely understood that they were the townsfolk most likely to have connections to friends, family, or business associates in Philadelphia. Still, he stopped short of opening his mouth in front of them, paralyzed by doubt and fear. Would they befriend him or betray him? Why should any white stranger risk his or her own reputation and safety to help a black tinner's assistant? And what would James Paul do if he caught him telling tales?[4]

These questions—and their dark, disillusioning answers—consumed Cornelius throughout his first fall and winter in Alabama. He understood now, as he could not have before, why so few African Americans escaped slavery in the Cotton Kingdom. Without help there was nothing to be done and nowhere to go. Cornelius knew almost no one outside of his master's small household, and must have intuitively understood that Tuscaloosa was hardly a hotbed of antislavery activity. On the contrary, most residents of this Black Belt boomtown—whether they had migrated from neighboring states or from farther afield—saw nothing to gain by debating human bondage or getting between a neighbor and his slave.[5]

Cornelius would spend more than six months trying and failing to find a person he thought he could trust. Then, out of the blue one day in April 1826, two white men he barely knew charged into his master's tin shop and asked him two questions point-blank: Is your name Sinclair? Were you kidnapped from Philadelphia last summer?[6]

Yes, he said, after thinking for a long time. Yes I am. Yes I was.

✢

Cornelius had seen these two men around town. One was Joshua Boucher, Tuscaloosa's Methodist minister. The other was Robert Kennon, the denomination's presiding elder for northern Alabama. That was about all he knew. To tell them the truth was an extraordinary risk. Slaveholders paid the salaries of these local clergymen. Yet here he was wagering his prospects for freedom on the hope that they would believe his story and help him get away.

In some ways, it was a canny bet. Whether Cornelius knew it or not, the Methodist Church had long enjoyed a reputation as a bastion of antislavery thought and activism. Founded in the 1730s by John Wesley, an English theologian and reformer, Methodism was an offshoot of Anglicanism. To differentiate their sect, its early disciples committed themselves to the radically egalitarian belief that everyone can forge a path to heaven. That populist position soon attracted converts on both sides of the Atlantic, including a great many enslaved southerners who began worshipping alongside their masters and overseers in racially segregated congregations. American Methodist leaders also denounced chattel slavery unequivocally during these early years of growth. In the 1780s, they tried several times to force slave-owning members to emancipate their human property or face expulsion.[7]

Unfortunately for Cornelius, all that was in the past. Though he could not have known it, by 1826, white Methodist opposition to slavery had been watered down to the thinnest gruel—at least in Alabama. Since the 1780s, every proposal to make slaveholding and church membership mutually exclusive had failed, shouted down by Methodists across the South who were unwilling to liberate their labor force without compensation. The same vocal southern rank and file had also persuaded the denomination's national body, the General Conference, to leave the matter to state and regional committees to decide.[8]

Once free to set their own ethical standards, southern Methodist leaders had quickly and quietly laid aside their scruples over slavery. In Alabama, the generation of radical firebrands who had ridden in during the territorial period (1798–1819) denouncing human bondage and preaching spiritual equality eventually passed on. Into their place slipped a new cohort of Methodist clergymen whose stance on slavery was vastly more moderate.[9]

Ministers of Joshua Boucher and Robert Kennon's generation were surrounded and often financially supported by slaveholders and knew better than to bite the hands that fed them. They were far less likely than their predecessors to rebuke men like James Paul for owning slaves and ever more likely to appease them. To avoid harassment, ostracism, or violence, Methodist clergy across the Deep South learned to limit their public remarks to inoffensive encouragements to masters to properly clothe, feed, and evangelize their enslaved workforce. Some of Boucher's and Kennon's colleagues even purchased a few slaves of their own. If Cornelius had known all this, he might not have unburdened himself so eagerly to Boucher and Kennon when they came calling.[10]

Fortunately, neither man's views on slaveholding fit this general pattern. Joshua Boucher was the son of one of the first Methodist itinerants to arrive in Alabama. Though he was only a few months into his maiden year as minister at Tuscaloosa's First

Methodist Church, he had already alienated many of the white worshippers in his flock. He had done so by accepting membership in a local masonic lodge, an exclusive fraternity that many Tuscaloosans looked on with suspicion, and by expressing the sorts of antislavery views that had been common in his father's day but that were now dangerously dated and out of step.[11]

Robert Kennon, the town's forty-year-old presiding elder, held broadly similar convictions, but he was far more popular than Boucher, who was ten years his junior. Kennon also had recently accepted masonic membership and he too had long been vexed by the slavery question. When talking to white congregants on that subject, he was no less determined than Boucher in "making [their] crooked ways straight." Still, Kennon was far more diplomatic, even subtle, in conversation. A family doctor by training, he was cheerful and mild mannered, and possessed a playful, youthful affect that most of his patients and parishioners found uncommonly disarming.[12]

Cornelius knew both these men by sight and had likely heard each of them speak at the Methodist meetinghouse over the previous winter. Mixed congregations in which black churchgoers sat at the back behind white worshippers were a common feature of evangelical churchgoing across the Deep South in the 1820s. It would not have been unusual for an enslaved tinner's assistant to attend Methodist Sunday services—whether or not his master accompanied him.[13]

But what were these men doing in James Paul's shop? Both Boucher and Kennon had reputations for working "for the elevation and salvation of the negroes, no less than the Caucasians." If they had not told him that they knew his name and his secret, Cornelius might have assumed that they had come into the shop to try to save his soul.[14]

In truth, it was his life and liberty that they had come to save. The local paper, the *American Mirror*, had just published a strange piece announcing the unexpected arrival in the editor's office of a bundle of documents sent from the mayor of Philadelphia. The contents of that folder asserted that the town tinner had recently bought a ten-year-old victim of interstate kidnapping from a notorious trafficker. The paper's editor, Thomas Davenport, a proslavery booster of considerable energy and talent, had printed Mayor Watson's accusations against James Paul in full. Eager to protect southern slavery's national reputation and distance it from any accusation of criminal impropriety, Davenport had encouraged his readers to rescue this boy from Paul's clutches and establish his legal freedom in court. Boucher and Kennon had come to the tin shop to do just that.[15]

James Paul was out when they arrived, so Cornelius spoke freely. He told Boucher and Kennon who he was. He told them that Paul thought him clumsy and lazy and that he was on the verge of selling him to someone else, and that there was no time to lose. Then he was silent and stood still as they compared the child in front of them to the dossier's description of Joseph Sinclair's missing son: a stoutly built mixed-race lad with "thin long fingers" and a "left eye smaller than the right." Certain there was no mistake, they ushered Cornelius away, "out of the possession of the said Paul" and toward Boucher's home to hide and rest. The same day, another of Paul's enslaved assistants escaped, making off in a different direction, never to be seen again.[16]

When Paul returned to the workshop and learned what had happened, he was apoplectic. Having interrogated what was left of his labor force, he marched over to Boucher's house the next morning to berate him. "I . . . lost two negroes last night," Paul bellowed. "I have reason to believe that you . . . & Dr. Kennon stole them—it is a pretty pass that you have left your religion & turned to kidnapping." Bold as brass, and entirely insensitive to the hypocrisy of that last charge, Paul demanded satisfaction. He was loud and angry, but Boucher gave no ground, and Cornelius kept out of sight. Paul left the minister's doorstep still shouting. "Kennon . . . and Boucher stole my negroes," he yelled to anyone within earshot.[17]

❖

A few days later, Boucher and Kennon took the boy before a justice of the peace to begin court proceedings to petition for his freedom. Under oath, Cornelius told the official—a slaveholder named James Weathered—that he was legally free and had been the victim of kidnapping, interstate trafficking, and unlawful enslavement and sale. Weathered took down the account in longhand before passing it back to the child to read over. It was in cursive and Cornelius probably struggled over some of the words and spellings. Finally satisfied that it was fair and true, he slowly scrawled out his name at the bottom.[18]

It had taken Cornelius six months to get this far, yet still the road ahead looked rocky and likely impassable. Though every southern state provided a legal mechanism for people held illegally as slaves to sue for their freedom—one of the only times an enslaved person could advance proceedings against a free white person—precious few ever saw justice. The grounds on which someone could base a petition were narrow, and formidable practical obstacles stood in the path of every would-be black litigant. In Alabama, state law required that a white person file the freedom suit on a black petitioner's behalf and post a $1,000 bond, the equivalent today of more than $20,000.[19]

Engineered to deter all except the most robust claims, these escape hatches were usually too narrow to wriggle through. What's more, the vast majority of potential plaintiffs were unaware that these laws even existed. In the years between 1800 and 1860, courts in four counties near Natchez, Mississippi, heard just thirty-one cases brought by black people claiming they had been kidnapped into slavery. Of those, judges and jurors threw out, discontinued, or denied almost half (fifteen of thirty-one). Their colleagues in Tuscaloosa and elsewhere across the slave South did much the same.[20]

The hurdles facing Cornelius were especially high. Just ten years old, he did not have the first clue how to navigate the intricacies of Alabama's legal system. Nor did he have any money to hire a lawyer. Despite his obvious intelligence and independence, he would have to rely on Boucher and Kennon not only to bring the suit against Paul on his behalf, but also to pay for an attorney to represent them all in court.[21]

The two men tried to raise that money by reaching out to members of the local Methodist congregation. They were looking for a person with deep pockets willing to challenge a fellow slaveholder's property rights. That was a tall order in a town like Tuscaloosa, but Dennis Dent, a thirty-year-old Methodist originally from Maryland, agreed to hear them out. Dent had made a small fortune investing in slaves and cotton and fancied himself a philanthropist. He had a history of opening his purse to the poor and needy. To persuade him to help, Kennon and Boucher probably persuaded Cornelius—who was about the same age as Dent's eldest son—to talk to him face-to-face. Evidently, Dent was moved by what he heard, because on April 29, he put up the massive bond that the law required for the suit to proceed.[22]

When the clerk of the state's traveling circuit court arrived in town that July, Boucher formally filed Cornelius's petition for freedom, only the second in Tuscaloosa County since statehood in 1819. The petitioners asked that Cornelius "be decreed free and released from slavery" and that he be awarded "wages for the time he had been held as a slave by said Paul." On July 27, the clerk issued a summons to Paul to appear before the court at its next session in October. Four days later, on August 1, Hiram Cochran, the sheriff of Tuscaloosa County, hand delivered that summons to the tin shop.[23]

Petitioners in other states sometimes holed up in the local jails for their own protection until their suits could be heard. Yet Cornelius spent that hot summer—his first in the Deep South—in the comparative comfort of Joshua Boucher's home. While he waited for October to arrive, Boucher and Kennon searched for a lawyer to argue the petition. They chose Seth Barton, a hard-drinking, hard-charging barrel of a man. Barton was new to town, one among a small army of attorneys to descend on Tuscaloosa when the state capital had relocated there from Cahaba earlier in the year. He knew how to work a jury and had won many more cases than he lost. Best of all, he had no qualms about taking on a black client, provided he got paid.[24]

It was Barton who told them that the petition's prospects would rest on whether they could find a respectable white person who not only had known Cornelius as a free person back in Philadelphia but also would be willing to come to Tuscaloosa to testify that fall. Neither Boucher nor Kennon (nor ten-year-old Cornelius) had seen this coming. In a letter the two Methodist leaders had written to Mayor Watson back in April, they had expressed confidence that the dossier of depositions they had acquired from the newspaper office would be enough to satisfy a judge and jury that Cornelius had been kidnapped and had every right to freedom.[25]

Now they had new information and an urgent new request.

Barton filed a motion to delay the hearing for six months while Boucher and Kennon wrote to Watson in Philadelphia asking him to send someone southward as soon as possible. For weeks they waited patiently for the cavalry to come. It never did. By the time Boucher and Kennon realized that their letter had been lost in the mail, Christmas had come and gone. In earnest, they wrote to Watson again in early 1827 pleading with him to dispatch "a living witness here by the second Monday [of] March," when the circuit court would return to town.[26]

Their letter arrived at the mayor's office in Philadelphia on February 9, 1827. This left Watson almost no time to find a white witness who would not only swear to the boy's legal freedom but also travel deep into slave country to do so. Finding someone who filled that bill was extremely difficult. The testimony of the people who knew Cornelius best—his parents and other members of the city's free black community—was inadmissible in southern courts. "Had the father of Sinclair been a competent witness in Alabama, none could have been more capable of proving him," an editorial in Philadelphia's *African Observer* magazine later lamented.[27]

Most white city residents did not know black kids like Cornelius nearly as well. As the *African Observer*'s editor, Enoch Lewis, explained, "Few white persons can accurately describe the particular marks of a black child, who may have grown up even under their own roof." The passage of time only compounded the problem. The physical toll taken upon their young bodies by the ordeal of enslavement, along with the more modest afflictions of puberty, could quickly transform some black children beyond recognition. A great many freedom suits faltered because well-meaning white allies found that they could not identify a child they had not seen for many months with the "unwavering certainty" required in court.[28]

Besides, the journey from Philadelphia to the Deep South was long, dangerous, and costly—enough to give pause to even the stoutest defender of black liberty. At least one white witness had died on an expedition just like this. As Enoch Lewis observed: "To travel a thousand miles or more, in search of a kidnapped child, would require a share of zeal which friendship or philanthropy does not always supply." Volunteers were rare and usually expected to be reimbursed in full for all their expenses. Others asked for danger money, leveraging their promise to testify in places like Tuscaloosa to extort inflated advance payments from the children's families or from the well-to-do members of an abolition society.[29]

Adam Traquair, the man Mayor Watson asked to give in-person testimony in support of Cornelius's petition for freedom, was different. He did not ask for any money from anyone up front and seems to have undertaken the mission out of a sense of civic duty. Traquair was a forty-five-year-old Scottish-born father of two who worked as a stonecutter and chimneypiece maker in Philadelphia. He lived on Filbert Street, just five city blocks from the Sinclair family. He frequently employed black laborers in his stone yard and knew Cornelius from the neighborhood. Traquair had been outraged by the abductions and told Mayor Watson that he was happy to go. He left hastily, most likely aboard the first ship bound for New Orleans, and then traveled onward overland into Alabama.[30]

❖

On Monday, March 12, 1827, Judge John Gayle opened the spring session of the Third Circuit Court in the back room of a Tuscaloosa hotel. Gayle was supposed to spend just a week in town, but there were more than two hundred civil cases on his docket. The makeshift courtroom teemed with plaintiffs, defendants, and witnesses coming and going as Gayle and his clerks tried to make headway, hearing some suits and appeals and dismissing or putting off a great many others.[31]

On the last day of the circuit's second week in Tuscaloosa—Friday, March 23—Judge Gayle wearily opened the proceedings of the 126th case in the docket, a petition for freedom. The day had been long in coming and Cornelius was anxious to get it over with. In theory, the process of petitioning for freedom was liberating and empowering, a rare chance for an enslaved person to speak truth to power and press a claim to personhood. In practice, it was probably terrifying, especially for a child. By then, Cornelius had been trying to hide from his former master, James Paul, for the better part of a year. The prospect of confronting him again—even with the sheriff and a bailiff present to protect him if need be—must have been distressing.[32]

Cornelius Sinclair's freedom suit against James Paul was heard in Alabama's Third Circuit Court on March 23, 1827, with Judge John Gayle presiding. The court's recently digitized records include a five-page summary of the suit and the verdict. (Courtesy of the Tuscaloosa Genealogical Society.)

Paul was still angry, insistent that he had been robbed and wronged by Boucher and Kennon, two of the town's leading men. Back in October, he had put those claims on the record, filing a suit against both of them that sought $1,000 in compensation for trespassing on his property and stealing his slave. In response, Boucher and Kennon had countersued Paul for defamation, demanding $5,000 in damages. Both suits were still pending.[33]

Paul walked into the hearing feeling confident. He was convinced that a jury composed in great part of his customers and fellow slaveholders would find no merit in Cornelius's petition for freedom. They would, if they had any sense, send the boy back to Paul's workshop as his slave. Although the child would be able to enter his own written testimony, Paul knew that the word of a white person carried vastly more weight in Alabama's courts than that of any black plaintiff, no matter how forlorn. So when Sion Perry, his attorney, prompted Paul to speak, he denied all wrongdoing and stuck by his story. He had, he said, bought this slave from Ebenezer Johnson eighteen months earlier in good faith, at a fair price, and with no inkling that Cornelius was contraband.[34]

Because of the boy's young age, Judge Gayle did not permit him to speak during the hearing, so his lawyer did most of the talking. Seth Barton began by reminding the jury that Paul had provided no white witnesses to corroborate his account of his dealings with the Johnsons. Then he entered into evidence the sworn testimony that Cornelius had given to the court official eleven months earlier in which he had described in detail his abduction, incarceration, forced migration, and unlawful sale. Next, Barton submitted the contents of Mayor Watson's dossier, including a copy of an arrest warrant and a grand jury indictment for Ebenezer Johnson, as well as depositions from the boy's former teacher, Caleb Kimber, and his father, Joseph Sinclair.[35]

Finally, he put Adam Traquair, his precious living witness, on the stand. Cornelius had grown taller and stronger, and was perhaps a little less stout than Traquair remembered. Yet when Barton asked him to identify the petitioner, he did not hesitate. He told the judge and the assembled jury that the youth who stood awkwardly before him was Joseph Sinclair's son, the same free black boy who had vanished from the streets of Philadelphia two summers ago. Judge Gayle then gave the jury their instructions and sent them into an anteroom to debate the suit's merits and decide the child's fate.[36]

This undated portrait of Judge John Gayle by an unknown artist was most likely painted after he retired from the bench, during one of his two terms (1831–35) as governor of Alabama. (Courtesy of the Alabama Department of Archives and History.)

Gayle himself seemed torn. The judge owned a cotton plantation in Cahaba, the state's former capital, as well as several enslaved workers. So he was reflexively protective of slaveholders' property rights and reluctant to get between a master and his slave. On the other hand, he understood what it was like for parents and children to be separated. His work on the Third Circuit kept him on the road for weeks at a time, away from his much younger wife and their several small children. Gayle was in his fourth year riding the circuit, but was thinking of quitting to spend more time with his family. Thankfully, this was not his case to decide. It would be up to the twelve jurors to reach the verdict and then live with its consequences.[37]

Jurors in freedom suits always faced difficult choices. They were typically loath to hand down verdicts that would antagonize slaveholders, stir up other enslaved people's hopes for liberty, or increase the size of the region's free black population. And so they rarely did. Yet this petition was different, and there were other factors to consider. For one thing, the defendant, James Paul, had few allies in the jury pool. He had sued many of his customers for unpaid debts over the years, and his litigiousness had made him plenty of enemies. His comeuppance seemed long overdue.[38]

Cornelius's lawyer, Seth Barton, certainly hoped that Paul's unpopularity might swing this case in his client's favor. Barton knew his audience and had worked hard during oral arguments to avoid turning the trial into a referendum on the legality or morality of southern slavery. Instead, he had focused jurors' attention on the boy's youth and the distress he had suffered because he had been unlawfully abducted. Playing for their sympathy, Barton had appealed to this twelve-person panel of local men to envision themselves as honorable Christians with the power to help a young soul in torment.[39]

A piece written before the hearing by Thomas Davenport, the editor of Tuscaloosa's *American Mirror*, had already prepared the ground for this type of legal strategy. In the pages of the *Mirror*, Davenport had characterized Cornelius as "an innocent, suffering victim of unhallowed cupidity." Davenport had also heaped praise on any townsfolk who might act to restore the child "to his anxious and disconsolate parents (both of whom live in Philadelphia) and to that freedom so dear to every American, and to which he, although of a different complexion, is no less entitled than ourselves." Free people kidnapped into slavery, Davenport had informed his subscribers ahead of jury selection, deserved justice and liberty regardless of their race.[40]

By Davenport's reckoning, this was just good business. Turning from lofty principles to pocketbook politics, his editorial tried to explain to would-be jurors that holding a free-born northerner in unlawful bondage a moment longer jeopardized every southerner's long-term economic interests. He made clear that the longevity of slavery as a system of labor in the Cotton Kingdom relied on interstate comity—the bonds of union that compelled officials in states like Pennsylvania to cooperate when southern slave catchers and bounty hunters crossed into their jurisdictions to seize black fugitives seeking sanctuary there.[41]

By 1827, those legal bonds between states in the North and states in the South were wearing thin. Outrage over the raids on free black communities staged by kidnapping crews like the Cannon-Johnson operation had spawned proposals for tough new personal liberty laws in mid-Atlantic states. Southerners had begun to fret that those laws might one day eviscerate interstate comity entirely and criminalize slave catching in Pennsylvania and elsewhere once and for all. To avoid that sort of constitutional catastrophe, southerners would have to work harder to placate their neighbors in the North. If southerners could restore kidnapping victims like Cornelius to their families, for instance, perhaps northerners might see such acts as gestures of good faith. Writing in the *American Mirror*, Thomas Davenport certainly hoped so:

> *If we could not have our brethren of the north harbor and protect our fugitive slaves who may escape thither, let us be prompt in restoring their free citizens who may be torn from them by the ruthless hand of lawless violence, and brought among us from the worst of motives, by wretches unworthy [of] the name of MAN. Such acts are of high national importance, inasmuch as they tend to beget a confidence and friendly feeling between the citizens of the North & South, which must have a powerful influence in strengthening the bonds of union, so essential to the peace, prosperity, and permanency of our happy confederacy.*

Returning a kidnapped northerner to liberty, Davenport argued, was in southerners' best interests. To deny Cornelius's petition for freedom seemed, to him at least, a perilously shortsighted decision. Given the glaring evidence in the boy's favor and the presence of a living witness to vouch for him, a finding against the child would only confirm emerging northern stereotypes about greedy, lawless southerners. By Davenport's reckoning, it could even accelerate legislative activity that might one day turn mid-Atlantic states into the sorts of fortresses in which fugitives from southern slavery could hide indefinitely.[42]

The twelve Tuscaloosan jurors got the message. They reached a verdict quickly, likely within the hour. Their foreman announced their unanimous decision that the petitioner was "born of free parents and is himself free" and as such "is entitled to be delivered from bondage." Judge Gayle then ordered that Cornelius be "discharged from the custody and controul of the said James Paul." He also told the defendant to pay the plaintiff's legal costs and to drop the trespass charges against the two Methodist clergymen. In turn, Boucher and Kennon agreed to abandon their slander suit against Paul. Then Judge Gayle moved on, turning to the particulars of the next case in his docket.[43]

✤

That evening, Boucher and Kennon wrote to Mayor Watson in Philadelphia to share the news. They were exultant. The twelve jurors had rejected Cornelius's claim for back wages, but had given him his freedom, deprived Paul of his most recently trained apprentice, and left him $300 out of pocket. The verdict, they told the mayor, "has afforded not a little pleasure to many of the benevolent of this place."[44]

All that remained was to send Cornelius home. That was easier said than done. The handful of other people who secured their liberty in similar suits sometimes languished in the custody of white allies for weeks, months, or even years before they could scrape together the dollars they needed to pay for their passage north. When Thomas Fitzgerald won his petition for freedom in Augusta, Georgia, in 1822, for instance, the boy walked out of slavery "with out a blanket or a suit of clothes" and not a cent to his name. A local doctor took him in, only to then send him out to work to earn "something for himself until arrangements can be made for sending him on."[45]

Cornelius was lucky. Adam Traquair made all the arrangements for him, and the two departed Tuscaloosa just days after the hearing. In New Orleans, they boarded a ship bound for Philadelphia, setting out on the same homeward voyage that Sam, Enos, and Alex had embarked upon ten months earlier. Like them, Cornelius had succeeded in surviving the Reverse Underground Railroad. Like them, he was returning home now as a living witness to its horrors. But it had been so long. Cornelius had not seen his parents for the better part of two years. To a child still shy of his twelfth birthday, it must have felt like a lifetime.[46]

Chapter 10

HUNTING WOLVES

Sᴀᴍ sᴄᴏᴍᴘ, ᴇɴᴏs ᴛɪʟɢʜᴍᴀɴ, and Alex Manlove arrived back in Philadelphia eleven months ahead of Cornelius Sinclair. On June 29, 1826, they pushed their way down the *Catharine*'s gangplanks and stepped onto one of the city's wooden wharves. The weather in Philadelphia that day was cool, and the skies were high and clear. June was one of the busiest times of year at the docks, and they were heaving that day, thronged by a "confused jumble of men, women and children, carts, coaches, and wheelbarrows." Sam, Enos, and Alex were alone in this crowd. They had arrived unannounced, and there was nobody there to meet them. The letter that Benjamin Morgan had written to inform Mayor Watson of their itinerary was still in Sam's pocket, waiting to be delivered. So the boys made their own way, tramping up the fifty-foot incline from the river onto the broad, freshly washed pavement of Market Street.[1]

From there the three of them most likely separated—their first time apart in months. Sam zigzagged the five blocks to Watson's office, asking directions here and there and passing one marble-stepped brick house after another. At city hall, he gave his name, turned over Morgan's letter, and asked to speak to the mayor. It was rare for a black person so young to be granted an audience, but Watson had spent months on Sam's case and beckoned him inside. They talked. Then Watson barked out instructions to his staff, laying plans for all three boys to give depositions under oath in front of witnesses the following morning. He also arranged for Sam—a runaway from West Jersey with nowhere else to go—to spend the night in an apartment in the debtors' prison on Arch Street, a few blocks west of the mayor's office.[2]

That evening, "a powerful Rain with thunder and Lightning fell" across the city. By then, Enos and Alex had each been home several hours. Enos, now eleven years old, bolted straight from the ship to the address where his mother and father, Hester and Elijah Tilghman, lived, while Alex, now nine, tore off in the direction of his parents' house on Elizabeth Street. What must those reunions have been like? Solomon Northup never forgot how his own heart had "overflowed with happiness" when he saw his family for the first time after more than a decade in slavery. His wife and children had run to him, tears streaming, and had hung upon his neck "overcome with emotion, and unable to speak."[3]

Enos and Alex had been away from their loved ones for a single year. But to children, a year is a lifetime. They were each a few inches taller than their parents remembered, and both lads had a bit less of the boy about them. They looked older, but also tired, hunger pinched, and wrung out. Perhaps it was their parents, brothers, and sisters who filled the stilted silence at first. Most likely, they told Alex and Enos about what their own ordeals had been like. Their lives too had been turned upside down and wrecked by what John Purnell and the Johnsons had done. They too had suffered a thousand trials and troubles in the days, weeks, and months since Alex and Enos had disappeared. It was important to acknowledge that, and to tell these boys just how worried they had been; to tell them that they had been missed and mourned, that they had been searched for, and that they had not been forgotten.[4]

✣

The next morning, June 30, was overcast but cool and pleasant. Sam walked the seven blocks from the debtors' prison to city hall under escort to give his deposition. Now sixteen, Sam was the oldest and most mature of the three boys, and Watson was hopeful that he would be savvy and specific enough to give him what he wanted: the dates, places, and names that could help him find, arrest, and convict Ebenezer Johnson and his gang of wolves. The mayor was eager to start the hunt.[5]

So too was Sam. He wanted to bear witness to the brutality he had seen and experienced. He wanted to see the Johnsons and their accomplices pay. He wanted this for himself—a small way for a young black fugitive to feel purpose and power. He also surely wanted it for the others—for Enos and Alex, for Cornelius, for Mary Fisher and Mary Neal, and of course for Joe, whose body lay buried in the black soil of Rocky Springs. Few riders on the Reverse Underground Railroad ever got a chance to tell their stories, let alone testify in open court like this. When they did, they usually seized it with both hands.[6]

The mayor's first-floor chambers were already packed when Sam arrived. Enos and Alex were seated alongside their relatives, friends, and former employers, who had all turned out in support. Sam spoke first. Apparently undaunted by the attention, he held forth for at least an hour, likely guided by prompts from Watson. He described his capture and incarceration, and then his coffle's torturous route from Philadelphia to Rocky Springs. He dredged up all the times, distances, and geographical information he had socked away during that long, fraught journey, and volunteered the names of seven gang members and accomplices. He also gave a clear physical description of John Purnell, the "small mulatto man" who had lured him out to the Navy Yard almost a year earlier.[7]

Sam surprised the court with how much he could remember. He was able to recall and repeat with surprising specificity at least half a dozen things that one or another of his captors had said in his presence over the ensuing months—a sure sign that many moments of that yearlong nightmare were seared in his memory. He piled detail upon detail, evidently eager to be believed and careful not to exaggerate. To prove that Ebenezer Johnson had "flogged him with a hand saw and with hickories in a most dreadful manner," Sam asked William Stewart, the mayor's clerk, to inspect his skull and upper body. The evidence Stewart found spoke for itself: "the back of this deponent and his head, were dreadfully scarred by the repeated beatings he had received," the clerk wrote in his notes.[8]

The text of Sam's final sworn statement ran to thirteen hundred words. The clerk's transcription does not survive in city records, but a few local papers copied it out for curious readers. Careful, precise, and deliberate, it is the longest and most comprehensive account of the lost boys' kidnapping and coerced migration, and the central source upon which this book is based. Enos, who was ten years old, and Alex, who was just nine, gave their own depositions later that day. They did not add much more, but their stories and their own haggard faces and frames confirmed the truth of everything Sam had said.[9]

❖

The boys' powerful testimony that morning revived Watson's stalled efforts to bring their kidnappers to justice. His courtroom was occupied by dozens of black constituents horrified by what they had heard, and the mayor really had no choice but to publicly vow that "no further effort on my part shall be wanting to procure the arrest and punishment of these men." He assured everyone present that he had already secured grand jury indictments against four of the boys' captors and had sent copies of those indictments to justice officials in Maryland, Delaware, Virginia, Alabama, and Mississippi, the five states in which he knew the gang operated.[10]

Privately, Watson doubted that there was anything more to be done. The kidnappers were professionals, wilier than wolves, and had already slipped through his fingers once. Back in March, two Delmarva residents had given him a tip that Ebenezer and Sally Johnson had returned to the peninsula from Rocky Springs, Mississippi, but by the time Watson had sent his high constable, Samuel Garrigues, to their Nanticoke neighborhood to look for them, they had gone again. They had returned to their hideout only long enough to grab their valuables and warn their partners and families that the sale to John Hamilton had gone wrong and that everyone should lie low.[11]

Watson would also fumble his next lead. It arrived on July 8, little more than a week after the boys' depositions, in a letter to the mayor from a magistrate in Woodbury, New Jersey, just across the river from Philadelphia. The magistrate, Job Brown, had seen press coverage of Sam's extraordinary witness testimony and had urgent news to share about John Purnell. Brown had heard from a free black farmhand that Purnell "is now and has been for some months past employed by a Farmer near this place." Purnell had even been overheard bragging about the money he had made the previous summer decoying city kids like Cornelius, Enos, and Alex into slavery.[12]

Watson surely knew that Purnell was a flight risk, but he still failed to respond decisively to this new tip-off. Rather than dispatch High Constable Garrigues to New Jersey immediately, Watson chose to write back to Brown for more information. Exchanging more letters back and forth took time, and almost two weeks passed before Garrigues met Brown at a tavern in Woodbury to assemble a posse to confront Purnell at his place of work. By then, Purnell had taken off, perhaps having guessed that one of his coworkers had turned him in.[13]

All summer the gang remained at large. Alex and Enos spent those weeks at home, while Sam remained in the debtors apartment at Arch Street Prison, a massive four-story hulk that also housed vagrants and suspects awaiting trial. Expecting to need him again, Mayor Watson had refused to turn over his star witness to his New Jersey owner, David Hill. He was concerned that Hill would beat the boy—or even sell Sam south—to punish him for his original escape. "Until I can make some arrangements with Mr. Hill," Watson wrote during Sam's second month in mayoral protection, the lad should remain in city custody "as well for his safety as that we may be assured of the benefit of his testimony against the felons, if we can find them."[14]

Summer inched into autumn with no arrests and no fresh leads. The only newsworthy development was the return to Delaware of Mary Fisher in late August. She had come to regret her decision to remain in John Hamilton's household after Sam, Enos, and Alex departed. Hamilton had treated Fisher well enough, but when he left the property in June "for the purpose of visiting his friends in the State of Tennessee," his overseer had turned on her. To punish Mary "for refusing to work," the overseer had "severely whipped" her and had threatened to hire out her labor "to the highest bidder," or perhaps even sell her as if she were a slave.[15]

Fisher had extricated herself from the grasp of one slave trader already and refused to surrender to this overseer to be sold. She fled the plantation at the end of June, seeking the protection of Hamilton's neighbor John Henderson. At her request, Henderson went to confront the overseer and to collect her things. Then he sent Fisher on to Benjamin Morgan, the New Orleans merchant who had helped the boys navigate that city's shipping terminal a few months earlier. She was terrified at the prospect of spending several weeks aboard ship, but allowed Morgan to book "a passage for her in the first vessel bound to Philadelphia."[16]

Mary Fisher arrived on Front Street sometime before September, but, unlike Sam, Enos, and Alex, steered clear of the court clerks and reporters who might have interviewed her. Instead, she turned in the other direction and walked out of history. Putting the mayor's office at her back, she set out for Old Duck Creek, the quiet village a few miles north of Dover, Delaware's modest capital city, where she hoped to find her husband, Charley, and their several children.

❖

Watson's investigation stagnated throughout the fall. As winter came on, it seemed on the verge of stalling out entirely. If the mayor took any action in the last six months of 1826, it left no trace in his surviving correspondence and drew no attention from the press. Then, in early January, Watson received a letter with an unfamiliar return address in Mississippi. Its authors—a wealthy, well-connected planter and a lawyer—enclosed a deposition. It was from another boy who claimed to have been kidnapped, coffled, and enslaved by the Johnson brothers and their accomplices.[17]

Peter Hook's story was chillingly familiar. A year or two earlier— Hook had been hazy about the dates—a man matching John Purnell's description had lured him away from his Philadelphia family and into the hold of a waiting sloop, along with four other black boys.

After a short sea voyage, their captors had marched them to Joseph Johnson's house on the Delmarva peninsula and chained them to a stake in its attic. Over the next six months that attic had filled to bursting with seven more boys, most of them apprentices, sweeps, or domestic servants, as well as two black women. When there was no room left, Joseph Johnson had led them in chains to the Nanticoke River, then across the Chesapeake Bay, through Virginia, and deep into North Carolina.[18]

Outside the town of Rockingham, Johnson struck a deal with two other slave traders, who then marched this fourteen-person caravan onward, eventually packaging them into smaller lots and selling them off to planters across the Deep South. Peter Hook ended up picking cotton on a plantation in Pike County in southern Mississippi, where he one day confided the fact of this "most cruel and complicated piece of villainy" to a neighbor's white servant. When that neighbor, David Holmes, heard Peter's story, he took him to a lawyer to get it down in writing. Then he sent this letter to Mayor Watson, whose exploits he had read about in the Natchez papers, to urge him to send out "some creditable person or persons" to identify Peter and the others and to redeem them all.[19]

Watson did as he was asked. In February 1827, he sent out teams of constables to take sworn statements from anyone who had known Peter Hook or any of the thirteen other stranded souls in this second cohort. After a few weeks of frantic work, Watson mailed several thick dossiers of testimony to Mississippi's attorney general, Richard Stockton, in hopes that he would again offer his assistance. Watson also beat the bushes for credible white witnesses willing to voyage south to identify these women and children and secure their return. He fed Philadelphia's newspapers story after story about his latest crusade, even promising city readers a five-hundred-dollar reward if they would volunteer to go to the South to do what Adam Traquair had done for Cornelius Sinclair. That first rescue mission had been a triumph, and Mayor Watson surely thought this second attempt to recover victims of kidnapping from the Deep South might turn out better still. This time, though, no one stepped forward to go there to testify, a grim reminder of just how rare such rescues were.[20]

❖

At the end of April, Watson got a tip about the whereabouts of John Purnell and Bill Paragee, the *Little John*'s skipper. This time the mayor did not hesitate. He immediately dispatched his best man, High Constable Samuel Garrigues, to investigate. Garrigues was thirty-four years old in 1827, the married father of two children—seventeen-year-old Sarah and ten-year-old Benjamin. He was from an immigrant Quaker family with a proud record of civil service and strong ties to the Pennsylvania Abolition Society. He had been the mayor's right-hand man—and the city's de facto chief of police—since Watson's first term in 1824. He was as sharp as a hunting dog, and over his three-year tenure as high constable had quickly earned a reputation as "chief among thief catchers."[21]

Garrigues went after Paragee first, intercepting the *Little John*'s erstwhile captain on board a pilot boat on the Delaware River. Mayor Watson chose to interrogate this old man personally, confronting him with a mass of "strong and decisive" evidence of his role as "an active conspirator" in all the recent kidnappings. Boxed in, Paragee "confessed the fact of his guilt." Then one of Garrigues's constables dragged him off to the jail on Arch Street to await what would surely be a death-penalty trial. Sam, whose testimony might soon send Paragee to the gallows, remained safely sequestered in the debtors' apartments on the other side of the Arch Street campus.[22]

Arch Street Prison, seen here in an undated watercolor painted by David Kennedy, comprised four stone cell blocks arrayed around a central hall. Sam was housed in the debtors' wing. The rest of the structure accommodated vagrants and prisoners awaiting trial. The city demolished the prison in 1837, soon after Eastern State Penitentiary opened. (Courtesy of the Historical Society of Pennsylvania.)

While Watson prepared for Paragee's trial, his high constable hurried off in pursuit of John Purnell, the man who had ensnared so many street kids with promises of work and food. Samuel Garrigues was on the hunt near the Nanticoke River out on the Delmarva peninsula when another tipster contacted the mayor with news that Purnell had been sighted in Baltimore and had since "shipp'd on board a Sch[ooner] bound to Boston."[23]

Watson had to scramble. Garrigues was two days' ride from the nearest major shipping terminal and unable to give chase to Purnell right away. The best plan Watson could think of was to send an urgent letter to Josiah Quincy, the mayor of Boston, asking him to seize Purnell when his ship arrived. So Watson did just that, and made a point of alerting Mayor Quincy and his men to the five-hundred-dollar reward they could claim if they took him.[24]

Boston is 150 nautical miles closer to Philadelphia than it is to Baltimore, a geographical advantage that meant that Watson's plea, sent by ship, reached Quincy just in time. The prospect of the reward money was enough to motivate the mayor's officers. They immediately began searching ships arriving from Baltimore for men who matched Purnell's description. They found him aboard the schooner *Sally Ann*, the third vessel they searched. On Sunday, May 27, 1827, Constable George Reed arrested him, led him to Mayor Quincy to be questioned, then tossed him into the Boston lockup until Pennsylvania officials could send along a formal rendition request and an agent to collect the prisoner.[25]

High Constable Garrigues arrived in Boston a few days later. He had been hunting for Purnell for the past several months and had traveled hundreds of miles. When he came to collect him from Mayor Quincy's men, it was the first time the two of them ever came face-to-face. Garrigues manacled his prisoner, and the pair left the city on a single horse, hastily bought for the purpose. He lodged Purnell in one local jail after another as they made their way southward via Providence and New York City. Garrigues was strong and broad chested and could be rough with prisoners, so much so that three months later a Philadelphia woman accused him of assault and battery. The opportunity to treat this child snatcher and trafficker as his own captive punching bag must surely have been appealing.[26]

❖

On Sunday, June 10, 1827, High Constable Garrigues rode in to Philadelphia with a handcuffed John Purnell in tow. Much had happened while he had been away. Nine days earlier, Bill Paragee had died in the Arch Street Prison before his case had reached trial. He had been quite old. If anyone suspected that he had cheated justice by committing suicide behind bars, no one said so publicly. The better news, as far as Watson and Garrigues were concerned, was the return from Tuscaloosa of Cornelius Sinclair, the fourth lost boy to be freed from deep southern slavery. Still only eleven years old, Cornelius had proved his maturity again and again in Alabama. Now that he was home, he was eager to confront Purnell and secure the man's conviction.[27]

Those proceedings began in earnest in the mayor's court on Wednesday, June 13, Purnell's fourth day back in the city. The courtroom was in the old statehouse, the building immediately adjacent to city hall. The room itself had formerly housed the Supreme Court of the United States, and it sat just across the corridor from the chamber in which delegates to the Second Continental Congress had debated independence in 1776. The mayor's court had exclusive jurisdiction over all criminal matters within city limits, and regularly

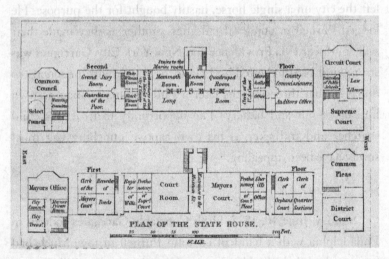

The locations of Mayor Joseph Watson's office and the mayor's court, where several members of the kidnapping crew were tried, are visible on this 1824 floor plan of city hall (left) and the old statehouse (center). Philadelphia in 1824; Or, A Brief Account of the Various Institutions and Public Objects in This Metropolis: Being a Complete Guide for Strangers, and An Useful Compendium for the Inhabitants. *Philadelphia, 1824. (Courtesy of the American Antiquarian Society.)*

heard cases involving larceny, forgery, assault and battery, fornication, and bastardy. Yet kidnapping trials were extremely rare, and the large room was soon "crowded to excess."[28]

After the usual bureaucratic recitations and swearings in, a clerk read the charges. They alleged that John Purnell, the meek-looking young man in the dock, was in fact "a principal agent in the atrocious kidnappings" that had taken place in Philadelphia in August 1825. Then, one by one, Sam, Alex, Enos, and Cornelius—the four survivors of those five abductions—each testified. Sam took the lead. He had told his story under oath before, and this time he snorted at his own naivete in having fallen for Purnell's talk of quick cash for unloading watermelons. It had been, Sam said, "a marvelously good joke."[29]

Cornelius spoke last. It was his first time in front of Mayor Watson, but his experience in Judge Gayle's court in Tuscaloosa earlier in the year had taught him what was expected and what was required. Unlike Sam, Cornelius did not think any of this was remotely funny. He laid out the whole grotesque story, and while that testimony is now lost, contemporary reactions to it suggest that he chose vivid images and graphic language to describe each act of violence done to him or in front of him. Everyone listened transfixed, and a reporter for *Poulson's* later confessed himself "particularly struck with the intelligence manifested by a little black boy, named St. Clair."[30]

Despite all the damning evidence against Purnell, the assembled jurors acquitted him. The court's records have not survived, except via newspaper accounts, but the verdict was most likely based on technical grounds, a reluctant acknowledgment of the fact that the site of these kidnappings, the Navy Yard, lay in Philadelphia County, several hundred feet south of the city's legal boundary. The yard was beyond the jurisdiction of the mayor's court, so Purnell was retried in the county court three days later, on June 16. At first he pleaded not guilty, though after the same parade of witnesses again made his guilt quite clear, he retracted that plea and admitted many of his crimes.[31]

This time, the twelve white male jurors found Purnell guilty on multiple counts of kidnapping—more than enough to bury him. Judge Edward King handed down the maximum possible sentence: forty-two years of hard labor in prison—a life sentence in all but name. A constable took Purnell away. At the Arch Street Prison that evening, staff processed him for intake, subjecting him to a degrading physical inspection not unlike those inflicted upon slaves at the points of sale in Natchez and New Orleans. A prison officer recorded that the state's newest unfree laborer was five feet three inches tall, of mixed race, and about twenty-six years old. He had a flat face, a distinctive hair mole on his chin, and crooked, scarred fingers on his left hand.[32]

As word of the court's verdict spread, newspapers across the northern states cheered Purnell's comeuppance. "This fellow's kidnapping days are over," whistled a commentator in *Niles' Weekly Register*. "Exemplary Punishment," ran one headline. "A Righteous Sentence," agreed another. Purnell would surely die in prison, a fitting retribution for the lifetime of captivity and hard labor he had tried to impose on Sam, Joe, Cornelius, Enos, Alex, and Mary Fisher.[33]

❖

Once behind bars, Purnell tried to remain a loyal soldier and at first refused to give up the hiding places of any of his bosses and associates. Frustrated, Mayor Watson reluctantly put the manhunt aside and instead tried to make progress finding and rescuing some of the women and children from his city still stuck in the slave South.

At the time of Purnell's trial, Watson was awaiting a reply to a letter he had sent to Philip Hickey, the owner of a large sugar plantation just south of Baton Rouge, Louisiana. The mayor had written to inquire after one of Hickey's slaves, a black child named James Dailey who had recently accosted a visiting merchant and confided that he had "been stolen away from Phila., about 12 or 18 months ago." The mayor had pleaded with Hickey to release the boy and had sent along copies of the depositions his constables had gathered from Dailey's loved ones in hopes that their testimonies of grief and loss would "produce the same feeling of indignation with you that it has excited here."[34]

They did not. In August, Watson received Hickey's blistering response. He professed to "sympathise with [the mayor's] indignation," but refused to release the boy, a slave he said he had bought fair and square. Hickey also dismissed the depositions, calling them "falsehoods" fabricated by militant free black activists "to cheat a slaveholder out of his property," and lambasted Watson as a meddling fool and "self styled philanthropist" who should leave well enough alone. The mayor could hardly believe his eyes and shot back a prickly reply in which he insisted that as Philadelphia's chief magistrate, he had a duty "to guard the rights and privileges of its inhabitants, even the most poor and humble of them." But it hardly mattered; Hickey had made it clear that he had no intention of cooperating.[35]

In a last-ditch attempt to liberate James Dailey, Mayor Watson sent Samuel Garrigues to the region that autumn to try to change Philip Hickey's mind. The high constable arrived in New Orleans at the end of November armed with more than one hundred depositions, letters, statutes, rulings, newspaper clippings, and maps. Watson had directed him to lobby Hickey and other planters there to rescue the rest of this second cohort of women and children. Dependable and dogged, Garrigues set to work. He spent the next three weeks shuttling back and forth between plantations in eastern Louisiana and western Mississippi trying to bargain with or bribe Hickey and the other masters he met.[36]

He got nowhere. Because Garrigues lacked credible white witnesses to vouch for the identities of the enslaved people in question, most of these slave owners brushed him off. So too did many local lawyers. Even those willing to help soon changed their minds after "receiv[ing] many threats for their interference." Richard Stockton, Mississippi's attorney general, had died in a duel earlier in the year, and without his patronage, Garrigues found it impossible to make progress. "It is all together an uphill business attended with many discouragements," he wrote to Watson at the end of his first week there.[37]

Garrigues returned to Philadelphia in early January 1828, humbled to have discovered the limits of his own power and ability. At his side were just three of the fourteen people he had been sent to save, all of them children. Two of them, Clem Coxe and Ephraim Lawrence, were fit and healthy and gave testimony to Mayor Watson before reuniting with their families. But the third child, fifteen-year-old Jim Dailey—the youth that Philip Hickey had initially refused to give up—returned to Philadelphia more bones than boy. Hickey had given him many "repeated whippings and blows" over the intervening months for having told his story to a stranger in the first place. By the time Garrigues had gotten to him, Jim was unable to walk, and Hickey had been happy to be rid of him. The child survived just eight days at home. A simple one-line autopsy report concluded that he "died of debility, resulting from improper food, neglect during illness, and severe treatment."[38]

✤

Watson and Garrigues spent what was left of the year trying to collar the rest of the Johnson gang. The results were disappointing. Ebenezer Johnson and his wife, Sally, had vanished. After returning from Rocky Springs in January 1826, they had sold their eighty-acre plot near the Nanticoke to a neighbor. They had pocketed the cash from that sale, then fled out of state, heading perhaps for their cabin in Ashville, Alabama. If they ever ventured north again, Mayor Watson was none the wiser.[39]

Joseph Johnson, the man the mayor believed to be "the well known head of the conspiracy," had also sold up and shipped out. After returning from North Carolina, Johnson had unloaded his house in Dorchester County, Maryland, onto his mother-in-law, Patty Cannon, executing the transfer on March 1, 1826. He then took the thousand dollars he raised in that sale and dropped off the map. Scattered, unconfirmed sightings over the next few years placed Johnson in New Orleans, Arkansas, and Florida. He returned to the Nanticoke perhaps just twice—in March 1827 and then again in December 1828—but easily evaded constables there. "If I could but lay my finger on him . . . ," a frustrated Watson lamented as the longest manhunt in the young nation's history ground on.[40]

Patty Cannon, Joseph Johnson's mother-in-law, was the only senior member of the gang to stay put. She moved into her son-in-law's large house and rented out her home to a tenant farmer. From her new headquarters, she attempted to keep the family business going. With two trusted hands, Purnell and Collins, now behind bars, she promoted Cyrus James, a young free black man who had long worked for her. Together they pared down the gang's operations to its core functions.[41]

To minimize the risk of arrest, their operatives briefly fell back, ceding the streets of Philadelphia for hunting grounds in towns and villages across the lower counties of the Delmarva peninsula. Volume suffered, though profits held steady, and demand for cheap black labor from planters farther south remained monstrously consistent. In May 1827, one woman did manage to escape from Cannon's attic and ran for the nearest constable, but there was only one minor arrest and conviction. Otherwise, Cannon's work went on without obstruction. In a report circulated among the nation's antislavery societies in 1828—during the gang's second year without Joseph Johnson at its helm—activists described Cannon's house as the Reverse Underground Railroad's "principal" depot on the peninsula.[42]

The year 1828 was almost over by the time Watson and Garrigues arrested Thomas Collins. Rotting away in the Arch Street Prison, John Purnell had finally begun to crack and had told them where to find his former accomplice, the white man who had forged the gang's fictitious bills of sale and helped to crew the *Little John*. In early October, Garrigues apprehended Collins somewhere out near the Nanticoke watershed where he had been "skulking" for some time, apparently "in constant dread of arrest from the persevering efforts used by the [Philadelphia] police." He stood trial in that city's county court on October 7. Sam, Cornelius, Alex, and Enos gave evidence against him. Like John Purnell before him, Thomas Collins pleaded not guilty, but the boys' testimony again convinced the jury otherwise, and Judge King sentenced him to another maximum sentence at hard labor. A constable carted him away.[43]

Two weeks after this latest courtroom drama, Joseph Watson's tenure as mayor came to an abrupt end when he lost his bid for a fifth one-year term to an ambitious state's attorney. His work on the boys' behalf had not been popular with most ordinary white

Pennsylvania Governor John Schulze (left) was the signatory on the warrant that High Constable Samuel Garrigues delivered to Boston Mayor Josiah Quincy (center) for the arrest and rendition of John Purnell. Judge Edward King (right), a magistrate in the Court of Quarter Sessions for Philadelphia County, passed sentence on both John Purnell and Thomas Collins. The artists, from left to right, are Jacob Eichholtz, Gilbert Stuart, and Montgomery P. Simons. (Left: Courtesy of the State Museum of Pennsylvania, Pennsylvania Historical and Museum Commission. Center: Courtesy of the Museum of Fine Arts Boston. Right: Courtesy of the Harvard Law School Library.)

Philadelphians, and he had surely known that his days in office were numbered. In a rare speech made to members of the city council during that last campaign—a speech that in retrospect reads like a eulogy for his political career—Watson talked at length about his long fight against the Cannon-Johnson crew. He claimed the lion's share of credit for redeeming Sam, Cornelius, Enos, Alex, and Mary Fisher. He also congratulated himself for bringing some of their kidnappers to justice, and for putting all the other operators of this Reverse Underground Railroad on the back foot, however briefly.[44]

Still, Mayor Watson knew there was much work left unfinished, and he confessed his sense of having otherwise failed and fallen short. Patty Cannon and the Johnsons, the leaders of this particular pack of predators, remained at liberty, while both Joe the sweep and James Dailey lay dead. Worst of all, so many of the other women and children that the gang had swallowed up over the years remained "doomed to slavery for life" somewhere in the Deep South. Watson did not know their exact whereabouts. All he really knew were their names. So he stood before his colleagues and constituents that day and recited each of those names slowly and clearly—as if reading from a roll of martyrs.[45]

Chapter 11

KIDNAPPERS ALL

ON THE FIRST day of April 1829, a tenant farmer plowing an orchard that had once belonged to Patty Cannon discovered a three-foot-long blue-painted wooden chest buried under topsoil. He dug it up and pried it open, hoping to find a forgotten stash of coins or cash inside. Instead, he found human remains—the doubled-over, decomposed body of a grown man.[1]

News of this grim discovery flew like wildfire around the Nanticoke watershed over the next few days. Everyone said the man had been killed in cold blood and that Patty Cannon, the orchard's previous owner, was responsible. Neighbors told investigators that the body belonged to "a Negro trader from Georgia, named Bell or Miller." Many could still remember him riding around their region several years earlier bragging to slave owners "that he had with him fifteen thousand dollars . . . to purchase [their] Negroes." It had long been an open secret, neighbors said, that Joseph and Ebenezer Johnson had murdered him for that money and that, with Patty Cannon's help, they had hidden his body somewhere on her property.[2]

Constables could not find either of the Johnson brothers. By

1829, they had long since left the Delmarva peninsula. So instead they arrested Cyrus James, Patty Cannon's second in command. They interrogated him for several days in the little brick jailhouse in Georgetown, Delaware. Under duress, James confirmed everything. He confessed to having seen the siblings shoot this swaggering slave buyer in the middle of dinner at Cannon's former home nine years earlier, in 1820.[3]

Desperate to strike a plea deal with prosecutors, Cyrus James then led them to three other secret burial sites in the same orchard plot. When officers dug down, they found more oak boxes and three more corpses. Two had belonged to a pair of black babies that Cannon and her crew had ripped away from mothers they planned to coffle southward. Each body showed signs of strangulation. The third had belonged to a boy no older than six whose skull had been battered in. James said Cannon had "knock[ed the boy] in the head with a billet of wood" because he was "bad" and would not shut up.[4]

The constables came for Patty Cannon on April 6. She was then living in Joseph Johnson's old house on the Maryland side of the state line. According to folklore, constables there had to chase her across the border into Delaware in order for that state's deputies to arrest her. However it happened, a week later, a three-judge panel presiding over twenty-three grand jurors indicted Cannon on four counts of murder. Homicide was a capital crime, so the judges announced that she would be tried before Delaware's Supreme Court when it met that October. In the meantime, deputies kept Cannon, who was by then "between 60 and 70 years of age" and, in the words of one local reporter, an "old hag," cuffed and captive in the Georgetown jail. This was hardly a high-security facility, and they worried that her old associates might try to break her out before the hangman could get to her, though no one ever came.[5]

On Monday morning, May 11, 1829, a jail worker found Cannon unconscious and unresponsive on the floor. She was dead. The coroner conducted a brief autopsy, but found no trace of foul play. A day or two later, the jailer buried Cannon's body in an unmarked pit in a corner of the yard near the whipping post.[6]

With Cannon dead and the Johnson brothers fled, only two gang members were still in custody. One was John Purnell, the man who had lured away Sam, Enos, and the others with promises of cash for work. The other was Thomas Collins, the former deckhand aboard the *Little John*, the sloop that had spirited them away from Philadelphia. Yet they too managed to evade the full measure of justice due to them. Having served less than six years of his forty-two-year sentence, Purnell died at the Walnut Street Penitentiary on March 26, 1833; the cause of his death went unrecorded.[7]

By then, Thomas Collins was on the verge of securing his own early release. Two years earlier, in April 1831, Collins had sent a letter to William Rawle, the president of the Pennsylvania Abolition Society, pleading for his help to secure a pardon. Collins was illiterate—or, as he put it, "totally destitute of all education." So he had dictated the letter to a fellow prisoner, filling it with fawning praise for Rawle and recasting the PAS's ongoing antislavery work as a far broader crusade to help victims of all manner of injustice.[8]

Collins told Rawle that he was as much a victim of injustice as any of the boys. He claimed that John Purnell and the Johnsons had duped him into helping them kidnap the five lads, that he had only "engaged in the business but the once," and that his job had been "only as a hand" and entirely nonviolent. In a letter to other PAS officers a month later, Collins continued his campaign. He talked at length about the ways that prison had changed him and pledged "to make all the amends to Society in my power" if released. The matter was urgent, he said, as his wife and children "are now perhaps starving for the want of my assistance."[9]

When Collins had been sentenced back in 1828, a writer in a Baltimore paper had scorned his prospects of ever earning any sort of pardon. But prisoners petitioned for conditional parole all the time, and Collins's pleas hit all the right notes. After some delay, Rawle endorsed Collins's petition for early release and sent it to the new governor of Pennsylvania, George Wolf. As governor, Wolf had a vested interest in demonstrating the power of the state's famous penitentiaries to rehabilitate those who passed through them, and he did not delay in approving this apparently penitent prisoner's request for clemency.[10]

Nine months after John Purnell's death, Thomas Collins collected his possessions from a warden. On December 30, 1833, he stepped through the gatehouse and disappeared around a corner.[11]

❖

The boys and their parents must have met all this news with disbelief. Five years earlier, they had cheered the arrest and conviction of Purnell and Collins and toasted the mayor of Philadelphia and his dogged high constable for dispersing and defeating the Cannon-Johnson gang. The optimists among them had even wagered that other conductors on the Reverse Underground Railroad still at large would soon be in custody, retreat, or retirement. "It is to be hoped that by the year of 1869, the trade of stealing children will be rendered unprofitable," predicted one white activist after calculating the year in which John Purnell's forty-two-year sentence would be up.[12]

In one sense, he was not far off. In 1865, the Thirteenth Amendment formally and finally abolished race-based slavery in the United States, obliterating the legal trade in slaves at the same time, putting most child snatchers and man stealers out of business. In every other sense, however, optimism surrounding the convictions of Purnell and Collins turned out to be horribly misplaced.

Neither man served out his full sentence, while the gang's leaders— Patty Cannon, Joseph Johnson, his brother Ebenezer, and sister-in-law Sally—all escaped justice. Nor did the Reverse Underground Railroad suddenly grind to a halt in the late 1820s as Mayor Watson's admirers had once hoped. Just the opposite. Fueled by strong demand, weak opposition, and rising racial tension in northern cities from New York to Cincinnati, this human trafficking network spread like a cancer over the next thirty years, infecting dozens of new sites and poisoning thousands of additional lives.[13]

Looking back, voters' decision to turn Mayor Watson out of office in 1828 was a turning point—a sign of changing times. His successor, George Mifflin Dallas, had his sights set on national office. He quickly tired of constituent service and sidelined or suspended other abduction investigations. Watson returned to civilian life and spent the next several years plugging away at half a dozen charitable projects to help his city's most vulnerable residents. A new job as a coal executive provided the funds for his philanthropy, but as a private citizen he soon discovered that he lacked the executive power to stop upstart new kidnapping operations from filling the void created when the Cannon-Johnson gang had been broken up. In 1836, a few months after the death of Samuel Garrigues, his formidable former high constable, Watson ran for mayor again, perhaps in hopes of reviving his antikidnapping crusade. It was not to be. He lost badly and died five years later at the age of fifty-seven.[14]

With Watson and Garrigues gone and their successors indifferent, professional kidnappers once again stalked the streets of Philadelphia unmolested by the long arm of the law. As Cornelius, Enos, and Alex tried to rebuild their lives, they found that they still had to be on their guard. Danger lurked down every alley. It is no coincidence that a man named George Alberti, a former city constable who would snatch away dozens of black children over the next three decades, first attracted local attention in May 1829, just five months after Watson left the mayor's office.[15]

Kidnappers of Alberti's generation were nothing if not ambitious. Many moved west in the 1830s and 1840s in search of fresh hunting grounds. The Gap Gang, which terrorized free black communities in and around Lancaster County, was just one of many loosely organized people-snatching collectives to haunt Pennsylvania's three-hundred-mile-long border with Maryland in this period. "Kidnappers seem to be prowling about all over the State, watching [for] their chance to pounce upon their prey," warned a writer in the *Pennsylvania Freeman* in 1844. "Our state is infested with them. . . . Let our colored friends beware and abolitionists be on the alert."[16]

This engraving from an antislavery almanac depicts four kidnappers abducting Peter John Lee, a free black man living in Westchester County, New York, in 1836. In a lengthy caption—below the headline "A Northern Freeman Enslaved by Northern Hands"—the almanac's editor reminded readers that atrocities like this were now all too common in free states. American Anti-Slavery Almanac for 1839, Boston, 1839. (Courtesy of the Library Company of Philadelphia.)

These parasites also started creeping into towns and cities farther north. As more cargo ships shuttled back and forth between New York and New Orleans, more free black children from lower Manhattan went missing—especially from the neighborhoods closest to the docks. By the 1830s, gangs like the Blackbirders and the Kidnapping Club had overrun that city. In January 1836, David Ruggles, an African American abolitionist, estimated that as many as five hundred black New Yorkers now fell victim to "these hyenas in human shape" every year, including many children who vanished "on their way to school."[17]

Nowhere was safe. Kidnappers crept around every corner of the expanding union in the 1830s and 1840s, including Michigan, Ohio, Indiana, and Illinois, the four free states newly carved from the Northwest Territory. Over a few months in 1844 and 1845, for instance, one crew stole away at least forty-four freemen and children from "abolition settlement[s]" in Illinois, stashing them aboard flatboats destined for Missouri, Arkansas, and Mississippi. "It is no unusual occurrence," a columnist for the *Chicago Western Citizen* lamented. Kidnapping "is increasing all along the border of the free states," agreed a writer for the *Cincinnati Gazette*.[18]

Antislavery activists struggled to keep up. "How many poor wretches are abducted in this way, God only knows!" bemoaned Benjamin Lundy in the pages of his newspaper, the *Genius of Universal Emancipation*. As Lundy knew from his own reporting, professional predators were becoming ever more adept at covering their tracks. Rather than try to steal away their kicking, screaming victims unobserved, ever more of them now posed as properly credentialed slave catchers and bounty hunters to get what they wanted. They would drag black people before bribable local magistrates and then wave around forged paperwork and lie under oath in hopes of securing removal certificates that would give them the legal authority to haul free black people out of state.[19]

Benjamin Lundy raised hell each time magistrates went along with this scam. Traffickers, he raged in 1830, were rampaging everywhere, using these and other sorts of subterfuges to steal away many "hundreds" of free black children and adults every year. Writing in 1839, Theodore Dwight Weld was even more alarmist. In his best-selling book *American Slavery As It Is*, he told readers that census data showing a surge in the size of the southern slave population was proof positive of the scale and scope of the Reverse Underground Railroad. Memoirs authored by former victims of this traffic, like Solomon Northup's *Twelve Years a Slave*, were only slightly more measured. Observers everywhere agreed that this underground operation was massive—and growing. "Kidnapping is the order of the day," sighed a resident of Richmond in 1850.[20]

✦

The economic and political forces fueling the growth of the Reverse Underground Railroad in the second quarter of the nineteenth century were obvious to anyone who cared to look. The Cotton Kingdom was expanding westward toward Texas in the 1830s and 1840s. At the same time, the Indian Removal program initiated by President Andrew Jackson was dispossessing tens of thousands of Native Americans of fertile acreage in Mississippi, Alabama, Georgia, and Florida, turning it over to white settlers. All those acres needed planting, supercharging the demand for slaves in the Deep South. Anyone who could sell black laborers to this next generation of American slaveholders could make a killing.[21]

Legal traders acted quickly so as not to miss out. Established slave dealers embraced new technologies like steamboats and railroads to increase their capacity, integrate their supply chains, and grow their sales. Isaac Franklin and John Armfield, the codirectors of one aggressive family firm, even purchased their own small fleet of slave ships to meet rising demand. By the end of the 1830s, Franklin and Armfield's agents regularly sent more than one thousand enslaved people from Alexandria to New Orleans each spring.[22]

No other operation ever grew quite as large. Still, by 1840, nearly twenty thousand black people a year made this legal forced migration, in either cargo holds or coffles. At least 10 percent were young children like the "ten naked negro boys, between six and twelve years of age tied together like puppies" that William Seward saw trudging along a Virginia road in 1835.[23]

Andrew Jackson, a slave owner and speculator, traded enslaved adults and children across state lines for decades prior to his presidency, a fact that several of his political opponents tried to exploit. A Brief Account of General Jackson's Dealings in Negroes, in a Series of Letters and Documents by His Own Neighbors, *New York, 1828. (Courtesy of the American Antiquarian Society.)*

Flush times for legal traders ensured that kidnappers too found eager buyers from Texas to Florida. "Kidnapping people of colour has long been practiced in this *free* country, and may be expected to continue, while slavery is continued," lamented Benjamin Lundy in the pages of the *Genius of Universal Emancipation*. "Where there are persons to purchase men as slaves, there will be no want of thieves to steal them from their homes for this purpose," agreed James Buckingham, a British visitor to the South in 1842.[24]

By then, kidnapping crews had begun to insinuate themselves into the sophisticated supply chains built by legal traders. Rather than drag their victims hundreds of miles to market, many of the kidnapping gangs active in the 1830s and 1840s chose to sell them off quickly, usually to agents of midsize slave-trading firms in Baltimore and Washington willing to dabble in the black market if the price was right. In 1825, Sam, Joe, Cornelius, Enos, and Alex had slogged their way southward in the custody of the same pack of outlaws who had abducted them. In contrast, in 1841, Solomon Northup would sail to New Orleans as the property of Theophilus Freeman, the co-owner of a largely legitimate slave-trading business who bought Northup from the two men who had first decoyed and drugged him.

As the bright lines that should have separated the legal domestic slave trade from the Reverse Underground Railroad grew ever more faded and blurred, these two long-entangled trading networks transformed the southern United States. They powered a massive economic expansion in the 1830s and 1840s, unleashing entrepreneurial energy that stimulated infrastructure investment and modernized markets. These twinned trades also succeeded in markedly broadening the base of slave ownership and consolidating the South's economic and political power. As a result, in the second quarter of the nineteenth century, wealthy proslavery southerners dominated all three branches of the federal government. Beholden only to their base, they brushed aside northern antislavery activists' pleas to properly police the legal interstate trade in slaves and repeatedly blocked nationwide antikidnapping legislation.[25]

❖

Northerners fumed about the rise of what they called the "Slave Power." But its political dominance in Washington concealed many lingering divisions and contradictions within the southern states. As the lost boys' time in Mississippi and Alabama (and briefly Louisiana) makes clear, slaveholders did not always march in lockstep, nor did every white person necessarily prosper as the South's economy surged. The region's rapid rise in the twenty-five years after 1825 produced both winners and losers, and white southerners spent years trying to reconcile their often diverse views on slavery, slave trading, and even kidnapping.

Consider John Hamilton and John Henderson. Before leaving office, Mayor Watson sent these Rocky Springs neighbors two engraved silver plates, each valued at $150 (more than $3,000 today). The plates were tokens of thanks, Watson explained, for the "humane and benevolent conduct" they had exhibited by working together to rescue Sam, Enos, Alex, and Mary Fisher "from the illegal bondage in which they were held." In truth, the whole affair had driven a wedge between the two men. By the time the plates reached Mississippi, Hamilton (the planter) and Henderson (the lawyer) were no longer on speaking terms. Hamilton's stalling to delay the boys' departure for Philadelphia and his overseer's later mistreatment of Mary Fisher had set these former friends on paths that would never cross again.[26]

John Hamilton would continue to drown in debt. Despite the booming economy, he could never get ahead of his creditors. Six of them, including a local bank, sued him between the fall of 1826 and the fall of 1828. Hamilton probably hocked his new silver plate almost immediately, but it was not enough to keep the bailiffs away. They sold off his oxen, steers, cows, and calves, as well as seven of his slaves—Lawrence, George, Peter, Isaac, Lotty, Sarah, and a little girl named Sereny. They also put up for sale 499 acres of Hamilton's best land. Even the elegant secretary desk from his plantation house ended up on the block.[27]

His fortunes collapsing, Hamilton hid in Tennessee in 1830 to avoid yet another creditor. A year later, he moved his family from Rocky Springs to Natchez. In that city's papers, he advertised for sale what remained of his cotton plantation, writing wistfully of the plot's potential as "first quality" land and admitting that he had failed to clear more than 15 percent of it. Yet no one came forward with a decent offer. The same for-sale notice turned up again three months later. That was the last time John Hamilton's name appeared in any southern newspaper. In February 1832, he was summoned to court to pay another outstanding debt, but he failed to appear. Someone told the judge that he had died.[28]

John Henderson, Hamilton's former friend, probably put his new silver plate on his mantel for all to see. He had been eyeing a career in politics, so welcomed the publicity generated by Mayor Watson's generous expression of thanks. A reliable defender of slavery, Henderson saw no contradiction in reminding local residents of his selfless efforts to thwart despicable kidnappers and restore their victims to liberty. Voters agreed and sent him to the Mississippi House of Representatives in 1827 and then to the state's upper chamber. In 1839, his fellow state legislators, most of them slaveholders, appointed him to the US Senate. In Congress, Henderson would repay his supporters by voting for the annexation of Texas to the union as a slave state in 1845, and later by leading an expedition to try to capture Cuba for the United States.[29]

Henderson died in 1857 a wealthy man, the master of more than fifty slaves, and the owner of a sprawling and prosperous plantation. At his memorial services, colleagues from the courts and from Congress lauded his "high moral courage" and tender concern for the oppressed. But his own son (and namesake) stood by and scoffed. John Henderson Jr. had been a small boy when his father had stepped in to help Sam, Enos, Alex, and Mary Fisher. As an adult, he loudly and publicly disavowed his politician father's proslavery positions and embraced radical abolitionism. During the Civil War, John Henderson Jr. spoke out against the Confederacy and in favor of full voting rights for black men. This was a dangerous platform for any southerner in the 1860s. He was murdered by a mob of racist city police in July 1866 after giving a speech in support of racial equality at a rally in New Orleans.[30]

Twists and turns almost as dark and dramatic also marked the lives of the three white southerners most directly involved in Cornelius Sinclair's struggle against slavery. One of those men was James Paul, the defendant in Cornelius's freedom suit. Paul had never been popular in Tuscaloosa, and the news that he had knowingly bought the life and labor of a free black child finally ruined his reputation there. He left town after losing the Sinclair case, taking with him at least four enslaved young men. He set up a new tin shop in Columbus, a smaller settlement just across the border in eastern Mississippi. In 1843, the Columbus sheriff arrested him on suspicion of having killed a slave of his who had tried to run away—and for having then burned the body to disguise his crime. Paul died in jail before he could face trial.[31]

Robert Kennon and Joshua Boucher, the Methodist ministers who had risked their reputations to help Cornelius file charges against James Paul, made two very different life choices in that suit's aftermath. Kennon never did anything so bold or brave again, and promised his fellow Tuscaloosans that he posed no threat to their rights as slaveholders. True to his word, Kennon limited his subsequent politicking to serving as a founding vice president of the Alabama Colonization Society, a controversial new organization that sought to strengthen slavery in the state by deporting its tiny free black population to Africa.[32]

The thought of that sort of complicity with the Slave Power would have turned Joshua Boucher's stomach. His own brush with the Reverse Underground Railroad had unsettled him deeply. At the end of 1826, he decided to leave the South for good. He told his superiors that he wanted nothing more to do with slavery and received a transfer to the Methodist circuit in Ohio, a free state.[33]

✢

Boucher's decision was powerful proof of the mark that Cornelius had made upon him, but it was perhaps the least significant legacy of the five boys' fight for freedom. That legacy was tangible, durable, and undeniably potent—especially in the free states. In Pennsylvania, their 1825 abduction spurred free black activists and their allies in the Pennsylvania Abolition Society to lobby for tougher laws to help Mayor Watson and High Constable Garrigues bring their kidnappers to justice. In early 1826, they took that fight to Harrisburg, the state capital, and in meetings with representatives there, repeatedly returned to the plight of these five children to personalize and humanize their cause. Legislators were evidently moved. The bill they signed into law that June gave mayors and constables across the state new tools and powers to police slave catchers and detain and interrogate suspected kidnappers. John Purnell, convicted in 1827, and Thomas Collins, convicted in 1828, were the first two suspects to be held, tried, and sentenced under the state's new personal liberty law.[34]

Southern slaveholders were infuriated by Pennsylvania's 1826 law and challenged it in federal court. In 1842, the US Supreme

Court struck it down. In a sweeping ruling, the justices declared all state-level personal liberty laws to be null and void, and demanded they be dismantled. Local lawmakers in New York, New Jersey, and Pennsylvania refused on point of principle and condemned the judgment as an assault on states' rights. In retaliation for such blatant defiance of federal power, southerners in Congress later pushed through the Fugitive Slave Act of 1850, a piece of federal legislation that deprived anyone remotely resembling a runaway slave of their right to a jury trial. This new law, which made it easier for kidnappers to disguise their work as legal slave catching, effectively declared open season on black families in the free states. It was so inflammatory and extreme that many historians regard it as the single most significant cause of the Civil War.[35]

The boys' long nightmare also injected fresh urgency into ongoing antislavery and antikidnapping work. For instance, in 1827, Benjamin Lundy, the indefatigable editor of the *Genius of Universal Emancipation* newspaper, gathered a dozen Maryland Quakers to set up the Baltimore Society for the Protection of Free People of Colour. Two years later, in 1829, the delegates to the American Convention of Abolition Societies, meeting in Washington, DC, formed a permanent "Committee on Kidnapping" to document the ongoing ravages of the Reverse Underground Railroad. Members of this new committee soon began to churn out regular reports and exposés. Their goal was to stir up northerners' fears that slavers were making a mockery of their region's status as free soil, a complaint that would later gain traction and emerge as a central pillar of the Republican Party's platform.[36]

Antislavery activists also learned some lasting lessons about how to court public opinion from the unprecedented publicity generated by the boys' ordeal. Theirs had been the first kidnapping in American history to be so obsessively reported and discussed. It had earned coverage in no less than forty-two newspapers and magazines in at least twenty-three cities in twelve states and the District of Columbia. Noticing that the boys' story had struck a nerve, antislavery activists retold it again and again over the following decades, mustering its macabre details as damning proof of southern slavery's insidious encroachment north of the Mason-Dixon Line.[37]

As a result, antislavery authors also began to put other black children at the center of their print campaigns. In hopes of attracting the same sort of publicity that the boys' case had commanded in the 1820s, activists who came of age in the 1830s crafted increasing numbers of nonfiction narratives and commentaries that focused on vulnerable young people violated by American slavery. Lydia Maria Child and Theodore Dwight Weld, the two most prominent antislavery writers of this generation, each clearly remembered what had happened to Sam, Cornelius, and the others and took the lead in a coordinated campaign to fill pamphlets, tracts, magazines, and newspapers with true tales of other black boys and girls ripped from their parents by kidnappers or legal slave traders. The result was an avalanche of sentimental propaganda that pulled powerfully at the heartstrings of northern white parents with sons and daughters of their own.[38]

Activists working in the lost boys' wake also pressed the language of kidnapping into expanded service. To try to rekindle the fury sparked in northern newspaper readers by the exploits of Patty Cannon, John Purnell, and the Johnson brothers, antislavery authors began describing all sorts of other stakeholders in American slavery as man stealers and child snatchers—that is, as kidnappers. One early adopter was Elizur Wright, the secretary of William Lloyd Garrison's Boston-based American Anti-Slavery Society. In the mid-1830s, Wright penned a series of newspaper columns under the title "Chronicles of Kidnapping in New York." In each one he described the largely legal activities of slave catchers in Manhattan using language designed to conjure the illegal operations of kidnappers on the Reverse Underground Railroad.[39]

Campaigners also began to use the same deliberate naming practices to impeach the domestic slave trade, repeatedly describing law-abiding businessmen like Franklin and Armfield as kidnappers or "nigger stealers." The same activists even tried to leverage the potent vocabulary of kidnapping to characterize slaveholding itself. As George Bourne argued in his illustrated *Picture of Slavery* in 1834, "He who claims a coloured child as his property, and nurtures and detains it in slavery, is equally a *man-thief* with the *negro-stealer* . . . Every coloured child born in his house, which he claims and holds as his property, is shamelessly kidnapped."[40]

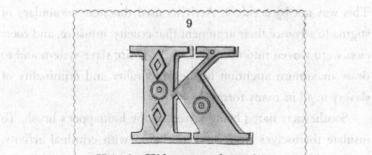

9

K is the Kidnapper, who stole
That little child and mother—
Shrieking, it clung around her, but
He tore them from each other.

In the second quarter of the nineteenth century, the language of kidnapping became a powerful weapon in the antislavery fight, used to characterize and denounce every type of enslavement. Hannah Townsend, The Anti-Slavery Alphabet, *Philadelphia, 1846. (Courtesy of the Library Company of Philadelphia.)*

Over time, more of Bourne's comrades began to say the same. Writing in 1855, on the eve of the trial of Solomon Northup's abductors, Henry Wright denounced the fifteen states in the union where slavery was still legal as a "Confederacy of Kidnappers" whose millions of victims would be liberated only by a full-fledged freedom war. There are, Wright wrote, "4,000,000 . . . kidnapped men, women, and children still under the American lash. Who will help to redeem them, and pay for their sufferings? Who can?"[41]

By then, a profound and permanent change had taken place in the language that many in the movement used to talk about and represent slavery. Words like "kidnapper" and "man stealer" were everywhere, their usage in print having doubled and tripled in the quarter century after 1825. Most antislavery authors now embraced "kidnap" as the preferred term to describe and denounce all sorts of instances in which black people were captured or held as slaves. This was not by accident. Activists used this new vocabulary of stigma to advance their argument that cruelty, injustice, and coercion were woven into the fabric of the entire slave system and to draw maximum attention to the immorality and criminality of slavery in all its many forms.[42]

Southerners hated being tarred by the kidnapper's brush. To insulate themselves from any association with criminal activity, legal traders launched face-saving public-relations campaigns beginning in the 1830s. Some took to the press to rebuke well-known kidnappers like George Alberti and the Gap Gang as loudly as possible. Others, like Franklin and Armfield, tried to elevate their image by allowing antislavery campaigners to inspect their depots and pore over their account books. A few proslavery spokesmen even tried in vain to persuade the northern reading public that Harriet Tubman and her fellow conductors on the Underground Railroad were the real kidnappers and man stealers.[43]

By the eve of the Civil War, the language of kidnapping had found its way into every corner of the slavery debate. It drew power and strength from the images of vulnerable children it readily brought to mind and allowed activists on both sides to paint their opponents as inhuman wretches who had no respect for individual consent, family integrity, states' rights, or the rule of law.

Conclusion

THE FIRST LAW
OF NATURE

T HE MORE ENERGY that white activists poured into their polemical print campaigns, the less time they found for kidnapping casework. The Baltimore Protection Society, founded in 1827, broke up two years later. The American Convention's Committee on Kidnapping also fizzled soon after, when members began to abandon it in favor of William Lloyd Garrison's newly formed American Anti-Slavery Society. By 1835, Benjamin Lundy's *Genius of Universal Emancipation* had shuttered too. Even the venerable Pennsylvania Abolition Society now took on fewer new cases.[1]

The timing of white activists' retreat from direct action was terrible. Free black people in the North were being squeezed from all sides in the 1830s. In Philadelphia, competition from immigrant job seekers arriving from Europe was narrowing African Americans' prospects as never before. Meanwhile, Democrats in the state legislature were drafting bills that would soon block black constituents from casting ballots in elections.[2]

Out on Philadelphia's streets, tension was rising. Watson and

Garrigues had both left office and their successors saw little to gain by protecting black nonvoters from harm. People who looked like Sam, Cornelius, Enos, and Alex now risked being jumped by bands of "rough looking white men and boys" looking for trouble. Soon enough, those brutal but isolated attacks gave way to waves of full-blown race riots in which hooligans torched black churches, schools, and homes and tortured or killed African American residents.[3]

Fearful for their lives, some black Philadelphians left the city in the late 1820s and early 1830s, heading for points north and west. Those recently arrived from slave states were the most likely to join this disillusioned exodus, and it is tempting to imagine Sam doing just that: reuniting with his parents and brothers in West Jersey, persuading them to walk out of slavery, and then setting out together on the long and dangerous journey toward Canada.[4]

Sadly, that's not what happened. Instead, Sam stayed put. He left his debtors' prison cell around the time he gave testimony at John Purnell's trial and then built a life for himself hiding in plain sight in the courts and alleys of Philadelphia's black neighborhoods. For years he kept his head down, but then, suddenly, there he is, caught in the middle of a race riot in the summer of 1835 "in which the fury of a mob was directed against the persons and property of the colored inhabitants."[5]

When a pack of white thugs fell upon him, Sam, now in his mid-twenties, gave as good as he got. He had to be pulled away by police and appeared in court that fall charged with three counts of assault. In a bizarre twist, one of his alleged victims turned out to be Thomas Shipley, a pacifist Quaker and PAS leader who had "disguised himself in such a manner as not to be recognized" to try to infiltrate the mob. When Shipley revealed his identity to the court, Sam might have presumed the charges would be dropped. But the state had other plans, and a jury of twelve white men quickly pronounced him guilty. The judge sentenced the young black man to thirteen months behind bars. A bailiff dragged him away. History loses sight of Sam afterward, and his name appears in no subsequent city directory, census record, or church membership list.[6]

✛

Enos, Alex, and Cornelius would also remain in Philadelphia, growing to manhood during this dark and dangerous time. To defend the way of life they had worked to build over the previous decades, members of embattled black communities in Philadelphia, New York, and elsewhere across the Northeast had to struggle mightily. They rebuilt churches, homes, and schools destroyed by white rioters. They created newspapers, libraries, literary societies, and lyceums. They also formed more than seventy-five new self-help and mutual-aid societies in Philadelphia alone between 1831 and 1838.[7]

Significantly, many of these groups sprang to life in response to the continued threat to black liberty posed by the conductors and station agents of the Reverse Underground Railroad. "We must look to our own safety and protection from kidnappers," David Ruggles told the *Liberator*'s many black readers in 1836, "remembering that 'self-defense is the first law of nature.'" By then, those readers had already set up several freedom-fighting clubs and organizations. The first of these was the Protecting Society for the Preventing of Kidnapping and Man-Stealing, a rapid-response unit organized by a small group of black elites in Philadelphia in 1827, in the wake of John Purnell's arrest. The society operated as an unofficial auxiliary of the whites-only Pennsylvania Abolition Society. It soon ran out of money, but during its short life, members succeeded in connecting lawyers on the society's acting committee with several "persons desirous of assistance in the recovery of their friends who have been kidnapped."[8]

David Ruggles set up the nation's first stand-alone black self-defense society a few years later. Founded in New York in 1835, Ruggles's Vigilance Committee quickly spawned copycat clubs in Philadelphia and across the mid-Atlantic states. These vigilance committees operated independently of lawyerly, all-white antislavery groups like the PAS and focused on community engagement and organizing. Members launched neighborhood watches, opened safe houses, posted notices warning local residents to be on the lookout for kidnappers and slave catchers, and rang bells when they spotted someone they suspected. In New York, Ruggles also published the name of every kidnapper he came across, producing in effect the nation's first most-wanted list.[9]

The next generation of black self-defense groups proved bolder still. For years, black vigilantes had lashed out at individual people of color they suspected of collaborating with kidnapping crews like the Cannon-Johnson ring and the Gap Gang. However, in the 1830s and 1840s, African Americans finally began to set upon white predators as well, a retaliation that marks a major escalation in their freedom fight. They would beat up slave catchers and kidnappers alike, refusing to differentiate between them. "Whether the kidnappers were clothed with legal authority or not, I did not care to inquire," William Parker, the leader of one armed posse in Chester County, Pennsylvania, later recalled. "Ourselves, our wives, our little ones, were insecure.... We felt that something must be done."[10]

The passage of the Fugitive Slave Law of 1850 only intensified the determination of Parker and his peers to use violence in defense of their liberty. The law's willfully proslavery provisions made it far easier for kidnappers to pass themselves off as legal slave catchers or bounty hunters, and spurred an enormous and terrifying wave of new abductions. Across the North, free black men and women fought this fresh onslaught with everything they had. As Henry Wright reported in the pages of the *Liberator* in October 1850, many African Americans had begun "arming themselves with pistols, bowie knives, and rifles, and learning to use them." One biracial group in Boston who called themselves the Anti-Man-Hunting League even met weekly to practice moves that members could use to seize, disarm, and restrain anyone they suspected of hunting black people.[11]

The Anti-Man-Hunting League was one of several new vigilante organizations formed in open defiance of the 1850 federal fugitive slave law. Between 1850 and 1859, these black and biracial neighborhood militias staged more than eighty rescue attempts—many of them violent, some of them successful.[12]

❖

There is every reason to wonder whether any of the three lost boys who grew up in Philadelphia ever joined the ranks of these militant self-defense groups. Cornelius, Enos, and Alex had taken their first steps toward antislavery activism by giving damning public testimony against their kidnappers and enslavers in 1826 and 1827. They may well have returned to this antislavery fight as adults, when friends or neighbors needed their help.

A great many of their contemporaries did just that. Later in life, black leaders like David Ruggles (b. 1810), William Wells Brown (b. 1814), Henry Highland Garnet (b. 1815), William Still (b. 1821), and William Parker (b. 1821) would each assert that their own careers in the cause had been catalyzed by personal encounters with kidnappers. The same was surely true for many among the massive army of silent soldiers in the free black self-defense movement who never rose to front-rank positions.[13]

Many free black leaders of the antebellum antislavery campaign joined that movement as a result of their own encounters with agents or survivors of the Reverse Underground Railroad. From left to right: William Wells Brown, Henry Highland Garnet, and William Still. (Left and right: Courtesy of the Library Company of Philadelphia. Center: Courtesy of the National Portrait Gallery, Washington, DC.)

Without more evidence, we cannot know for sure whether Cornelius, Enos, or Alex joined one of these vigilante groups. Membership was often secret, and hundreds of people moved in and out of these loose networks from year to year. Most free black freedom fighters were, after all, only part-time paramilitaries. They had jobs to work and families to feed. In time, so too would Cornelius, Enos, and Alex, and none of them ever achieved the level of financial independence and comfort needed to pursue antislavery activist work full-time.

Cornelius was the only one among them who knew how to read and write. He might once have been able to land a job in a store or a print shop, two of the few places where his hard work back at the Adelphi School would be useful. Yet those positions were slipping out of reach in the 1830s and 1840s, as antiblack hostility grew and African Americans' access to jobs with prospects shrank. Most black men who grew up when he did had to make

do with menial work: sawing wood, whitewashing walls, or picking rags—three dirty, poorly paid jobs that white men insisted
were beneath them. Cornelius avoided that fate when his father
helped him find a position as a porter instead. The work kept him
on his feet hauling goods around the city every day and paid pennies, but Cornelius was evidently industrious. At the age of twenty-
two, the last time his name turns up in surviving records, he opened
an account at the Philadelphia Savings Fund Society, a sure sign
that he had his eyes fixed on the future.[14]

Enos and Alex found the ever-shrinking job market just as difficult to navigate. Enos's former employer, Samuel Murray, regarded
him as "quite stupid" and refused to take him back to train him as a
master sweep. Lacking skills and with his father still often absent at
sea, Enos soon fell into bad company. In March 1828, constables

THE WOOD-SAWYER.   (96)   THE WHITEWASHER.   (14)   THE RAG-PICKER.   (82)

*Sawing wood, whitewashing walls, and collecting rags for reuse were among the jobs
available for poor, unskilled free black men in antebellum Philadelphia.* City Characters; or, Familiar Scenes in Town. Illustrated with Twenty-Four Designs, *Philadelphia, 1851. (Left and right: Courtesy of the American Antiquarian Society. Center:
Courtesy of the Library Company of Philadelphia.)*

arrested and charged him on two counts of petty larceny. He was not yet fifteen, so he served just two days behind bars. After that, his trail is difficult to follow. Perhaps he made his way by picking pockets, breaking and entering, or fencing stolen goods. Or perhaps he found honest work, married well, and settled down.[15]

Alex would do just that—though it took him years. He had hated school, never learning to read or write, and spent his working life doing manual labor of one kind or another. He went to sea in 1837, just before his eighteenth birthday, toiling as a deckhand on the same New Orleans to Philadelphia route that he had traveled a decade earlier. It was dangerous work, as black seamen still risked being seized and sold into slavery if they set foot on shore in southern port cities. Alex had no intention of being kidnapped and enslaved again, so he quit as soon as he could. By the time he was twenty-eight, he was back in Philadelphia doing odd jobs and living in a tiny back-alley apartment that he shared with seven other people. A few years later, he married another native Philadelphian, a free black woman named Mary. They had four children together, two of whom survived to adulthood. Alex would live until 1869, just long enough to see slavery in the United States destroyed in the carnage of the Civil War.[16]

❖

Making the best of lives as hard as these was in itself a way to do important antislavery work. To find moments of grace in the midst of struggle and loss was difficult and harrowing—but essential. To build lives that reveled in liberty and that refused to buckle in the face of oppression was to assert a vision of the United States in which free black people had a permanent home and an unshakable right to remain. This was vital activism, no less significant in African Americans' ongoing fight for equality than any subsequent petition or public protest.[17]

Of course, Sam, Joe, Cornelius, Enos, and Alex had already left an extraordinary mark. Whether they knew it or not, their ordeal clearly and directly advanced the cause of racial justice in America. Their courage helped free black people see that vigilance and violence were powerful tools to fight slavery and defend their liberty. Their sufferings also reshaped the antislavery movement by demonstrating the emotional power of placing the sorrows of separated families and tormented children center stage. Most immediately, their abduction spurred passage of a tough new personal liberty law in Pennsylvania that ratcheted up tensions between the North and the South, driving the country ever closer to the racial reckoning of civil war.

ACKNOWLEDGMENTS

LIVING WITH THESE five boys for so long has given me a lot of time to think about children, parents, and families—including my own. I first came across their story in 2011 during a visit to the Library Company of Philadelphia, my favorite place to work. At the time, my wife and I were thinking about starting a family. The thought of a child like ours falling into the hands of people like John Purnell, Joseph Johnson, and Patty Cannon left me choking back tears in a rare-book room in the middle of the day. Now, almost a decade later, we have two young daughters. The thought that anyone could take our children from us—and that we might be powerless to stop them—still tears at me in a primal, elemental way. Families belong together.

My own family is close but far-flung. I've spent my adult life in the United States, so I treasure the love, care, and support of my parents and sister back in Britain all the more. My wife Monica's wonderful American family has made the separation easier to bear. So too does she, while our children, Ruby and Rosie, make every day in our house a joy—an exhausting, hilarious joy. I am so pleased to be able to show Ruby, our encourager-in-chief, that this book is now finally finished. Monica, more than anyone else, made this possible. She is my first, last, and best reader, the reader whose opinion matters to me most. She also covered my many absences for many years. We both know what I owe her.

I was on the road a long time doing research for this book, and it's a blissful act of closure to here thank the many archivists, librarians, and curators who fielded my pestering questions. They include Judy Bolton, Jennie Claybrook, Chris Densmore, Karie Diethorn, Connie King, Cindy Knight, Catherine Medich, Mimi Miller, Jackie Penny, and Matt Turi. Particular thanks to John Boyd, Emily Deal, Carolyn Wiggins, and the rest of the team of volunteer conservators and digitizers at the Tuscaloosa Genealogical Society, without whom much of Cornelius's story would have been lost in the decay of a damp attic. The same goes for Weckea Lilly, Reg Pitts, and Joe Stuart, three gifted genealogists and researchers who double- and triple-checked my work as I tried, mostly in vain, to keep up with the boys on their journey into adulthood after their return to Philadelphia.

Poking around in archives in so many states up and down the country required a great deal of financial support, and I am pleased to be able to acknowledge this little book's many generous benefactors, including the American Antiquarian Society, the American Philosophical Society, the Central New York Humanities Corridor, Duke University Special Collections, the Historical Society of Pennsylvania, the Huntington Library, the Library Company of Philadelphia, the John W. Kluge Center at the Library of Congress, the Massachusetts Historical Society, the Schomburg Center at the New York Public Library, the North Caroliniana Society, the Virginia Historical Society, and the University of Maryland. The National Endowment for the Humanities—the beleaguered government agency that does so much with so little—funded this project not once but twice, and I could not be prouder to be associated with its programs and professional staff.

Every road warrior hits roadblocks, and I'm in the debt of all the scholars who have shared their own smarts and some of their own sources over the years to help me get back on track. Among them were Jeff Bolster, George Boudreau, Corey Brooks, Al Brophy, Mary Daggett, Andrew Diemer, Elliott Drago, Daniel Dupre, Rob Gamble, Jim Gigantino, Sarah Gronningsater, Scott Heerman, Leon Jackson, Stephanie Jones-Rogers, Natalie Joy, Elise Kamerer, Scott Marler, Skip Medairy, James Miller, Sharon Moore, Christen Mucher, Kathryn Olivarius, Paul Polgar, Jayne Ptolemy, Adam Rothman, Josh Rothman, Calvin Schermerhorn, Rebecca Scott, Samantha Seeley, Billy Smith, Sharon Sundue, Phil Troutman, William Wagner, and Kim Welch.

Shepherding this book into production was also the work of many hands. Many seminar participants and conference goers heard bits and pieces along the way and shared excellent ideas, and many more friends and colleagues read drafts as the book took shape. They include the members of my writing group, which meets in windowless storerooms around campus every two weeks, as well as four current and former doctoral students, Dusty Dye, Nicole Mahoney, Ashley Towle, and Rachel Walker. During the final push, I got valuable feedback on the entire manuscript from more than two dozen expert readers, among them Julia Bell, Nik Berry, Chris Bonner, Will Cavert, Alexandra DeLaite, Connie King, Nadine Knight, Pete McKean, Whitney Martinko, Amanda Moniz, Jess Roney, Jason Sharples, Adam Rothman, and the magnificent Jane Kamensky.

Finding visual images to illuminate the boys' journey along the Reverse Underground Railroad was downright difficult, and I'm grateful to Heather Moore, Marie Lamoureux, Ann McShane, and the dozen other reproduction and permission managers at the many archives whose rich collections helped me to illustrate this story. That goes double for Caitlin Burke at the University of Maryland's GIS and Geospatial Services Center, who custom built the book's maps. My gratitude too to the editors of the *Journal of the Early Republic*, *Slavery & Abolition*, and *History Compass* for the chance to flesh out some of my arguments in earlier, stand-alone articles, and to Katherine Flynn, my splendid agent, and Dawn Davis, my no-nonsense editor. Both Katherine and Dawn found something in this story in its early days and worked hard to push it into print.

Finally, the warmest of thanks to Phil Soergel, the chair of the Department of History at Maryland; to Gail Russell and Lisa Klein, two of the department's amazing professional staff; and to the several talented undergraduate students who worked on parts of this project with me over the years. My friends in the department, including Janna Bianchini, Chris Bonner, Holly Brewer, Clare Lyons, and Mike Ross, have also been generous with their time and advice and have set the bar so very high in their own work. My only regret is that our dear colleague Ira Berlin did not live to see this day. I miss him. He was the best of us.

NOTES

Introduction: THE REVERSE UNDERGROUND RAILROAD

1. Edward G. Gray, "The First Partition: The Troubled Origins of the Mason-Dixon Line," in *The American Revolution Reborn*, ed. Patrick Spero and Michael Zuckerman (Philadelphia: University of Pennsylvania Press, 2016), 272–75 (quote on 275).
2. William J. Switala, *The Underground Railroad in Pennsylvania* (Mechanicsburg, PA: Stackpole Books, 2001); David W. Blight, ed., *Passages to Freedom: The Underground Railroad in History and Memory* (Washington, DC: Smithsonian Books, 2004); Keith P. Griffler, *Front Line of Freedom: African Americans and the Forging of the Underground Railroad in the Ohio Valley* (Lexington: University Press of Kentucky, 2004); Larry Gara, *The Liberty Line: The Legend of the Underground Railroad* (Lexington: University Press of Kentucky, 1961).
3. Writing in 1987, historian Julie Winch was the first to draw the comparison between the trade in kidnapped free black people and the Underground Railroad. Julie Winch, "Philadelphia and the Other Underground Railroad," *Pennsylvania Magazine of History and Biography* 111, no. 1 (January 1987): 3–25.
4. "Enabling Freedom," *National Underground Railroad Freedom Center*, accessed June 17, 2018, http://freedomcenter.org/enabling-freedom; *Underground*, Internet Movie Database, accessed June 17, 2018, www.imdb.com/title/tt4522400.
5. The only significant scholarly treatment of the trade in kidnapped people of color is Carol Wilson, *Freedom at Risk: The Kidnapping of Free Blacks in America, 1780–1865* (Lexington: University Press of Kentucky, 1994).
6. Solomon Northup, *Twelve Years a Slave* (New York: Penguin, 2013), 12–55.
7. Steven McQueen, dir., *12 Years a Slave* (Century City, CA: Fox Searchlight Pictures, 2013), DVD.

Chapter 1: SANCTUARY CITY

1. Isaac Harvey, diary entry, August 9, 1825, Isaac Harvey Papers, Historical Society of Pennsylvania, Philadelphia (hereafter cited as Harvey Papers).

2. Tyrone Power, *Impressions of America During the Years 1833, 1834, and 1835*, 2 vols. (London, 1836), 1: 189.

3. "Kidnapping," *African Observer: A Monthly Journal, Containing Essays and Documents* (February 1827): 38.

4. Candice L. Harrison, "The Contest of Exchange: Space, Power, and Politics in Philadelphia's Public Markets, 1770–1859" (PhD diss., Emory University, 2008), 89, 108, 120, 123, and 168.

5. Power, *Impressions of America*, 1: 192; John Finch, *Travels in the United States of America and Canada Containing Some Account of Their Scientific Institutions, And . . . An Essay on the Natural Boundaries of Empires* (London, 1833), 76–77 and 91–92.

6. "Kidnapping," *African Observer*, 39; "William Pettigon, alias Bill Paragee," *Washington Whig* (Bridgeton, NJ), June 2, 1827.

7. "Kidnapping," *African Observer*, 39–40.

8. Ibid., 40.

9. Ibid.

10. William B. Roatch, deposition, February 16, 1826, item 274, Joseph Watson Papers, 1824–1828, Historical Society of Pennsylvania, Philadelphia (hereafter cited as JWP).

11. John Henderson to Joseph Watson, January 2, 1826, item 262, JWP.

12. "Kidnapping," *African Observer*, May 1827, 139. Contemporaries estimated Joe's age as being between fourteen and sixteen, depending on the date of their testimony. In a 2016 essay, I incorrectly asserted that Joe was just six years old in 1826. I regret the error. Richard Bell, " 'Thence to Patty Cannon's': Gender, Family, and the Reverse Underground Railroad," *Slavery & Abolition* 37, no. 1 (December 2016): 661–79.

13. Minutes, Tuscaloosa County Circuit Court Sitting in Chancery 1826–1829, Tuscaloosa County Courthouse, Tuscaloosa, Alabama, March 12, 1827, 182 (hereafter cited as TCCC); "Kidnapping," *African Observer*, 139.

14. Henderson to Watson, January 2, 1826, item 262, JWP; James J. Gigantino II, *The Ragged Road to Abolition: Slavery and Freedom in New Jersey, 1775–1865* (Philadelphia: University of Pennsylvania Press, 2015), 7.

15. James P. Snell, comp., *History of Hunterdon and Somerset Counties, New Jersey, with Illustrations and Biographical Sketches of Its Prominent Men and Pioneers* (Philadelphia, 1881), 506; Gigantino, *The Ragged Road*, 7; Phyllis B. D'Autrechy, ed., *Some Records of Old Hunterdon County, 1701–1838* (Trenton, NJ: Trenton Printing Company, 1979), 230–31; Abstract of List of Documents, March 10, 1826, item 274, JWP; John W. Hamilton to Watson, January 27, 1826, item 272, JWP. Sam's birth does not appear in the incomplete list of slave births in Hunterdon County compiled by Phyllis B. D'Autrechy.

16. Gigantino, *The Ragged Road*, 7; D'Autrechy, *Some Records*, 171 and 196–98.

17. Abstract of List of Documents, March 10, 1826, item 274, JWP.

18. Gigantino, *The Ragged Road*, 95; Phyllis B. D'Autrechy, ed., *More Records of*

Old Hunterdon County, 2 vols. (Flemington, NJ: Hunterdon County Historical Society, 2000), 2: 116. There were 178 slaves in Hunterdon County in 1830 according to the census. D'Autrechy, *Some Records*, 204.

19. D'Autrechy, *More Records*, 2: 116; Israel Hendrickson, deposition, February 17, 1826, item 274, JWP. David and Maria Hill had twelve children in all. For a family tree, see William H. Mitchell to Hiram E. Deats, September 3, 1925, Hill Genealogical File, Hunterdon County Historical Society, Flemington, NJ.

20. Gigantino, *The Ragged Road*, 282–85; D'Autrechy, *Some Records*, 105 and 144.

21. Abstract of List of Documents, March 10, 1826, item 274, JWP.

22. Gigantino, *The Ragged Road*, 7 and 118–21. In Trenton, state legislators talked openly and excitedly about plans to forcibly relocate New Jersey's free black population to West Africa.

23. In 1780, Quaker legislators in Pennsylvania had led the charge to pass the new nation's first statewide gradual emancipation law, which set race slavery in the state on a path to extinction within a generation.

24. Gigantino, *The Ragged Road*, 122–23.

25. Eric Foner, *Gateway to Freedom: The Hidden History of the Underground Railroad* (New York: W. W. Norton, 2015), 4; Elwood L. Bridner Jr., "The Fugitive Slaves of Maryland," *Maryland Historical Magazine* 66, no. 1 (1971): 36–38. Vagrancy dockets from the mid-1790s suggest that three out of every five arriving migrants had come from one or another of the slave states of the Upper South. While most were fugitives, some were manumitted people.

26. Erica Armstrong Dunbar, *A Fragile Freedom: African American Women and Emancipation in the Antebellum City* (New Haven, CT: Yale University Press, 2008), 4; Leonard P. Curry, *The Free Black in Urban America, 1800–1850: The Shadow of the Dream* (Chicago: University of Chicago, 1981), 256. One survey of data from the 1790s found that the vast majority of the city's free black population (eleven out of every twelve people) had been born somewhere other than Philadelphia, most of them into slavery. Likewise, an 1838 survey found that one in four black households contained at least one family member who had been born a slave. Gary B. Nash, *Forging Freedom: The Formation of Philadelphia's Black Community, 1720–1840* (Cambridge, MA: Harvard University Press, 1988), 134–35; Theodore Herschberg, "Free Blacks in Antebellum Philadelphia: A Study of Ex-Slaves, Freeborn, and Socioeconomic Decline," *Journal of Social History* 5, no. 2 (1971): 192.

27. John C. Fitzpatrick, ed., *The Writings of George Washington*, 39 vols. (Washington, DC: US Government Printing Office, 1939), 29: 78–79.

28. Daniel E. Meaders, comp., *Kidnappers in Philadelphia: Isaac Hopper's Tales of Oppression, 1780–1843* (New York: Garland, 1994), 179; Richard S. Newman, "'Lucky to Be Born in Pennsylvania': Free Soil, Fugitive Slaves and the Making of Pennsylvania's Anti-Slavery Borderland," *Slavery & Abolition* 32, no. 3 (September 2011): 418. On a visit to the Baltimore Almshouse in 1831, Alexis de Tocqueville and Gustave de Beaumont encountered an African American man rendered insane by his fear of the slave trader Austin Woolfolk. "The

Negro of whom I speak," de Tocqueville observed, "imagines that this man sticks close to him day and night and snatches away bits of his flesh." Alexis de Tocqueville, *Journey to America*, ed. J. P. Mayer, trans. George Lawrence (Westport, CT: Greenwood Press, 1981), 159–60. So acute was this terror that when slave catchers did occasionally come knocking, several cornered runaways cut their throats rather than surrender their freedom and return to slavery. Meaders, *Tales of Oppression*, 18, 262, and 305–7; Herbert Aptheker, ed., *A Documentary History of the Negro People in the United States*, 2 vols. (New York: Citadel Press, 1969), 1: 73; "Liberation!" *Niles Weekly Register* (Baltimore), May 19, 1821.

29. Meaders, *Tales of Oppression*, 21.

30. Dunbar, *Fragile Freedom*, 4; Herschberg, "Free Blacks," 197–98; Sam Bass Warner Jr., *The Private City: Philadelphia in Three Periods of its Growth* (Philadelphia: University of Pennsylvania Press, 1968), 126–27; Julie Winch, "Self-Help and Self-Determination: Black Philadelphians and the Dimensions of Freedom," in *Antislavery and Abolition in Philadelphia: Emancipation and the Long Struggle for Racial Justice in the City of Brotherly Love*, ed. Richard Newman and James Mueller (Baton Rouge: Louisiana State University Press, 2011), 78–79; Curry, *The Free Black*, 49–50 and 75–76. For a useful map, see Nash, *Forging Freedom*, 168.

31. "Report on Female Wages," in *Miscellaneous Essays*, ed. Mathew Carey (Philadelphia, 1830), 267; Herschberg, "Free Blacks," 199.

32. Herschberg, "Free Blacks," 199; Nash, *Forging Freedom*, 148–49; Emma Jones Lapsansky, "South Street Philadelphia, 1762–1854: 'A Haven for Those Low in the World'" (PhD diss., University of Pennsylvania, 1975), 124. On the city's black elite, which numbered about one thousand persons in 1820, see Julie Winch, *Philadelphia's Black Elite: Activism, Accommodation, and the Struggle for Autonomy, 1787–1848* (Philadelphia: Temple University Press, 1988).

33. Henderson to Watson, January 2, 1826, item 262, JWP; Wilson, *Freedom at Risk*, 40–41; W. Jeffrey Bolster, *Black Jacks: African American Seamen in the Age of Sail* (Cambridge, MA: Harvard University Press, 1997), 158–60, 171–72, 200–201, and 236. By 1820, black sailors filled more than 20 percent of all berths on ships registered in Philadelphia. As a result, the city itself was home to 140 black women for every 100 black men, a demographic phenomenon that left one in five black families to get by without a male head of household. A decade later, little more than three-quarters of black households contained two parents. Herschberg, "Free Blacks," 194.

34. American Convention of Abolition Societies, *Minutes of the Eighteenth Sessions of the American Convention for Promoting the Abolition of Slavery* (Philadelphia: 1823), 13; Priscilla Ferguson Clement, "The Philadelphia Welfare Crisis of the 1820s," *Pennsylvania Magazine of History and Biography* 105, no. 2 (April 1981): 150–65; Nash, *Forging Freedom*, 142 and 173–77. "There appears to exist, in the lower class of white laborers in this city, a very bitter hostility to the colored people," a canny visitor from Connecticut observed in 1835. Ethan

Allen Andrews, *Slavery and the Domestic Slave Trade in the United States. In a Series of Letters Addressed to the Executive Committee of the American Union for the Relief and Improvement of the Colored Race* (Boston, 1836), 30.

35. Nash, *Forging Freedom*, 142, 154–55, 173–81, 210–14, 246–47, and 273; Karl Bernhard, Duke of Saxe-Weimar-Eisenach, *Travels Through North America During the Years 1825 and 1826*, 2 vols. (Philadelphia, 1828), 1: 227. As early as 1813, agitated petitioners to the Pennsylvania State Assembly had demanded tougher control on black migration, swearing that the streets of Philadelphia now teemed with "4000 runaway negroes," most of them "public nuisances." Quoted in Paul J. Polgar, "Standard Bearers of Liberty and Equality: Reinterpreting the Origins of American Abolitionism" (PhD diss., CUNY Graduate Center, 2013), 219.

36. Edward Raymond Turner, *The Negro in Pennsylvania, 1639–1861* (New York: Arno, 1969), 144–45; Nash, *Forging Freedom*, 146.

37. "The Following Is an Account of the Religious Denominations of Coloured People in the City of Philadelphia," *Juvenile Magazine*, July 1, 1813, 21; Winch, "Self Help," 82.

38. Aptheker, *A Documentary History*, 1: 113–14; Nash, *Forging Freedom*, 109, 210–11, and 273.

39. Caleb Kimber, deposition, item 274, JWP; Elise Kammerer, "To Uplift Their Race: Free Black Education and Antislavery Activity in Early National Philadelphia" (PhD diss., University of Cologne, 2016), 140.

40. Kammerer, "Free Black Education," 111–45; Harry S. Silcox, "Delay and Neglect: Negro Public Education in Antebellum Philadelphia, 1800–1860," *Pennsylvania Magazine of History and Biography* 97, no. 4 (October 1973): 444–64.

41. Kammerer, "Free Black Education," 111–45; Silcox, "Delay and Neglect," 444–64; Edward Whiteley, *Philadelphia Directory and Register, for 1821* (Philadelphia, 1821). Education among free people of color in Philadelphia varied according to income and occupation. In 1849, only 7 percent of black almshouse residents could read even a little, and only five in one hundred could "write sufficient to affix their signatures." *A Statistical Inquiry Into the Condition of the People of Colour, of the City and Districts of Philadelphia* (Philadelphia, 1849), 25.

42. Abstract of List of Documents, March 10, 1826, item 274, JWP; "$20 Reward," *United States Gazette* (Philadelphia), November 11, 1825; Henderson to Watson, January 2, 1826, item 262, JWP.

43. Abstract of List of Documents, March 10, 1826, item 274, JWP; Pennsylvania Abolition Society, *The Present State and Condition of the Free People of Color, of the City of Philadelphia and Adjoining Districts, As Exhibited by the Report of a Committee of the Pennsylvania Society For Promoting the Abolition of Slavery Etc* (Philadelphia, 1838), 9–10.

44. Janet Harrison Shannon, "African-American Childhood in Early Philadelphia," in *Multiculturalism: Roots and Realities*, ed. C. James Trotman (Bloomington: Indiana University Press, 2002), 197.

45. Paul A. Gilje and Howard B. Rock, "'Sweep O! Sweep O!': African-American Chimney Sweeps and Citizenship in the New Nation," *William and Mary Quarterly* 51, no. 3 (July 1994): 507–38; George Lewis Phillips, *American Chimney Sweeps: An Historical Account of a Once Important Trade* (Trenton, NJ: Past Times Press, 1957).

46. By 1825, the trade was facing an uncertain future as patented new sweeping machines began to appear. Gilje and Rock, "'Sweep O! Sweep O!,'" 529.

47. "$20 Reward"; Phillips, *American Chimney Sweeps*, 63; Henderson to Watson, January 2, 1826, item 262, JWP; An Indenture of Apprenticeship, October 28, 1823, item 274, JWP.

48. For the kidnapping of another apprentice sweep, see *Minute Book of the Acting Committee, 1810–1822*, reel 5, August 11 and September 8, 1818, Papers of the Pennsylvania Abolition Society 1748–1979, Historical Society of Pennsylvania, Philadelphia (hereafter cited as PAS).

Chapter 2: BLACK HEARTS

1. "$20 Reward." Purnell's other aliases included Spencer Francis and James Morris.

2. For adult victims of kidnapping, see, for example, "The Kidnappers," *Poulson's American Daily Advertiser* (Philadelphia), June 3, 1818; "Reported for the Democratic Press," *Commercial Advertiser* (New York), July 9, 1819; "A Serious Affray," *Relf's Philadelphia Gazette*, September 23, 1819. For complaints to the mayor of Philadelphia about "groups of black boys at the corner of the streets," see Anonymous to Watson, January 16, 1825, item 79, JWP.

3. "Kidnapping," *Genius of Universal Emancipation* (Baltimore), January 28, 1826; J. Williams, Daniel Mason, and Gallaudette Oliver to Watson, September 5, 1824, item 475, JWP; Isaiah Sadler, deposition, September 13, 1824, item 476, JWP; American Convention of Abolition Societies, *Minutes of the Proceedings of the Eighth Convention of Delegates From the Abolition Societies Established in Different Parts of the United States . . .* (Philadelphia, 1803), 11.

4. Shane White, "Freedom's First Con: African Americans and Changing Notes in Antebellum New York City," *Journal of the Early Republic* 34, no. 3 (Fall 2014): 400–409; Michael LeBlanc, "The Color of Confidence: Racial Con Games and the Logic of Gold," *Cultural Critique* 73, no. 1 (Fall 2009): 3; David W. Maurer, *The Big Con: The Story of the Confidence Man and the Confidence Game* (Indianapolis, IN: Bobbs Merrill, 1940), 147–48 and 171; Karen Halttunen, *Confidence Men and Painted Women: A Study of Middle-Class Culture in America, 1830–1870* (New Haven, CT: Yale University Press, 1982), 1–32; Stephen Mihm, *A Nation of Counterfeiters: Capitalists, Con Men, and the Making of the United States* (Cambridge, MA: Harvard University Press, 2007), 92. For a more broadly conceived account of the fluidity and instability of this thriving "counterfeit economy" and the role of petty entrepreneurs, see Brian P. Luskey and Wendy A. Woloson, eds., *Capitalism by Gaslight: Illuminating the Economy of Nineteenth-Century America* (Philadelphia: University of Pennsyl-

vania Press, 2015), especially the essays by Will B. Mackintosh, Brendan P. O'Malley, Corey Goettsch, and Craig B. Hollander. On the first use of the term "confidence man," see Johannes Dietrich Bergmann, "The Original Confidence Man," *American Quarterly* 21, no. 3 (Autumn 1969): 560–77.

5. Peter Still, *The Kidnapped and the Ransomed: The Narrative of Peter and Vina Still After Forty Years of Slavery* (Philadelphia: Jewish Publication Society of America, 1970), 27; "Kidnapping," *Relf's Philadelphia Gazette*, October 2, 1818; "A Serious Affray." See also Richard Bell, "Counterfeit Kin: Kidnappers of Color, the Reverse Underground Railroad, and the Origins of Practical Abolition," *Journal of the Early Republic* 38, no. 2 (Summer 2018): 199–230.

6. "Female Kidnappers!!!!" *Poulson's American Daily Advertiser* (Philadelphia), June 1, 1818; "To the People of Color," *Baltimore Patriot & Mercantile Advertiser*, August 13, 1821. See also Bell, "'Thence to Patty Cannon's,'" 661–79.

7. "Look Out," *Relf's Philadelphia Gazette,* May 22, 1822.

8. Job Brown to Watson, July 5, 1826, item 72, JWP; Humanitas, *Reflections Upon Slavery, with Recent Evidence of Its Inhumanity Occasioned by the Melancholy Death of Romain, a French Negro* (Philadelphia, 1803), 25; "Kidnapping"; Lydia M. Child, *Isaac T. Hopper: A True Life* (Boston, 1854), 70. For evidence that Purnell was married with children, see "On Sunday Afternoon," *Connecticut Herald* (New Haven), June 5, 1827.

9. "Communication," *Baltimore Patriot & Mercantile Advertiser*, July 26, 1817; Carol Wilson, "Active Vigilance Is the Price of Liberty: Black Self-Defense Against Fugitive Slave Recapture and Kidnapping of Free Blacks," in *Antislavery Violence: Sectional, Racial, and Cultural Conflict in Antebellum America*, eds. John R. McKivigan and Stanley Harrold (Knoxville: University of Tennessee Press, 1999), 108–27. These conversations between black parents and their children are analogous to "the talk," the conversation that modern-day parents of color have with their sons about dealing with the police. I am grateful to Emily Clark for suggesting this comparison.

10. Meaders, *Tales of Oppression*, 93–94; "Kidnapping." While these vigilance networks were largely informal in the 1810s and 1820s, the records of the Pennsylvania Abolition Society contain a tantalizing reference to the existence of a "black abolition society" that was focused on kidnapping and that worked on the front lines in 1817. *Minute Book of the Acting Committee, 1810–1822*, reel 5, December 11, 1817, PAS.

11. Aptheker, *Documentary History*, 1: 73–74; Jesse Torrey, *A Portraiture of Slavery in the United States, Proposing National Measures for the Education and Gradual Emancipation of the Slaves, Without Impairing the Legal Privileges of the Possessor: And a Project of Colonial Asylum for Free People of Color Including Memoirs of Facts on the Interior Traffic in Slaves, and on Kidnapping*, 2nd ed. (Ballston Spa, NY, 1818), 84–85. The state subsequently sought the death penalty for John Read, but he was instead eventually convicted of manslaughter and sentenced to nine years behind bars. See also Benjamin Drew, *A North-side View of Slavery. The Refugee; Or, the Narratives of Fugitive Slaves in Canada Related by Themselves.*

With an Account of the History and Condition of the Colored Population of Upper Canada (Boston: J. P. Jewett, 1856), 34–39 and 102; "Kidnapping."

12. Meaders, *Tales of Oppression*, 21 and 310. See also J. W. Loguen, *The Reverend J. W. Loguen, As a Slave and As a Freeman: A Narrative of Real Life* (New York: Negro Universities Press, 1969), 12–13; "Kidnappers"; "From the Morristown Herald. Man Stealing," *Poulson's American Daily Advertiser* (Philadelphia), July 9, 1819; *Minute Book of the Acting Committee, 1822–1842*, reel 5, November 1822, PAS. In 1819, an outraged writer in the same paper urged those accosted by kidnappers to "resolve to put their oppressors to death [at] the first opportunity." "Obligation of Contracts," *Niles Weekly Register* (Baltimore), June 12, 1819.

13. "York, June 21. A Riot," *Relf's Philadelphia Gazette*, June 24, 1825. York was home to the second-largest free black community in Pennsylvania. See also "Serious Affray," *Franklin Gazette* (Philadelphia), January 3, 1820; "Kidnapping"; Torrey, *Portraiture of Slavery*, 97; "Philadelphia."

14. For black writers' denunciations of kidnappers of color in this period, see Bell, "Counterfeit Kin."

15. Todd A. Herring, "Kidnapped and Sold in Natchez: The Ordeal of Aaron Cooper, a Free Black Man," *Journal of Mississippi History* 60, no. 1 (Winter 1998): 341–53; "Kidnapping," *Easton Gazette*, September 4, 1824.

16. On the history of the Pennsylvania Abolition Society, see Edward Needles, *An Historical Memoir of the Pennsylvania Society, for Promoting the Abolition of Slavery; The Relief of Free Negroes Unlawfully Held in Bondage, and for Improving the Conditions of the African Race, Compiled From the Minutes of the Society and Other Official Documents by Edward Needles and Published by Authority of the Society* (Philadelphia, 1848); Richard S. Newman, *The Transformation of American Abolitionism: Fighting Slavery in the Early Republic* (Chapel Hill: University of North Carolina Press, 2002), 16–106.

17. Child, *Isaac T. Hopper*, 23–24 and 46–47.

18. Ibid., 33–34 and 206–7; Margaret Hope Bacon, *Lamb's Warrior: The Life of Isaac T. Hopper* (New York: Thomas Y. Crowell, 1970), 59; Meaders, *Tales of Oppression*, 118.

19. Wilson, *Freedom at Risk*, 87; Turner, *Negro in Pennsylvania*, 211–12; *Minute Book of the Acting Committee, 1800–1824*, reel 1, June 27, 1816, and April 30, 1821, PAS. Established to provide aid to former Caribbean slaves who faced deportation and reenslavement, the PAS only began to handle domestic kidnapping cases in the mid-1790s. Needles, *Historical Memoir*, 24; Richard S. Newman, "The Pennsylvania Abolition Society and the Struggle of Racial Justice" in *Antislavery and Abolition*, 130.

20. *Minute Book of the Acting Committee, 1810–1822*, reel 5, September 5, 1820, PAS; Newman, " 'Lucky to Be Born in Pennsylvania,' " 418–19. See also Meaders, *Tales of Oppression*, 47–48.

21. Pennsylvania General Assembly, *Journal of the Senate of the Commonwealth of Pennsylvania, Which Commenced at Lancaster, the Third Day of December, in the*

Year of Our Lord, One Thousand Eight Hundred and Eleven ... (Lancaster, PA, 1812), 109, 186, and 214–15; Newman, "The Pennsylvania Abolition Society," 122 and 131; Matthew Mason, *Slavery and Politics in the Early American Republic* (Chapel Hill: University of North Carolina Press, 2006), 140–41. On the hidden transcripts associated with black lobbying efforts, see Samantha Seeley, "The Politics of Protection in the Early Republic" (paper presented at the Human Trafficking in Early America Conference, Philadelphia, PA, April 24, 2015), 9–10. At the behest of the PAS, the American Convention of Abolition Societies articulated a concomitant commitment to anti-kidnapping work in the early 1820s. American Convention for Promoting the Abolition of Slavery, *Minutes of the Seventeenth Session of the American Convention for Promoting the Abolition of Slavery, and Improving the Condition of the African Race, Convened at Philadelphia* (Philadelphia, 1821), 29.

22. *Minute Book of the Acting Committee, 1822–1842*, reel 5, September 24, 1822, PAS. During its brief three-year existence, the Maryland Protection Society, which often received cash donations from Baltimore's free black community, also claimed a number of similar successes. In 1818, it reported having "rescued more than sixty human beings" from unlawful slavery over the two years prior. T. Stephen Whitman, *The Price of Freedom: Slavery and Manumission in Baltimore and Early National Maryland* (New York: Routledge, 2000), 81.

23. *Minute Book of the Acting Committee, 1800–1824*, reel 1, March 29, 1821, PAS; Newman, *The Transformation of American Abolitionism*, 69; Wilson, *Freedom at Risk*, 94 and 102.

24. Unknown to Daniel Mifflin, December 16, 1810, Loose Correspondence, incoming, 1796–1819, reel no. 12, PAS; "Kidnapping!" *Poulson's American Daily Advertiser* (Philadelphia), July 24, 1817.

25. "Kidnapping"; Humanitas, *Reflections on Slavery*, 22–24; Bacon, *Lamb's Warrior*, 2.

26. "Boy Lost," *Poulson's American Daily Advertiser* (Philadelphia), August 13, 1825.

27. Ibid.

Chapter 3: MIDNIGHT LAND

1. Isaac Harvey, diary entry, August 10, 1825, Harvey Papers; George Henry, *Life of George Henry. Together with a Brief History of the Colored People in America* (Freeport, NY: Books for Libraries Press, 1971), 49; "Almanack," *Poulson's American Daily Advertiser* (Philadelphia), August 10, 1825.

2. Bolster, *Black Jacks*, 171; "A Morning's Walk in the State of Delaware," *Analectic Magazine*, October 1, 1818. "Delmarva" is a twentieth-century locution. There was no commonly used name for the peninsula before about 1920.

3. Jarena Lee, *Religious Experience and the Journal of Mrs. Jarena Lee* (Philadelphia, 1849), 21; Samuel Hazard, ed., *Register of Pennsylvania, Devoted to the Preservation of Facts and Documents*, 9 vols. (Philadelphia, 1831–35), 1: 67–68;

John Melish, *Travels in the United States of America, in the Years 1806 & 1807, and 1809, 1810, & 1811*, 2 vols. (Philadelphia, 1812), 1: 177–78.

4. "More Kidnapping," *Commercial Advertiser* (New York), January 30, 1827; "A Kidnapper Taken," *Easton Gazette* (Maryland), June 24, 1820; *Minute Book of the Acting Committee, 1810–1822*, reel 5, May 11, 1819, PAS.

5. John Palmer, *Journals of Travels in the United States of North America, and in Lower Canada, Performed in the Year 1817* (London, 1818), 18–19; Melish, *Travels in the United States of America*, 1: 177–78; Power, *Impressions of America*, 1: 196–97; Finch, *Travels in the United States*, 76–77 and 91–92. Sunrise on Thursday, August 11, 1825, was at 5:12 a.m.

6. Finch, *Travels in the United States*, 91–92; Tracey L. Bryant and Jonathan R. Pennock, *The Delaware Estuary: Rediscovering a Forgotten Resource* (Newark: University of Delaware Sea Grant College, 1976), 7. Other children kidnapped by Purnell and Johnson earlier that same summer later remembered having somehow caught a glimpse of the Henlopen lighthouse as the *Little John* had rounded this cape. "Kidnapping," 43–44.

7. "Kidnapping," 40; unidentified newspaper clipping, item 274A, JWP; Henry, *Life of George Henry*, 49; George H. Gibson, ed., "William P. Brobson Diary, 1825–1828 (Part I)," *Delaware History* 15, no. 1 (April 1972): 78–79.

8. "Kidnapping," 40; Bernard John Medairy, *The Notorious Patty Cannon and Her Gang of Kidnappers on the Eastern Shore* (Towson, MD: B. Medairy, 1995), 143.

9. Medairy, *The Notorious Patty Cannon*, 144; "Kidnapping," 40–41 and 43–44.

10. "Kidnapping," 43–44.

11. Johnson had bought the unimproved plot for $150 four years earlier, in 1822, using proceeds from prior abductions and slave slaves. Hal Roth, *Now This Is the Truth . . . and Other Lies: Tales from the Eastern Shore . . . and More* (Vienna, MD: Nanticoke Books, 2005), 104; Medairy, *The Notorious Patty Cannon*, 123. When Johnson sold it to his mother-in-law in 1826, he valued the house and the land on which it sat at $1,000, an extraordinary price tag for all but the largest private dwellings on the Eastern Shore. Medairy, *The Notorious Patty Cannon*, 153; Hal Roth, *The Monster's Handsome Face: Patty Cannon in Fiction and Fact* (Vienna, MD: Nanticoke Books, 1998), 48.

12. Gabrielle M. Lanier, *The Delaware Valley in the Early Republic: Architecture, Landscape, and Regional Identity* (Baltimore: Johns Hopkins University Press, 2005), 80–84; Harold B. Hancock, *The History of Sussex County, Delaware* (Rehoboth Beach, DE: self-published, 1976), 64; "Black Marylanders 1820: African American Population by County, Status & Gender," Legacies of Slavery in Maryland, Archives of Maryland, accessed June 19, 2018, http://slavery.msa.maryland.gov/html/research/census1820.html.

13. Lorena S. Walsh, "Slave Life, Slave Society, and Tobacco Production in the Tidewater Chesapeake, 1620–1820," in *Cultivation and Commerce: Labor and the Shaping of Slave Life in the Americas*, eds. Ira Berlin and Philip D. Morgan (Charlottesville: University of Virginia Press, 1993), 170–99; Calvin Schermerhorn, *Money over Mastery, Family over Freedom: Slavery in the Antebellum Upper*

South (Baltimore: Johns Hopkins University Press, 2011). While selling slaves out of state was common in Maryland, it was less so in Delaware, due to laws passed in 1787 and 1819 that privileged manumission over slave trading.

14. Frederick Douglass, *My Bondage and My Freedom* (New York: Barnes and Noble, 2005), 223; Schermerhorn, *Money over Mastery*, 13–15; Marie Jenkins Schwartz, *Born in Bondage: Growing Up Enslaved in the Antebellum South* (Cambridge, MA: Harvard University Press, 2000), 91; William S. McFeely, *Frederick Douglass* (New York: Simon & Schuster, 1991), 55; Preston, *Young Frederick Douglass* (Baltimore: Johns Hopkins University Press, 1980), 74–78. "Is there a town on the Eastern Shore of Maryland, or in Delaware," one Baltimore-based antislavery editor asked in 1822, "which has not been visited by negro buyers, and the ears of whose inhabitants have not been assailed by the cries of the oppressed?" "To the Editor," *Genius of Universal Emancipation* (Baltimore), March 1822, 142.

15. Schermerhorn, *Money over Mastery*, 38; Walsh, "Slave Life," 197–98. The combined free black populations of Dorchester and Sussex counties grew by 50 percent in the twenty years after 1800, reaching 12,958 by 1820. John A. Munroe, *History of Delaware*, 5th ed. (Newark: University of Delaware Press, 1954), 99; Lanier, *Delaware Valley*, 99–100.

16. Robert Goodloe Harper, *A Letter from Gen. Harper, of Maryland, to Elias B. Caldwell, Esq., Secretary of the American Society for Colonizing the Free People of Colour, in the United States, with their own consent* (Baltimore, 1818); Lanier, *Delaware Valley*, 98–99; Gordon E. Finnie, "The Antislavery Movement in the Upper South Before 1840," *Journal of Southern History* 35, no. 3 (1969): 321–24.

17. Hancock, *Sussex County*, 65; Barbara Jeanne Fields, *Slavery and Freedom on the Middle Ground: Maryland during the Nineteenth Century* (New Haven, CT: Yale University Press, 1985), 35; Patience Essah, *A House Divided: Slavery and Emancipation in Delaware, 1635–1865* (Charlottesville: University of Virginia Press, 1996), 108–28; Ira Berlin, *Slaves Without Masters: The Free Negro in the Antebellum South* (New York: Pantheon, 1974), 101; Philanthropos, *Address to the Inhabitants of the State of Delaware* (n.p., 1843), 16–17; John Parrish, *Remarks on the Slavery of Black People; Addressed to the Citizens of the United States* (Philadelphia, 1806), 14; Harold B. Hancock, "William Yates's Letter of 1837: Slavery and Colored People in Delaware," *Delaware History* 14 (April 1971), 208–11. Legislators also effectively outlawed interracial marriage.

18. Lanier, *Delaware Valley*, 76–79. Between 1797 and 1825, no significant antislavery society existed in Maryland. For unsuccessful attempts to establish durable antislavery societies on the Delmarva peninsula south of Wilmington, see John A. Munroe, *Federalist Delaware, 1775–1815* (New Brunswick, NJ: Rutgers University Press, 1954), 217–18; Kenneth L. Carroll, "Voices of Protest: Eastern Shore Abolition Societies, 1790–1820," *Maryland Historical Magazine* 84, no. 1 (Winter 1989): 350–58; Finnie, "The Antislavery Movement," 320–25. Founded by Quaker merchants, manufacturers, and lawyers in Wilmington in 1800, the Delaware Abolition Society never attained the profile its founders

had envisioned. While it survived until the 1830s, its officers consistently struggled to raise the funds needed to significantly advance its legislative agenda. Its
limited lobbying efforts in support of a gradual abolition law received the cold
shoulder from most non-Quakers in the Delaware legislature and faced active
obstruction from delegates representing slaveholders in Sussex County. Such
setbacks frustrated abolition society members, and many drifted away from
the organization over time, "yielding to the weight of discouragement." *Minute
Book of the Acting Committee, 1801–1819*, Abolition Society of Delaware, PAS,
88; Monte A. Calvert, "The Abolition Society of Delaware, 1801–1807," *Delaware History* 10, no. 4 (October 1963): 295–320; Essah, *House Divided*, 60–62.

19. Douglass, *My Bondage*, 59.

20. "American Intelligence," *Federal Gazette and Philadelphia Evening Post*, September 7, 1789. See also Daniel Boorstin, ed., *Delaware Cases, 1792–1830*, 3
vols. (St. Paul, MN: West Publishing, 1943), 2: 68–69, 124–26, and 169–71;
Minute Book of the Acting Committee, 1801–1819, Abolition Society of Delaware, PAS, 12 and 21.

21. Berlin, *Slaves Without Masters*, 160. A legal coffle of forty slaves could sell for
more than $30,000 in cash, enough specie to sometimes render lame the horses
tasked with carrying it all. Michael Tadman, *Speculators and Slaves: Masters,
Traders, and Slaves in the Old South* (Madison: University of Wisconsin Press,
1989), 19 and 22. On the carrying costs (food, shelter, clothing), see John Komlos and Bjorn Alecke, "The Economics of Antebellum Slave Heights Reconsidered," *Journal of Interdisciplinary History* 26, no. 3 (Winter 1996): 438–39;
Herman Freudenberger and Jonathan B. Pritchett, "The Domestic United
States Slave Trade: New Evidence," *Journal of Interdisciplinary History* 21, no.
3 (Winter 1991): 462–63. For contemporary recognition of the Reverse Underground Railroad's parasitical relationship to the legal domestic slave trade, see
American Convention of Abolition Societies, *Minutes of the Twentieth Session
of the American Convention for Promoting the Abolition of Slavery and Improving
the Condition of the African Race, Convened at Philadelphia* (Baltimore, 1827),
50. For the prior occupations of men arrested for kidnapping, see Account of
Prisoners Received into the Maryland Penitentiary, S275 Record Set, Maryland State Archives, Annapolis, Maryland.

22. *Governor's Register, State of Delaware* (Wilmington: Public Archives Commission of Delaware, 1926), 105, 131, 134, 144, 146, 151, 154, and 163. For a sampling of other kidnapping activity on the peninsula in this period, see "Trade
in Negroes," *Niles Weekly Register* (Baltimore), July 19, 1817; "Kidnapping!"
Republican Star, or, Eastern Shore General Advertiser (Easton, MD), July 29,
1817; "Kidnappers," *Niles Weekly Register* (Baltimore), June 6, 1818; "Look out
for the Kidnappers," *Delaware Gazette* (Wilmington), March 20, 1827; Torrey,
Portraiture of Slavery, 84–85; Unknown to Enoch Lewis, July 26, 1825, Miscellaneous Papers, Meeting for Sufferings, Friends Historical Library, Swarthmore College, Swarthmore, Pennsylvania (hereafter cited as FHL).

23. "Intelligence," *Genius of Universal Emancipation* (Baltimore), May 1822; *Laws*

of the State of Delaware, 2 vols. (New-Castle, DE, 1797), 2: 1093–95. On Maryland, see Jeffrey R. Brackett, *The Negro in Maryland: A Study of the Institution of Slavery* (New York: Negro Universities Press, 1969), 184–86.

24. Robert H. Gudmestad, *A Troublesome Commerce: The Transformation of the Interstate Slave Trade* (Baton Rouge: Louisiana State University Press, 2003), 156; Helen Black Stewart, "The Negro in Delaware to 1829" (master's thesis, University of Delaware, 1940), 44; *Governor's Register, State of Delaware*, 105, 131, 134, 144, 146, 151, 154, 163, 208, and 224. The Delaware governor also occasionally remitted fines assessed on convicted kidnappers; for instance, *Governor's Register, State of Delaware*, 183 and 228. For the Eastern Shore of Maryland, see Jennifer Hull Dorsey, *Hirelings: African American Workers and Free Labor in Early Maryland* (Ithaca, NY: Cornell University Press, 2011), 93–94. For contemporary commentary on the effect of this ingrained antiblack bias upon jury decisions, see "Trial for Kidnapping," *Genius of Universal Emancipation* (Baltimore), February 1822.

25. William H. Williams, *Slavery and Freedom in Delaware, 1639–1865* (Wilmington, DE: Scholarly Resources, 1996), 239; M. Sammy Miller, "Legend of a Kidnapper," *The Crisis*, April 1975, 118–19; "$200 Reward," *Delaware Gazette and Peninsula Advertiser* (Wilmington), May 13, 1818. In Delaware, exceptions to the prohibition on black testimony against white suspects were granted on a case-by-case basis. Wilson, *Freedom at Risk*, 87; Essah, *House Divided*, 122; Lanier, *Delaware Valley*, 78.

26. Torrey, *Portraiture of Slavery*, 82; Calvert, "The Abolition Society of Delaware," 310.

27. Berlin, *Slaves Without Masters*, 100.

28. "To the Editor," *Genius of Universal Emancipation* (Baltimore), March 1822, 141. Lundy was reprinting a letter from a resident of Queen Anne's County, Maryland, originally published in the *Baltimore American* in 1816. Other observers rendered this trade in smuggled persons in more visceral terms, referring to it as a plague or a pestilence and describing men like Johnson and Purnell as prowling predators or "beasts of prey." Torrey, *Portraiture of Slavery*, 82; "Kidnappers," *National Advocate* (New York), June 7, 1819.

29. Torrey, *Portraiture of Slavery*, 95. For similar commentaries from Eastern Shore residents and visitors in this period, see "A Morning's Walk in the State of Delaware"; American Convention of Abolition Societies, *Minutes of the Proceedings of the Fifteenth American Convention for Promoting the Abolition of Slavery and Improving the Condition of the African Race Assembled at Philadelphia* (Philadelphia, 1817), 13.

30. *Minute Book of the Acting Committee, 1801–1819*, Abolition Society of Delaware, PAS, 67, 100–101, 136, and 140; American Convention of Abolition Societies, *Minutes, Constitution, Addresses, Memorials, Resolutions, Reports, Committees and Anti-Slavery Tracts*, 3 vols. (New York: Bergman, 1969), 3: 815. Between 1816 and 1818, members of the Delaware Abolition Society organized a series of petitions complaining to legislators that those responsible for this "iniquitous

traffic" were "disgracefully prosecuted" and mustered more than a thousand signatures. *Minute Book of the Acting Committee, 1801–1819*, Abolition Society of Delaware, PAS, 13; Race and Slavery Petitions Project, University of North Carolina at Greensboro, accessed June 18, 2018, https://library.uncg.edu/slavery /petitions/history.aspx, PARs 10381612, 10381701, 10381705-17, 10381802, and 10381809-18. In 1817, members collected another 450 signatures demanding changes to state laws to better "punish the inhuman practice of kidnapping." *Minute Book of the Acting Committee, 1801–1819*, Abolition Society of Delaware, PAS, 144–45. State legislators rarely debated these petitions, and officers of the Delaware Abolition Society soon concluded that "Congress alone" had the power to suppress this interstate black market. *Minute Book of the Acting Committee, 1801–1819*, Abolition Society of Delaware, PAS, 155–56.

31. Torrey, *Portraiture of Slavery*, 82; William McMann to Lewis, July 18, 1825, Miscellaneous Papers, Meeting for Sufferings, FHL; Dean, "Free Negro in Delaware," 18–19.

32. "Kidnapping," 40.

33. Ibid.

Chapter 4: IN-LAWS AND OUTLAWS

1. Unidentified newspaper clipping, item 274A, JWP; Roth, *The Monster's Handsome Face*, 48; Calvin W. Mowbray and Maurice D. Rimpo, *Close-ups of Early Dorchester County History* (Silver Spring, MD: Family Line, 1987), 53.

2. *Minute Book of the Acting Committee, 1800–1824*, reel 1, November 30, 1819, PAS; Medairy, *The Notorious Patty Cannon*, 154–55.

3. [John M. Clayton?], *The Narrative and Confessions of Lucretia P. Cannon Who Was Tried, Convicted, and Sentenced to Be Hung at Georgetown, Delaware, with Two of Her Accomplices Containing an Account of Some of the Most Horrible and Shocking Murders and Daring Robberies Ever Committed by One of the Female Sex* (New York, 1841), 23. In the twentieth century, a host of magazine feature writers imagined the Cannon place—which no longer stands—as a raucous, open-all-hours tavern, a popular spot for legal slave traders and for black market traffickers to carouse and compare notes. In reality, it was far more homely. It received few unexpected visitors and likely served no other commercial function than as a place to stash stolen children destined for sale as slaves in the Deep South. For commentary on this process of mythologizing, see Roth, *Now This Is the Truth*, 125–27.

4. Clayton, a Delaware lawyer and future secretary of state and chief justice, was involved in two failed efforts to bring the Cannons and the Johnsons to justice in 1821 and 1822. On Clayton, see Joseph P. Comegys, *Memoir of John M. Clayton* (Wilmington: Historical Society of Delaware, 1882); Carole C. Marks, *Moses and the Monster and Miss Anne* (Urbana: University of Illinois Press, 2009), 37–39; Roth, *The Monster's Handsome Face*, 34; "Kidnappers and Murderers," *Daily National Intelligencer* (Washington, DC), May 27, 1837. On the

pamphlet and its genre conventions, see Dawn Keetley, "Victim and Victimizer: Female Fiends and Unease Over Marriage in Antebellum Sensational Fiction," *American Quarterly* 51, no. 2 (1999): 344–84; Thomas M. McDade, "Lurid Literature of the Last Century: The Publications of E. E. Barclay," *Pennsylvania Magazine of History and Biography* 80, no. 4 (1956): 452–67. Printed and published in 1841, Clayton's pamphlet has stoked two centuries of lively public interest in Cannon's criminal career. She has been the subject of countless newspaper and magazine features, as well as plays, poems, and at least five novels, all of which draw on Clayton's highly misleading 1841 pamphlet to a greater or lesser degree. Even today, fascination with Cannon endures. Titillated tourists still show up at the crossroads near her former address on the Delaware-Maryland border and visit the local museum, where a very unsettling animatronic Cannon sits rocking back and forth. On Patty Cannon's real origins, see Medairy, *The Notorious Patty Cannon*, 1–17; Roth, *Now This Is the Truth*, 46–52.

5. Medairy, *The Notorious Patty Cannon*, 7; Roth, *Now This Is the Truth*, 48.

6. Medairy, *The Notorious Patty Cannon*, 186; "Kidnappers and Murderers"; Roth, *The Monster's Handsome Face*, 185–91 and 197–98.

7. Medairy, *The Notorious Patty Cannon*, 16–18; Robert Wilson, *The Massie/Massey and Related Families* (Taftsville, VT: Robert E. Wilson, 2002), Appendix 2; George V. Massey, comp., *James Cannon of Nanticoke and Descendants Including the Allied Families of Cordry, Adams, Hooper, Obier and Ward* (n.p., 1948), 11–12; Caroline County Land Records, 1804–1809, May 3, 1808, book 1: 94–99, Maryland State Archives, Annapolis, Maryland.

8. Medairy, *The Notorious Patty Cannon*, 21–24. There is fragmentary evidence that Jesse Cannon manumitted one of the enslaved people in his household in 1792 and was the subject of a freedom suit brought by another black person in 1803.

9. Medairy, *The Notorious Patty Cannon*, 21–24.

10. Ibid., 35–38; Roth, *The Monster's Handsome Face*, 50–52.

11. *Minute Book of the Acting Committee, 1800–1824*, reel 1, August 26, 1815, PAS; "State vs. H. Brereton and J. Griffith, Murder, Sussex County," March 1813, Sussex County Court of Oyer and Terminer, 1823–1829, Delaware State Archives, Dover, Delaware, 1–4. Brevington was convicted for shooting to death a South Carolina slave dealer on a road not far from the Cannon house. On Brevington and his father, Robert, a Lewes blacksmith who also worked with Jesse Cannon in this period, see Medairy, *The Notorious Patty Cannon*, 25–26, 35–45, 55–60, and 187; *Minute Book of the Acting Committee, 1800–1824*, reel 1, July 27, 1812, PAS; *Governor's Register, State of Delaware*, 87, 101.

12. Medairy, *The Notorious Patty Cannon*, 60 and 187; Boorstin, *Delaware Cases*, 2: 621–22; "Kidnappers and Murderers."

13. Medairy, *The Notorious Patty Cannon*, 61–74, 132, 140, and 153–54; Watson to Hamilton and Henderson, March 10, 1826, item 275, JWP. Brittania Johnson later married Jesse Cannon Jr.

14. Medairy, *The Notorious Patty Cannon*, 78–80, 154–55, and 162–63; *Minute Book of the Acting Committee, 1800–1824*, reel 1, June 24, 1817, PAS; Wilson, *Freedom at Risk*, 21–23; Torrey, *Portraiture of Slavery*, 81–82; Roth, *The Monster's Handsome Face*, 183–85. A tax assessment conducted in 1816 listed forty-one members of the Cannon family in Sussex County alone, including the coroner and the tax assessor himself. *Governor's Register, State of Delaware*, 140. For the Cannon family tree, see Massey, *James Cannon of Nanticoke*. For Isaac and Jacob Cannon, see William Morgan, Journal 1752–1853, Delaware State Archives, Dover, Delaware; Robert B. Hazzard, *The History of Seaford: From Its First Survey and Plotting in 1799 to the Completion of the Delaware Railroad in 1856* (Seaford, DE: Sussex Printing, 1961), 9–29; Lanier, *Delaware Valley*, 88–89; J. Thomas Scharf, *History of Delaware, 1609–1888*, 2 vols. (Port Washington, NY: Kennikat Press, 1888), 1: 1281 and 1305.

15. "Look Out for the Kidnapper," *Poulson's American Daily Advertiser* (Philadelphia), May 18, 1819; Loose Correspondence, incoming, 1796–1819, reel 12, June 28, 1819, PAS; *Minute Book of the Acting Committee, 1810–1822*, reel 5, May 11, 1819, PAS; *Minute Book of the Acting Committee, 1810–1822*, reel 5, May 15, 1819, PAS; *Minute Book of the Acting Committee, 1810–1822*, reel 5, June 15, 1819, PAS; *Minute Book of the Acting Committee, 1810–1822*, reel 5, July 6, 1819, PAS; *Minute Book of the Acting Committee, 1810–1822*, reel 5, November 24, 1819, PAS; *Minute Book of the Acting Committee, 1800–1824*, reel 1, November 30, 1819, PAS; "Reported for the Democratic Press," *Commercial Advertiser* (New York), July 9, 1819.

16. "Reported for the Democratic Press"; *Minute Book of the Acting Committee, 1800–1824*, reel 1, November 30, 1819, PAS.

17. *Minute Book of the Acting Committee, 1800–1824*, reel 1, November 30, 1819, PAS.

18. Ibid.

19. Ibid.

20. Ibid.

21. According to one of Johnson's neighbors, "Joe Johnson is a man of much cunning . . . and has an army of Little Rascals that will give him information of the approach of any officer." Jesse Green to Watson, March 12, 1826, item 178, JWP.

22. *Governor's Register, State of Delaware*, 137; *Minute Book of the Acting Committee, 1800–1824*, reel 1, November 30, 1819, PAS. For other contemporary claims as to their invulnerability, see Isaac Gibbs to B. L. Lear, January 5, 1816, HR14A-C17.4, Box 15, Papers of Select Committee to Inquire into the Existence of an Inhuman and Illegal Traffic in Slaves . . . in the District of Columbia, National Archives, Washington, DC, 8: 1–2; Watson to Hamilton and Henderson, March 10, 1826, item 275, JWP; James Rogers to Watson, February 14, 1826, General Reference Folder #706, Delaware State Archives, Dover (hereafter cited as GRF).

23. Court of General Sessions, November 1825, Sussex County, Delaware State Archives, Dover, 1–3; "More Kidnapping," *Easton Gazette* (Maryland), May

24, 1823; Rogers to Watson, February 14, 1826, GRF; "More Kidnapping," *Easton Gazette* (Maryland), July 27, 1822; Robert S. Starobin, *Blacks in Bondage: Letters of American Slaves* (New York: M. Wiener, 1994), 111; "Kidnapping," *Genius of Universal Emancipation* (Baltimore), February 25, 1826. On Ebenezer Johnson, see Green to Watson, February 28, 1826, item 177, JWP; Wilson, *Freedom at Risk*, 28–29; Medairy, *The Notorious Patty Cannon*, 154; Dick Carter, *The History of Sussex County* (Millsboro, DE: Delmarva News and Delaware Coast Press, 1976), 25; "On Monday Morning," *Easton Gazette* (Maryland), July 23, 1821; "Kidnapping," *New-York Gazette & General Advertiser*, September 6, 1821. For glimpses of Joseph Johnson's entanglements with Delmarva courts, see Session Dockets, Court of General Sessions, Sussex County, Delaware, Delaware State Archives, Dover, 36, 44, 57–63, 65–66, 86, 88–89, 92–93, 95–98, 100–102, and 331 (hereafter cited as CGS); Medairy, *The Notorious Patty Cannon*, 109–30. In May 1822, jurors found Johnson guilty of kidnapping twelve people, many of them children. The governor remitted the maiming of his ear, but the Sussex County sheriff lashed and pilloried him on June 4, 1822. *Governor's Register, State of Delaware*, 183–85. One of the prosecuting lawyers, apparently recruited by the PAS, was John M. Clayton, the likely author of the 1841 pamphlet mythologizing Patty Cannon's criminal history. "Kidnappers and Murderers"; Comegys, *John M. Clayton*, 31–32.

24. Wilson, *Freedom at Risk*, 31; Michael Morgan, *Delmarva's Patty Cannon: The Devil on the Nanticoke* (Charleston, SC: History Press, 2015), 28–35; Medairy, *The Notorious Patty Cannon*, 78–80, 132, and 179–87; "Murders in Sussex," *Delaware Gazette and American Watchman* (Wilmington), April 17, 1829; Session Dockets, CGS, 85 and 87–90; *Governor's Register, State of Delaware*, 216; "A Horrible Development," *Niles Weekly Register* (Baltimore), April 25, 1829.

25. Session Dockets, CGS, 92; Medairy, *The Notorious Patty Cannon*, 107 and 130; Roth, *The Monster's Handsome Face*, 222–23. A comprehensive 1835 survey of the inmates of eight major prisons in Pennsylvania, New York, Maryland, Delaware, and Virginia found not a single female kidnapper serving time behind bars. A study of judicial cases relating to the slave trade concluded the same. William Crawford, *Report on the Penitentiaries of the United States* (Montclair, NJ: Paterson Smith, 1969); Helen Tunncliff Catterall, ed., *Judicial Cases Concerning American Slavery and the Negro: Cases From the Courts of New England, the Middle States and the District of Columbia* (New York: Octagon Books, 1968). See also *Governor's Register, State of Delaware*, 224.

26. Sydney Greenbie and Marjorie Barstow Greenbie, *Anna Ella Carroll and Abraham Lincoln: A Biography* (Manchester, ME: University of Tampa Press, 1952), 24; Unknown to Enoch Lewis, July 26, 1825, Miscellaneous Papers, Meeting for Sufferings, FHL.

27. "To the People of Color," *Baltimore Patriot & Mercantile Advertiser*, August 13, 1821. On Thomas Collins, see Sentence Docket, 1825–1835, County Prison, Philadelphia City Archives, Philadelphia, Pennsylvania, 172 (hereafter cited

as County Prison). On Jacob Purnell, see unidentified newspaper clipping, item 274A, JWP. By some estimates the gang comprised "about 30 men" in these years. On its scale and composition see Medairy, *The Notorious Patty Cannon*, 155–61.

28. "Kidnapping," *Niles Weekly Register* (Baltimore), April 10, 1824; "To the People of Color," *Baltimore Patriot & Mercantile Advertiser*, August 13, 1821; Session Dockets, CGS, 66; "It Was Not Without Reluctance," *New York National Advocate*, April 1, 1824; *Minute Book of the Acting Committee, 1810–1822*, reel 5, August 22 1820, PAS; Mayor's Court Docket, September 1820, Philadelphia City Archives, Philadelphia, Pennsylvania, 277 (hereafter cited as PCA).

29. Receiving Docket, 1825–1828, County Prison, #107; "On Sunday Afternoon," *Connecticut Herald* (New Haven), June 5, 1827.

30. Medairy, *The Notorious Patty Cannon*, 161.

31. Isaiah Sadler, deposition, September 13, 1824, item 476, JWP; "More Kidnapping," *Easton Gazette* (Maryland), May 14, 1823. The gang also sometimes used the nearby homes of Jesse Cannon Jr. and Ebenezer Johnson as safe houses. "Black List," *Genius of Universal Emancipation* (Baltimore), April 28, 1827; Watson to Hamilton and Henderson, March 10, 1826, item 275, JWP.

32. American Convention of Abolition Societies, *Minutes of the Adjourned Session of the Twentieth Biennial American Convention for Promoting the Abolition of Slavery, and Improving the Condition of the African Race, Held at Baltimore, Nov. 1828* (Philadelphia, 1828), 21–24.

33. For the date, see J. F. Wright and G. Wright to Watson, February 15, 1826, item 274, JWP.

34. Isaac Harvey, diary entry, August 18, 1825, Harvey Papers; Deborah Norris Logan, diaries, Historical Society of Pennsylvania, Philadelphia, 99.

35. Charles Fleming, deposition, February 23, 1826, item 274, JWP; Eleanour Blackiston, deposition, February 23, 1826, item 274, JWP; Eben Blackiston to Watson, March 10, 1826, item 23, JWP; Hamilton to Watson, January 27, 1826, item 272, JWP; "Kidnapping," *Easton Gazette* (Maryland), February 16, 1826. Two local men later alleged that one of Fisher's assailants was "Thomas Galloway of Kent County, Delaware," who had then sold her to Ebenezer Johnson and provided him with a fake bill of sale. Wright and Wright to Watson, February 15, 1826, item 274, JWP.

36. Kidnapping," 39–41; Smith, "Notes and Documents," 323; Winch, "Other Underground Railroad," 12. On the gang's history of slave stealing, see Medairy, *The Notorious Patty Cannon*, 123–25; "More Kidnapping," *Commercial Advertiser* (New York), January 30, 1827.

37. Morgan, *Delmarva's Patty Cannon*, 49–52; Scharf, *History of Delaware*, 1: 1305. Two local men who lived very close to the ferry later recalled seeing the group arrive there, though they put the date two days earlier, "about the 16th of August." Wright and Wright to Watson, February 15, 1826, item 274, JWP. The ferry was owned by Jacob and Isaac Cannon, who in-

herited the business from their parents. Roth, *The Monster's Handsome Face*, 189–93.

38. Medairy, *The Notorious Patty Cannon*, 144; Roth, *The Monster's Handsome Face*, 183–85. One of the children aboard later asserted that the sloop was the *Little John*, though an older boy said the second vessel was much larger. Unidentified newspaper clipping, item 274A, JWP.

Chapter 5: THE BEATEN WAY

1. Henry, *Life of George Henry*, 19–20.
2. Frederick Douglass, *Narrative of the Life of Frederick Douglass, an American Slave* (New York: Penguin, 1986), 106; Henry, *Life of George Henry*, 28. For examples of kidnapping vessels intercepted on the Chesapeake Bay, see "Kidnappers and Flesh-Dealers," *National Advocate* (New York), August 22, 1817; Andrews, *Domestic Slave Trade*, 181–85.
3. "Kidnapping," 39–41; Erik J. Hofstee, "The Great Divide: Aspects of the Social History of the Middle Passage in the Trans-Atlantic Slave Trade" (PhD diss., Michigan State University, 2001), 58 and 97; David Richardson, "Shipboard Revolts, African Authority, and the Atlantic Slave Trade," *William & Mary Quarterly* 58, no. 1 (January 2001): 76. For Solomon Northup's abandoned plan to stage a revolt, see Northup, *Twelve Years*, 40–43.
4. Northup, *Twelve Years*, 35–36; Hofstee, "The Great Divide," 92.
5. For evidence in support of Norfolk as the most likely landing place, see "For the Easton Gazette. More Kidnapping," *Easton Gazette* (Maryland), May 24, 1823; Adam Rothman, *Slave Country: American Expansion and the Origins of the Deep South* (Cambridge, MA: Harvard University Press, 2005), 198; Herring, "Kidnapped and Sold," 348.
6. Morris Birkbeck, *Notes on a Journey in America, From the Coast of Virginia to the Territory of Illinois* (London, 1818), 7; Charles William Janson, *The Stranger in America, 1793–1806* (New York: Press of the Pioneers, 1935), 333–34; Isaac Weld, *Travels Through the States of North America, and the Provinces of Upper and Lower Canada, During the Years 1795, 1796, and 1797* (London, 1799), 97–100.
7. "For the Easton Gazette. More Kidnapping"; Tommy Bogger, *Free Blacks in Norfolk, Virginia, 1790–1860: The Darker Side of Freedom* (Charlottesville: University of Virginia Press, 1997), 100–101; Herring, "Kidnapped and Sold," 348.
8. On price differentials, see Gudmestad, *Troublesome Commerce*, 11; William Calderhead, "The Role of the Professional Slave Trader in a Slave Economy: Austin Woolfolk, a Case Study," *Civil War History* 23, no. 3 (September 1977): 202; Roger Ransom and Richard Sutch, "Capitalists Without Capital: The Burden of Slavery and the Impact of Emancipation," *Agricultural History* 62, no. 3 (Summer 1988): 153. On the gang's prior overland marches, see "Kidnapping," 47–48; Levina Johnson to Isaac Johnson, Loose Correspondence,

incoming, 1820–1849, 1857, 1859–1863, reel 13, July 7, 1824, PAS; "More Kidnapping," *New York Commercial Advertiser*, January 30, 1827.

9. Rothman, *Slave Country*, 198; Freudenberger and Pritchett, "New Evidence," 462.

10. Steven Deyle, *Carry Me Back: The Domestic Slave Trade in American Life* (New York: Oxford University Press, 2005), 98–99 and 153; Jim Barnett and H. Clark Burkett, "The Forks of the Road Slave Market at Natchez," *Journal of Mississippi History* 63, no. 3 (September 2001): 170–71; Todd Ashley Herring, "Natchez, 1795–1830: Life and Death on the Slavery Frontier" (PhD diss., Mississippi State University, 2000), 222. For a comparison of transportation costs by land and sea, see Philip Troutman, "Slave Trade and Sentiment in Antebellum Virginia" (PhD diss., University of Virginia, 2000), 52.

11. Legal traders who traveled overland and sold their slaves in the Deep South could make about sixty dollars per head after expenses. On transportation costs, provisions, and profitability, see Calderhead, "Austin Woolfolk," 199–202; Deyle, *Carry Me Back*, 121–22; Charles Sackett Sydnor, *Slavery in Mississippi* (Gloucester, MA: Peter Smith, 1965), 149; Jonathan B. Pritchett, "Interregional Slave Trade and the Selection of Slaves," *Journal of Interdisciplinary History* 28, no. 1 (Summer 1997): 63–64; Robert Evans Jr., "Some Economic Aspects of the Slave Trade, 1830–1860," *Southern Economic Journal* 27, no. 4 (April 1961): 335–37; Freudenberger and Pritchett, "New Evidence," 473–74; Komlos and Alecke, "Slave Heights Reconsidered," 441–43.

12. "Kidnapping," 39–41. On driver wages and other financial incentives, see Evans, "Economic Aspects," 330–31.

13. "Kidnapping," 39–41.

14. Charles D. Lowery, "The Great Migration to the Mississippi Territory, 1798–1819," *Journal of Mississippi History* 30, no. 3 (August 1968): 173–92; William O. Lynch, "The Westward Flow of Southern Colonists Before 1861," *Journal of Southern History* 9, no. 3 (August 1943): 316–17.

15. Angela Pulley Hudson, *Creek Paths and Federal Roads: Indians, Settlers, and Slaves and the Making of the American South* (Chapel Hill: University of North Carolina Press, 2010), 126; Deyle, *Carry Me Back*, 19–27; Joan E. Cashin, *A Family Venture: Men and Women on the Southern Frontier* (New York: Oxford University Press, 1991). For boosterism, see, for instance, Ebenezer Harlow Cummins, *A Summary Geography of Alabama* (Philadelphia, 1819).

16. Rothman, *Slave Country*, 34–35 and 177.

17. Deyle, *Carry Me Back*, 38 and 56–57; Tadman, *Speculators and Slaves*, 12–21. Despite the federal ban on importing enslaved people from overseas, slavers would continue to smuggle modest numbers of foreign-born captives into ports like New Orleans until the 1820s. Rothman, *Slave Country*, 193–96.

18. Edward Ball, "Retracing Slavery's Trail of Tears," *Smithsonian*, November 2015, accessed June 17, 2018, www.smithsonianmag.com/history/slavery-trail-of-tears-180956968; Tadman, *Speculators and Slaves*, 23–45. Between 1790 and 1860, more than one million enslaved people made this massive interstate mi-

gration, a number twenty times greater than the number of Natives forcibly relocated during the era of Indian Removal. Schermerhorn, *Money over Mastery*, 67.

19. Tyre Glen to Isaac Jarratt, November 2, 1832, Isaac Jarratt Papers, Southern Historical Collection, University of North Carolina, Chapel Hill; Schermerhorn, *Money over Mastery*, 13; Steven F. Miller, "Plantation Labor Organization and Slave Life on the Cotton Frontier: The Alabama-Mississippi Black Belt, 1815–1840," in *Cultivation and Culture*, 159; Freudenberger and Pritchett, "New Evidence," 454. Legal slave traders regularly sold children the same ages as these five boys; the Johnsons and other kidnappers specialized in doing so. Cheaper to feed, less likely to run or to fight, and easier to control, coerce, and intimidate than adult males, black boys were the staple of the Reverse Underground Railroad. International smugglers who brought slaves into New Orleans from Cuba and elsewhere in the Caribbean in the early nineteenth century also favored children. On the smugglers' preferences for children, see Benjamin N. Lawrance, *Amistad's Orphans: An Atlantic Story of Children, Slavery, and Smuggling* (New Haven, CT: Yale University Press, 2014), 35–36 and 149; Paul Lovejoy, "The Children of Slavery—The Transatlantic Phase," *Slavery & Abolition* 27, no. 2 (August 2006): 202; Hofstee, "Great Divide," 66 and 100. Adult women were also in high demand, and in New Orleans, at least, they fetched only a few dollars less than men of equivalent age. Women fit and able to bear children, as both Mary Fisher and Mary Neal likely were, often commanded a premium. Tadman, *Speculators and Slaves*, 141–42; Laurence J. Kotlikoff, "Structure of Slave Prices in New Orleans," *Economic Inquiry* 17, no. 4 (October 1979): 502.

20. Frederick W. Seward, ed., *Autobiography of William H. Seward, From 1801 to 1834, with a Memoir of His Life, and Selections From His Letters From 1831 to 1846* (New York, 1877), 271; Ira Berlin, *The Making of African America: The Four Great Migrations* (New York: Viking, 2010), 15; Theodore Dwight Weld, *American Slavery As It Is: Testimony of a Thousand Witnesses* (New York, 1839), 76.

21. Walter Johnson, *Soul by Soul: Life Inside the Antebellum Slave Market* (Cambridge, MA: Harvard University Press, 1999), 60–62; Tadman, *Speculators and Slaves*, 73–77.

22. Basil Hall, *Travels in North America, in the Years 1827 and 1828*, 3 vols. (Edinburgh, 1829), 3: 197; Deyle, *Carry Me Back*, 146–47; Ball, "Slavery's Trail of Tears."

23. Edward E. Baptist, *The Half Has Never Been Told: Slavery and the Making of American Capitalism* (New York: Basic Books, 2014), 2. The Johnsons married the previous summer. Henderson to Watson, January 2, 1826, item 262, JWP.

24. In good weather and without lengthy stopovers or delays, an experienced slave driver could deliver a coffle from Norfolk to Natchez in about ten weeks, though the average overland travel time was 106 days. Freudenberger and Pritchett, "New Evidence," 470–72.

25. Damian Alan Pargas, *Slavery and Forced Migration in the Antebellum South*

(New York: Cambridge University Press, 2015), 111; John Owen, *John Owen's Journal of His Removal From Virginia to Alabama in 1818*, ed., Thomas McAdory Owen (Baltimore, 1897), 9; William C. Davis, *Way Through the Wilderness: The Natchez Trace and the Civilization of the Southern Frontier* (New York: Harper-Collins, 1995), 51.

26. All journey times and distances between Norfolk and Tuscaloosa are adapted from Owen, *John Owen's Journal*. On travel routes, see Thomas Perkins Abernethy, *The Formative Period in Alabama, 1815–1828* (Montgomery, AL: Brown, 1922), 80–81.

27. "Kidnapping," 39–41; Saxe-Weimar Eisenach, *Travels through North America*, 2: 14, 23–25, and 30; Carl David Arfwedson, *The United States and Canada in 1832, 1833, and 1834*, 2 vols. (London, 1834), 1: 360–63.

28. Hudson, *Creek Paths*, 126; Charles Lyell, *A Second Visit to the United States of North America*, 2 vols. (New York, 1849), 2: 69; Rhoda Coleman Ellison, *Bibb County, Alabama: The First Hundred Years, 1818–1918* (Tuscaloosa: University of Alabama Press, 1984), 16; Cashin, *Family Venture*, 57.

29. Andrews, *Domestic Slave Trade*, 104; Tadman, *Speculators and Slaves*, 75; Thomas Hamilton, *Men and Manners in America*, 2 vols. (Edinburgh, 1833), 2: 257.

30. Owen, *John Owen's Journal*, 4–11; Hudson, *Creek Paths*, 125–28; Hamilton, *Men and Manners*, 2: 253–77. Two months later, one traveler's carriage overturned eight times along a similar route. Saxe-Weimar Eisenach, *Travels through North America*, 2: 14–23 and 27–28.

31. Greenbie and Greenbie, *Anna Ella Carroll*, 28–29.

32. Nathaniel Southard, *Why Work for the Slave?* (New York, 1838), 2; "Messrs. Crutcher & Stockton," *Port Gibson Correspondent* (Mississippi), September 7, 1826; John Brown, *Slave Life in Georgia: A Narrative of the Life, Sufferings, and Escape of John Brown, a Fugitive Slave, Now in England* (London, 1855), 20. The Johnsons likely owned a pocket-size map book to help with route planning and navigation. See, for example, Daniel Hewett, *The American Traveller; Or, National Directory, Containing An Account of All the Great Post Roads and Most Important Cross Roads in the United States . . .* (Washington, DC, 1825).

33. Brown, *Slave Life*, 18–19; Edward E. Baptist, " 'Cuffy,' 'Fancy Maids,' and 'One-Eyed Men': Rape, Commodification, and the Domestic Slave Trade in the United States," *American Historical Review* 106, no. 5 (December 2001): 1619–50; Johnson, *Soul by Soul*, 56–57 and 62–63. Historians have yet to uncover clear evidence that slave traders raped any of the men or boys in their custody, but that may say more about the types of sources that survive and the stigma surrounding victim testimony than it does about lived experience. Thomas Foster, "The Sexual Abuse of Black Men Under American Slavery," *Journal of the History of Sexuality* 20, no. 3 (September 2011): 448.

34. Deyle, *Carry Me Back*, 252; Pargas, *Slavery and Forced Migration*, 115; George Tucker, *Letters From Virginia, Translated From the French* (Baltimore, 1816), 31; Weld, *American Slavery As It Is*, 70 and 76. See also Melish, *Travels in the United States of America*, 2: 94–95.

35. Frederic Bancroft, *Slave Trading in the Old South* (Baltimore: J. H. Furst, 1931), 283–86; Brown, *Slave Life*, 15–16; Johnson, *Soul by Soul*, 64 and 70–77; Deyle, *Carry Me Back*, 270; Tucker, *Letters From Virginia*, 30–31; Pargas, *Slavery and Forced Migration*, 115–20; Ira Berlin, *Generations of Captivity: A History of African-American Slaves* (Cambridge, MA: Harvard University Press, 2003), 173.

36. Charles Ball, *Slavery in the United States: A Narrative of the Life and Adventures of Charles Ball* (New York, 1837), 84; Weld, *American Slavery As It Is*, 69. The cost of food for coffle slaves was between twenty-five and thirty-four cents per day per slave. Freudenberger and Pritchett, "New Evidence," 473.

37. Seward, *William H. Seward*, 271; Loguen, *Narrative*, 13–14; Pargas, *Slavery and Forced Migration*, 112; Deyle, *Carry Me Back*, 146–47. For a sampling of the sorts of places in which travelers on these roads camped, see Owen, *John Owen's Journal*, 4–11.

38. Baptist, *Never Been Told*, 23–24; Johnson, *Soul by Soul*, 60–65.

39. Ball, *Narrative*, 70; W. H. Robinson, *From Log Cabin to Pulpit; Or Fifteen Years in Slavery* (Eau Claire, WI: James A. Tifft, 1913), 44; David L. Lightner, *Slavery and the Commerce Power: How the Struggle Against the Interstate Slave Trade Led to the Civil War* (New Haven, CT: Yale University Press, 2006), 10.

40. Owen, *John Owen's Journal*, 4–11.

41. Cummins, *Geography of Alabama*, 18–19; Gideon Lincecum, "Autobiography of Gideon Lincecum," *Publications of the Mississippi Historical Society* 8 (1905): 464–65; Tuscaloosa Genealogical Society, *Pioneers of Tuscaloosa County, Alabama, Prior to 1830* (Tuscaloosa, AL: Tuscaloosa Genealogical Society, 1981), 2–3; Matthew William Clinton, *Tuscaloosa, Alabama, Its Early Days, 1816–1865* (Tuscaloosa, AL: Zonta Club, 1958), 28–32. Market Street is now Greensboro Avenue. Broad Street is now University Boulevard.

42. Smith, *Reminiscences*, 183–88 (quotation on 186).

43. Robert Cook from James Paul, Book A, Deed Records, Tuscaloosa County Courthouse, Tuscaloosa, Alabama; Abernethy, *Formative Period*, 175; Johnson, *Soul by Soul*, 7–8 and 79. It is possible that Paul already owned one or two enslaved craftsmen who assisted in the workshop, but the purchase of this swathe of cotton acreage meant that he was now in the market for many more.

44. Minutes, TCCC, March 12, 1827, 185; Henderson to Watson, January 2, 1826, item 262, JWP.

45. Minutes, TCCC, March 12, 1827, 185; "Tuscaloosa (Ala.) April 22," *Woodville Republican* (Mississippi), April 22, 1826. All things being equal, a boy's age determined his market value. In 1830 (in New Orleans, at least), a ten-year-old like Cornelius should have fetched 60 percent of the sale price of a prime male hand, or about $600. Pritchett, "Selection of Slaves," 57; Daina Ramey Berry, *The Price for Their Pound of Flesh: The Value of the Enslaved, From Womb to Grave, in the Building of a Nation* (Boston: Beacon Press, 2017), 83; Wendell Holmes Stephenson, *Isaac Franklin: Slave Trader and Planter of the Old South. With Plantation Records* (Baton Rouge: Louisiana State University Press, 1938), 90. If the boy had apprenticed in a skilled trade, he could be worth even more.

Chapter 6: THE BODY IN THE WAGON

1. Pargas, *Slavery and Forced Migration*, 118–19.

2. "Kidnapping," 39–41; Margaret Clevenger, "Ashville: Old, New, and Lovely," *Alabama Heritage*, Summer 2010, 18–19.

3. "Kidnapping," 39–41; Mattie Lou Teague Crow, *History of St. Clair County (Alabama)* (Huntsville, AL: Strode Publishers, 1973), 20.

4. Outbreaks of yellow fever raged in Natchez, Mississippi, and in nearby Port Gibson for much of October.

5. Freudenberger and Pritchett, "New Evidence," 463–67. Traveling in the fall also made it easier for coffle slaves to adjust to the climate of the Deep South. Sydnor, *Slavery in Mississippi*, 149.

6. Ball, *Narrative*, 85; Lincecum, "Autobiography," 469; Johnson, *Soul by Soul*, 119. For a contemporary comparison to the grooming of animals for sale, see Andrews, *Domestic Slave Trade*, 151.

7. Northup, *Twelve Years*, 47–48; Johnson, *Soul by Soul*, 119; Felix Hadsell, Memoir, c. 1905, Historic Natchez Foundation, Natchez, Mississippi, 1.

8. Watson, *Narrative*, 10; Brown, *Slave Life*, 20; Northup, *Twelve Years*, 47; Johnson, *Soul by Soul*, 120–21. "Us was made to clean ourselves an' dress up," recalled Anne Maddox, a former Virginian slave sold in Alabama when she was just thirteen. Pargas, *Slavery and Forced Migration*, 122–23.

9. Johnson, *Soul by Soul*, 137–49. On the repellent sexual dimensions of male buyers' inspections of young black women, see Pargas, *Slavery and Forced Migration*, 122–23.

10. Northup, *Twelve Years*, 47; Deyle, *Carry Me Back*, 137 and 162; Johnson, *Soul by Soul*, 46–47, 129–39, and 179–81. Fraud laws were ambiguous and largely unenforced. Only traders in Louisiana were legally required to provide warranties, but, even then, medical problems and a long list of preexisting physical and character conditions were exempted as grounds for return.

11. Gudmestad, *Troublesome Commerce*, 98–101.

12. "Kidnapping," 37–39; Johnson, *Soul by Soul*, 119 and 129.

13. "Kidnapping," 39–41; "Kidnapping," *Port Gibson Correspondent* (Mississippi), June 8, 1826; Deyle, *Carry Me Back*, 106–11.

14. Owen, *John Owen's Journal*, 9; Deyle, *Carry Me Back*, 125–26.

15. Theodore Dwight Weld and James A. Thome, *Slavery and the Internal Slave Trade in the United States of North America* (London, 1841), 61; Deyle, *Carry Me Back*, 254–58. For other examples of violent revolt on southern roads, see "Washington PA, Feb. 2, Murder," *Relf's Philadelphia Gazette*, February 8, 1828; Sydnor, *Slavery in Mississippi*, 156–57; Baptist, *Never Been Told*, 24; Gudmestad, *Troublesome Commerce*, 46 and 140–41; Lightner, *Slavery and the Commerce Power*, 11.

16. Gudmestad, *Troublesome Commerce*, 3, 62–86, and 148–68; Tadman, *Speculators and Slaves*, 179–201; Deyle, *Carry Me Back*, 138. Austin Woolfolk, the leading legal trader in the 1820s, was reported to have blown the whistle on fellow traders who trafficked in kidnapped free people, and when Joshua Leavitt, an anti-

slavery activist, confronted John Armfield with evidence that two of his personal chattels had been acquired improperly, he offered an abject apology.

17. "Kidnapping," 37–42; "To the Editor of the Democratic Press," *Democratic Press* (Philadelphia), January 25, 1827; "Kidnapping," *Port Gibson Correspondent* (Mississippi), June 8, 1826.

18. "Kidnapping," 39–41; Baptist, *Never Been Told*, 14; Johnson, *Soul by Soul*, 59 and 68–69; Andrews, *Domestic Slave Trade*, 142 and 165.

19. Unidentified newspaper clipping, item 274A, JWP.

20. "Kidnapping," *Port Gibson Correspondent* (Mississippi), June 8, 1826; "Kidnapping," 39–41. For behavior symptomatic of Stockholm syndrome in an eight-year-old child who went through a similar ordeal in the mid-1820s, see Jeffrey Stewart, ed., *Narrative of Sojourner Truth* (New York: Oxford University Press, 1991), 52–54.

21. G. W. Featherstonhaugh, *Excursion Through the Slave States* (New York: Negro Universities Press, 1968), 124; Judith Kelleher Schafer, *Slavery, the Civil Law, and the Supreme Court of Louisiana* (Baton Rouge: Louisiana State University Press, 1994), 99–100; Jeff Forret, *Race Relations at the Margins: Slaves and Poor Whites in the Antebellum Southern Countryside* (Baton Rouge: Louisiana State University Press, 2006), 22–23.

22. Ball, *Narrative*, 100; Deyle, *Carry Me Back*, 254–62. For suicide attempts among slaves caught in the interstate trade, see Torrey, *Portraiture of Slavery*, 79–80; Weld, *American Slavery As It Is*, 50 and 89; Pargas, *Slavery and Forced Migration*, 84–85.

23. James Taylor Carson, *Searching for the Bright Path: The Mississippi Choctaws From Prehistory to Removal* (Lincoln: University of Nebraska Press, 1999), 72–73; Saxe-Weimar Eisenach, *Travels through North America*, 2: 24–25; Hudson, *Creek Paths*, 140; Barbara Krauthamer, *Black Slaves, Indian Masters: Slavery, Emancipation, and Citizenship in the Native American South* (Chapel Hill: University of North Carolina Press, 2013), 27–28.

24. Hamilton, *Men and Manners*, 2: 260.

25. Natalie Joy, "Finding Refuge in the Wigwam: Native Americans and the Underground Railroad" (paper presented at the Washington Early American Seminar, College Park, MD, May 6, 2017); Josiah Henson, *An Autobiography of the Reverend Josiah Henson* (Reading, MA: Addison-Wesley Publishing, 1969), 66; Daniel H. Usner, "American Indians on the Cotton Frontier: Changing Economic Relations with Citizens and Slaves in the Mississippi Territory," *Journal of American History* 72, no. 2 (September 1985): 310.

26. Joy, "Finding Refuge in the Wigwam," 2; Krauthamer, *Black Slaves, Indian Masters*, 6–7; Donna L. Akers, *Living in the Land of Death: The Choctaw Nation, 1830–1860* (East Lansing: Michigan State University Press, 2004), 23–24. The 1830 federal census counted 17,963 Choctaws.

27. Krauthamer, *Black Slaves, Indian Masters*, 3–7; Carson, *Bright Path*, 71; Dawn Peterson, "Domestic Fronts in the Era of 1812: Slavery, Expansion, and Familial Struggles for Sovereignty in the Early-Nineteenth-Century Choctaw South,"

in *Warring for America: Cultural Contests in the Era of 1812*, eds. Nicole Eustace and Fredrika J. Teute (Chapel Hill: University of North Carolina Press, 2017), 386–418. In 1801, in the Treaty of Fort Adams, the Choctaws ceded 2.5 million acres of land to appease white settlers. They ceded an additional 5 million acres in 1820 in the Treaty of Doak's Stand (which was subsequently renegotiated). Arthur H. DeRosier Jr., *The Removal of the Choctaw Indians* (Knoxville: University of Tennessee Press, 1970), 53–69. Travelers through the Choctaw territory in the early 1820s reported seeing several hundred African slaves tending more than three thousand acres of cotton crops. Several hundred more were at labor at other tasks: they herded livestock, cleared forests, planted corn, and built bridges, roads, and houses. Even though the absolute number of slaves in the territory was small by southern standards, more and more Choctaws were becoming accustomed to calculating their personal wealth by counting their slaves, and several more now made their living as slave traders. Carson, *Bright Path*, 80–82; Krauthamer, *Black Slaves, Indian Masters*, 4–5, 17, and 42; Christina Snyder, *Slavery in Indian Country: The Changing Face of Captivity in Early America* (Cambridge, MA: Harvard University Press, 2010), 180–92.

28. Arthur H. DeRosier Jr., "Pioneers with Conflicting Ideals: Christianity and Slavery in the Choctaw Nation," *Journal of Mississippi History* 21 (July 1959): 186; Krauthamer, *Black Slaves, Indian Masters*, 23; Joy, "Finding Refuge in the Wigwam," 3–4 and 15.

29. "Kidnapping," 39–41; John Marrant, *A Narrative of the Lord's Wonderful Dealings with John Marrant, a Black*, 4th ed. (London: 1785), 19; DeRosier, "Pioneers," 186.

30. "Kidnapping," 39–41. Almost a year later, Sam's head was still deeply and visibly scarred.

31. James A. Crutchfield, *The Natchez Trace: A Pictorial History* (Nashville, TN: Rutledge Hill Press, 1985), 123–25.

32. "Kidnapping," 39–41. See also Pargas, *Slavery and Forced Migration*, 119; Robinson, *From Log Cabin to Pulpit*, 42–44; Weld, *American Slavery As It Is*, 70.

33. "Kidnapping," 39–42; "Messrs. Crutcher & Stockton," *Port Gibson Correspondent* (Mississippi), September 7, 1826; Henderson to Watson, January 2, 1826, item 262, JWP; Smith, "Notes and Documents," 324.

34. "Messrs. Crutcher & Stockton."

35. Katy McCaleb Headley, comp., *Claiborne County, Mississippi: The Promised Land* (Port Gibson, MS: Claiborne County Historical Society, 1976), 86–87; Bud Steed, *The Haunted Natchez Trace* (Charleston, SC: Haunted America/History Press, 2012), 39.

36. "Negroes for Sale," *Port Gibson Correspondent* (Mississippi), October 12, 1826.

37. Henderson to Watson, January 2, 1826, item 262, JWP; "Mississippi," *Daily National Intelligencer* (Washington, DC), May 29, 1826; Miller, "Plantation Labor Organization," 158.

38. "Kidnapping," *Port Gibson Correspondent* (Mississippi), June 8, 1826; Henderson to Watson, January 2, 1826, item 262, JWP. An outbreak of yellow fever

that fall in nearby Natchez, the region's largest slave-trading center, may explain Hamilton's willingness to buy slaves from a roadside vendor visiting Rocky Springs. "Yellow Fever in Natchez," *Port Gibson Correspondent* (Mississippi), October 6, 1825.

39. "Weather," *Natchez Ariel* (Mississippi), December 25, 1825.

40. "Kidnapping," *Port Gibson Correspondent* (Mississippi), June 8, 1826.

41. Ibid.; Henderson to Watson, January 2, 1826, item 262, JWP.

42. Ibid.

43. Ibid.

Chapter 7: THE HALFWAY HOUSE

1. "Kidnapping," *Easton Gazette* (Maryland), February 26, 1826; "Kidnapping," *Port Gibson Correspondent* (Mississippi), June 8, 1826.

2. Henderson to Watson, January 2, 1826, item 262, JWP; "E. F. Johnston vs. J. W. Hamilton," February Term, 1826, Chancery Court, Peace and County Court, 1803–1829, Port Gibson, Mississippi, Family History Library, Salt Lake City, Utah (hereafter cited as PGCC).

3. Ibid.

4. Henderson to Watson, January 2, 1826, item 262, JWP.

5. "Kidnapping," *Port Gibson Correspondent* (Mississippi), June 8, 1826; Henderson to Watson, March 20, 1826, item 264, JWP; Green to Watson, February 28, 1826, item 177, JWP.

6. Loguen, *Narrative*, 14–16. See also Weld, *American Slavery As It Is*, 89. For a surprising and successful intervention in similar circumstances, see "Kidnapping," 43–44.

7. David Child, "The Domestic Slave Trade," *American Anti-Slavery Reporter* 1, no. 7 (1834): 103; Everett Dick, *The Dixie Frontier: A Social History of the Southern Frontier From the First Transmontane Beginnings to the Civil War* (New York: Knopf, 1948), 54.

8. Henderson to Watson, January 2, 1826, item 262, JWP. Courts across the region prosecuted slave stealers relentlessly. A law in neighboring Louisiana passed in 1819 prescribed "imprisonment at hard labor for not less than two years or more than twenty years for any person convicted of stealing a slave or helping a slave to run away." Schafer, *Slavery, the Civil Law*, 92.

9. "Messrs. Crutcher & Stockton."

10. Watson to William Rawle, Loose Correspondence, incoming, 1820–1849, 1857, 1859–1863, reel 13, July 4, 1826; "Kidnapping," *Port Gibson Correspondent* (Mississippi), June 8, 1826. See also "Messrs. Crutcher & Stockton."

11. Henderson to Watson, January 2, 1826, item 262, JWP. In his own letter to the mayor of Philadelphia, mailed twenty-four days later, Hamilton did many of the same things, ultimately naming twenty-three individuals. Hamilton to Watson, January 27, 1826, item 272, JWP.

12. Henderson to Watson, January 2, 1826, item 262, JWP.

13. "Doctor G. Keirn," *Port Gibson Correspondent* (Mississippi), April 28, 1821.

14. *Biographical and Historical Memoirs of Mississippi*, 2 vols. (Spartanburg, SC: Reprint Co., 1978), 1: 907; Smith, "Notes and Documents," 324.

15. "Probate Notice," *Port Gibson Correspondent* (Mississippi), December 6, 1823; "Various Items," *Port Gibson Correspondent* (Mississippi), January 22, 1824; *Memoirs of Mississippi*, 1: 907; Cashin, *Family Venture*, 34; Headley, *Claiborne County*, 54–55. Daniel Webster once called John Henderson the greatest land lawyer the United States had ever produced.

16. Irene S. Gillis and Norman E. Gillis, *Mississippi 1820 Census* (Baton Rouge, LA: n.p., 1963), 60; "Rocky Spring Celebration," *Port Gibson Correspondent* (Mississippi), July 8, 1824. See also Rhoda M. Love, "The Grand Old Man of Northwest Botany: Louis F. Henderson (1853–1942)," *Pacific Northwest Quarterly* 91, no. 4 (Fall 2000): 183–99; *Memoirs of Mississippi*, 1: 907. For Henderson's early forays into state politics representing Claiborne County in the Mississippi legislature, see "Kidnapping," *Port Gibson Correspondent* (Mississippi), June 8, 1826; "Election Returns," *Natchez Ariel* (Mississippi), August 17, 1827.

17. Cashin, *Family Venture*, 33–39, 44; Sydnor, *Slavery in Mississippi*, 47; Herring, "Natchez, 1795–1830," 200 and 207. For more on Hamilton's presence in Natchez in this period, see Christopher Morris, *Becoming Southern: The Evolution of a Way of Life, Warren County and Vicksburg, Mississippi, 1770–1860* (New York: Oxford University Press, 1995), 66; Miscellaneous John W. Hamilton Debt Suits, 1813, Historic Natchez Foundation, Natchez, Mississippi (hereafter cited as HNF).

18. Miscellaneous John W. Hamilton Debt Suits, 1814–1815, HNF; Cashin, *Family Venture*, 64–68.

19. Cashin, *Family Venture*, 64; Kathryn Meyer McAllister Olivarius, "Necropolis: Yellow Fever, Immunity, and Capitalism in the Deep South, 1800–1860" (DPhil diss., University of Oxford, 2016), i, ii, 4, and 24–25. During a yellow fever outbreak in Natchez in October 1825, one person died every day on average, including several medical men. "The Yellow Fever," *Port Gibson Correspondent* (Mississippi), October 27, 1825.

20. Olivarius, "Necropolis," 24 and 61–72; Headley, *Claiborne County*, 55; Miscellaneous John W. Hamilton Debt Suits, 1823, HNF; Judgments, 1823–1831, Circuit Court of Mississippi, 210, 285-87, HNF. There are no further mentions of Hamilton's son in subsequent records; hence the deduction that he died.

21. Cashin, *Family Venture*, 39–44, 59, and 62; "Rocky Spring Celebration," *Port Gibson Correspondent* (Mississippi), July 8, 1824; Ancestry.com, *United States General Land Office Records, 1776–2015* (Provo, UT: Ancestry.com Operations, Inc., 2008), documents 775 and 976. Hamilton likely had to displace and pay off squatters occupying the land that was above the high-water mark and had at least two natural springs. Dick, *Dixie Frontier*, 54–55; "For Sale," *Port Gibson Correspondent* (Mississippi), December 16, 1825.

22. "Valuable Land for Sale," *Statesman and Gazette* (Natchez, MS), March 9, 1831; Cashin, *Family Venture*, 40. At some point between 1824 and 1831,

Hamilton and his enslaved laborers also constructed a storehouse and several other outbuildings and dug two wells.

23. "Kidnapping," *Port Gibson Correspondent* (Mississippi), June 8, 1826. The price of cotton had been falling precipitously ever since the Panic of 1819 and bottomed out below seventeen cents per pound in December 1825, leaving debtors like Hamilton to despair about their diminished ability to pay back their creditors and stave off foreclosure. Rothman, *Slave Country*, 187; Daniel S. Dupre, *Transforming the Cotton Frontier: Madison County, Alabama, 1800–1840* (Baton Rouge: Louisiana University Press, 1997), 50–51, 55–56, 66–67, and 99; "Cotton," *Natchez Ariel* (Mississippi), December 19, 1825; "Cotton," *Natchez Ariel* (Mississippi), March 24, 1826. A survey of service records and pension applications reveals that several dozen John Hamiltons served in the armed forces at some point or other during the War of 1812, though none at the rank of colonel and none from Tennessee. What's more, the man who rescued Sam in December 1825 was a resident of Natchez, Mississippi, for the duration of the war. See Ancestry.com, US, *War of 1812 Service Records, 1812–1815* (Provo, UT: Ancestry.com Operations, Inc., 1999).

24. "T. Gibson & Co.," *Port Gibson Correspondent* (Mississippi), October 12, 1826; "Sheriff's Sales," *Port Gibson Correspondent* (Mississippi), October 12, 1826; "Debt Suit," *Port Gibson Correspondent* (Mississippi), October 12, 1827; "T. Gibson vs. John W. Hamilton," *Port Gibson Correspondent* (Mississippi), March 31, 1827.

25. Miller, "Plantation Labor Organization," 158–59 and 162; Headley, *Claiborne County*, 4.

26. "E. F. Johnston vs. J. W. Hamilton," February Term, 1826, PGCC.

27. Ibid.

28. Ibid.; Headley, *Claiborne County*, 55.

29. Sharla M. Fett, *Recaptured Africans: Surviving Slave Ships, Detention, and Dislocation in the Final Years of the Slave Trade* (Chapel Hill: University of North Carolina Press, 2017), 55 and 80–81; Kwok B. Chan and David B. Loveridge, "Refugees 'in Transit': Vietnamese in a Refugee Camp in Hong Kong," *International Migration Review* 21, no. 3 (Autumn 1987): 746 and 755; Faith R. Warner, "Social Support and Distress Among Q'eqchi' Refugee Women in Maya Tecún, Mexico," *Medical Anthropology Quarterly* 21, no. 2 (June 2007): 193.

30. Henderson to Watson, January 2, 1826, item 262, JWP. Watson's note to Henderson does not survive.

31. "To the Editor of the American Daily Advertiser," *Poulson's American Daily Advertiser* (Philadelphia), February 13, 1826; Abstract of List of Documents, March 10, 1826, item 274, JWP.

32. "Kidnapping!" *Poulson's American Daily Advertiser* (Philadelphia), July 24, 1817.

33. "Kidnapping," 37–39.

34. "To the Editor of the American Daily Advertiser."

35. "Kidnapping!" *Poulson's American Daily Advertiser* (Philadelphia), July 24, 1817; "Messrs. Crutcher & Stockton."

36. Northup, *Twelve Years*, 53; Deyle, *Carry Me Back*, 247.
37. Joshua Raybold, deposition, February 7, 1826, item 274, JWP; Hester Tillman, deposition, February 4, 1826, item 274, JWP.
38. John Raymon, deposition, February 4, 1826, item 274, JWP; Caleb Carpenter, deposition, February 4, 1826, item 274, JWP.
39. William Warwick, deposition, February 6, 1826, item 274, JWP; Joseph Middleton, deposition, February 6, 1826, item 274, JWP; James McCann, deposition, February 4, 1826, item 274, JWP; Thomas Earle, deposition, February 6, 1826, item 274, JWP; Caleb Kimber, deposition, February 6?, 1826, item 274, JWP.
40. David Hill, deposition, February 17, 1826, item 274, JWP; Israel Hendrickson, deposition, February 17, 1826, item 274, JWP; Charles Ewing, declaration, February 17, 1826, item 274, JWP; John Lawber, deposition, March 15, 1826, item 274, JWP; Mary Clark, deposition, March 8, 1826, item 274, JWP; Benjamin Coombe, deposition, March 10, 1826, item 274, JWP. Verifying Mary Fisher's identity took longer than the others and required Watson to send out a second public plea in late February seeking testimony that could prove her claim to freedom.
41. "To the Editor of the American Daily Advertiser"; Rogers to Watson, February 14, 1826, GRF; *Minute Book of the Acting Committee, 1810–1822*, reel 5, April 6, 1819, PAS. Watson wrote the press release on February 9, four days before it first appeared in print. It was subsequently reprinted in other Philadelphia papers and also in Baltimore (February 15) and Washington, DC (February 17), and in the next issue of Philadelphia's monthly antislavery journal, the *Genius of Universal Emancipation*. The press release included a copyedited transcription of Henderson's January 2 letter to which Watson had added specific landmark information (e.g., "under Red Lion") to help Philadelphia readers better identify locations and addresses.
42. Wright and Wright to Watson, February 15, 1826, item 274, JWP; James Gaskins to Watson, February 19, 1826, item 176, JWP; Green to Watson, February 28, 1826, item 177, JWP. A fourth letter arrived from Thomas Garrett, an antislavery activist living in Wilmington, Delaware. He asked Mayor Watson if the Mary Fisher named in news reports was actually Charity Fisher, a twenty-four-year-old free black woman who had disappeared from Wilmington the previous October, leaving her nine-month-old son, Mathew. She was not. Thomas Garrett to Watson, February 20, 1826, GRF.

Chapter 8: THE LIFEBOAT

1. Watson, warrant, February 17, 1826, item 274, JWP; Grand Jury, true bill, March 1826, item 274, JWP; Court of Quarter Sessions Docket and Index, 1824 to 1826, 1826 to 1828, 1828 to 1831, Philadelphia City Archives, Philadelphia, Pennsylvania, 18: 321. See also Joshua S. Taylor, certification of conviction, February 22, 1826, item 274, JWP.

2. Watson to Hamilton and Henderson, March 10, 1826, item 275, JWP; Watson to Hamilton and Henderson, March 15, 1826, item 276, JWP; Watson to Hamilton, February 24, 1826, item 273, JWP.

3. Watson to Hamilton, February 24, 1826, item 273, JWP; "Tuscaloosa (Ala.) April 22," *Woodville Republican* (Mississippi), April 22, 1826; Hamilton to Watson, May 17, 1826, item 277, JWP.

4. Watson to Hamilton and Henderson, March 10, 1826, item 275, JWP. For the list of contents, see Abstract of List of Documents, March 10, 1826, item 274, JWP. On March 15, Watson sent along three more depositions attesting to the free status of Mary Fisher.

5. Watson to Hamilton and Henderson, March 10, 1826, item 275, JWP.

6. "Joseph Watson, Esq.," *Daily Chronicle and General Advertiser* (Philadelphia), April 12, 1841. See also "Philadelphia," *Commercial Advertiser* (New York), October 19, 1825.

7. "Alderman Watson," *National Advocate* (New York), April 24, 1824; Smith, "Notes and Documents," 317–18.

8. Smith, "Notes and Documents," 318.

9. "The United States Gazette," *Ithaca Journal* (New York), March 2, 1825. In May 1828, Watson received an engraved silver goblet from the Farmers Bank of Reading in gratitude "for his zeal and effective exertions in the destruction of an extensive Combination of Counterfeiters." "Reward of Merit," *Baltimore Gazette and Daily Advertiser*, May 31, 1828. On counterfeiting and law enforcement in this period, see Mihm, *Nation of Counterfeiters*, 103–56.

10. J. Williams, Daniel Mason, and Gallaudette Oliver to Watson, September 5, 1824, item 475, JWP. See also Bell, "Counterfeit Kin."

11. Papers relating to the case of Nicholas Young, American Convention of 1826, reel 28, December 31, 1825, PAS.

12. During the American Revolution, Watson's father, Isaac, was fined for "nonperformance of tour of duty when called out"; that is, for his pacifist refusal to take up arms. For Watson's family history, see Jane W. T. Brey, *A Quaker Saga: The Watsons of Strawberryhowe, the Wildmans, and Other Allied Families from England's North Counties and Lower Bucks County in Pennsylvania* (Philadelphia: Dorrance, 1967), xxv, 10, 146–47, 194, and 299. Incomplete records suggest that Watson and his wife forfeited good standing when they "married out of unity"—that is, when they failed to properly announce their intention to wed at a monthly meeting—and it is notable that he is buried in an Episcopal burial ground.

13. Joseph J. Lewis, *A Memoir of Enoch Lewis* (West Chester, PA, 1882), 83; *Centennial Anniversary of the Pennsylvania Society* (Philadelphia, 1875), 51–66; Elliott Drago, "Neither Northern nor Southern: The Politics of Slavery and Freedom in Philadelphia, 1820–1847" (PhD diss., Temple University, 2017), 104–5; Brey, *The Watsons*. Enoch Lewis set up the *African Observer*, a journal proudly committed to slavery's extinction, two years into Watson's tenure as mayor.

14. *Second Report of the Provident Society for the Employment of the Poor, Presented at the Meeting, January 10, 1826* (Philadelphia, 1826), 5. This Asylum for Lost Children was an outgrowth of the work of the Philadelphia Provident Society, a charity set up in 1824 to provide job opportunities to the indigent. Watson served as its founding vice president. *First Report of the Provident Society for the Employment of the Poor, Presented at the Meeting, January 11, 1825, with An Appendix* (Philadelphia, 1825).

15. "Kidnapping," 45.

16. Watson to Hamilton and Henderson, March 10, 1826, item 275, JWP; "Kidnapping," 45–46.

17. "Messrs. Crutcher & Stockton"; "Various," *Port Gibson Correspondent* (Mississippi), July 28, 1827; Watson to Benjamin Morgan and Joseph Bennet Eves, March 20, 1826, item 1, Watson Correspondence, 1826–1846, Louisiana State University Special Collections, Baton Rouge (hereafter cited as JWC). The "humane persons" Watson referred to were likely the officers of the Quaker-led Pennsylvania Abolition Society, who had been following the case since February. Watson to Rawle, Loose Correspondence, incoming, 1820–1849, 1857, 1859–1863, reel 13, July 4, 1826, PAS; "From the American Daily Advertiser," *Port Gibson Correspondent* (Mississippi), September 7, 1826.

18. Henderson to Watson, March 20, 1826, item 264, JWP. See also "Messrs. Crutcher & Stockton."

19. Henderson to Watson, April 17, 1826, item 265, JWP; Henderson to Watson, May 5, 1826, item 266, JWP; Henderson to Watson, May 8, 1826, item 267, JWP.

20. Henderson to Watson, May 5, 1826, item 266, JWP.

21. "Richard Stockton Jr., Esq," *Port Gibson Correspondent* (Mississippi), July 7, 1821; "Richard Stockton Jr.," *Port Gibson Correspondent* (Mississippi), January 27, 1825; James D. Lynch, *The Bench and Bar of Mississippi* (New York, 1881), 92.

22. "Kidnapping," 41–42.

23. Henderson to Watson, May 8, 1826, item 267, JWP; *Minute Book of the Acting Committee, 1825–1847*, reel 2, June 7, 1826, PAS; Watson to Rawle, Loose Correspondence, incoming, 1820–1849, 1857, 1859–1863, reel 13, July 4, 1826, PAS.

24. *Minute Book of the Acting Committee, 1825–1847*, reel 2, June 7, 1826, PAS. See also Hamilton to Watson, May 17, 1826, item 277, JWP; Morgan to Watson, May 29, 1826, Haverford College, Special Collections Library, Haverford, PA (hereafter cited as HSC).

25. Henderson to Watson, May 8, 1826, item 267, JWP; Hamilton to Watson, May 17, 1826, item 277, JWP; Estwick Evans, *A Pedestrious Tour, of Four Thousand Miles, Through the Western States and Territories, During the Winter and Spring of 1818* (Concord, NH: 1819), 218–19.

26. Gudmestad, *Troublesome Commerce*, 18 and 24–25; Herring, "Natchez, 1795–

1830," 213. On a visit to Natchez in 1817, Henry Fearon counted no less than fourteen flatboats tied up below the bluff, each one bulging with slaves for sale. Joel Gray Taylor, "Negro Slavery in Louisiana" (PhD diss., Louisiana State University, 1952), 36. The Deep South was full of Philadelphia-area transplants, many of whom rose to become leading men in legal, financial, and governmental circles. Keenly conscious of their shared heritage, this émigré community intermarried frequently, went into business with one another, and did all they could to ease the transition for later arrivals from eastern Pennsylvania and its environs. Fletcher M. Green, *The Role of the Yankee in the Old South* (Athens: University of Georgia Press, 1972), 5 and 7; Daniel Kilbride, *An American Aristocracy: Southern Planters in Antebellum Philadelphia* (Columbia: University of South Carolina Press, 2006); Lowery, "The Great Migration"; Cashin, *Family Venture.*

27. Henderson to Watson, May 8, 1826, item 267, JWP; Hamilton to Watson, May 17, 1826, item 277, JWP; Robert Gudmestad, *Steamboats and the Rise of the Cotton Kingdom* (Baton Rouge: Louisiana State University Press), 20. On the *Feliciana*, see "Notes and Abstracts," *American Engineer*, March 6, 1885, 118; Emerson W. Gould, *Fifty Years on the Mississippi; Or, Gould's History of River Navigation* (St. Louis, 1889), 206; Morgan to Watson, May 29, 1826, HSC.

28. Gudmestad, *Steamboats*, 56–57.

29. Rashauna Johnson, *Slavery's Metropolis: Unfree Labor in New Orleans During the Age of Revolutions* (New York: Cambridge University Press, 2016), 1–2.

30. Morgan to Watson, May 29, 1826, HSC; Jared William Bradley, ed., *Interim Appointment: W.C.C. Claiborne Letter Book, 1804–1805* (Baton Rouge: Louisiana State University Press, 2002), 282–98. Morgan had even made a failed run for mayor.

31. Gould, *Fifty Years*, 231; "For Philadelphia," *Louisiana State Gazette* (New Orleans), May 8, 1826; Morgan to Watson, May 29, 1826, HSC; Henderson to Watson, May 8, 1826, item 267, JWP.

32. Morgan to Watson, May 29, 1826, HSC; Henderson to Watson, May 8, 1826, item 267, JWP; Schafer, *Slavery, the Civil Law*, 99–100.

33. "Huzzah for Pennsylvania," *Port Gibson* (Mississippi), October 23, 1819; George J. Leftwich, "Robert J. Walker," *Publications of the Mississippi Historical Society* 6 (1902): 360; James P. Shenton, *Robert John Walker: A Politician From Jackson to Lincoln* (New York: Columbia University Press, 1961), 11.

34. "Kansas Territory, Slavery," *Mississippian and State Gazette* (Jackson) June 23, 1854. There were, in the words of the biographer of one quintessential southern transplant, "no limits on the potential success of Yankees who avoided condemning the South's ways." Robert A. May, *John A. Quitman: Old South Crusader* (Baton Rouge: Louisiana State University Press, 1985), 25.

35. Joshua D. Rothman, *Flush Times & Fever Dreams: A Story of Capitalism and Slavery in the Age of Jackson* (Athens: University of Georgia Press, 2012), 7–11 and 34; Dick, *Dixie Frontier*, 233; Thomas D. Clark and John D. W. Guice,

Frontiers in Conflict: The Old Southwest, 1795–1830 (Albuquerque: University of New Mexico Press, 1989), 93 and 188–89; Cashin, *Family Venture*, 46; Thomas Ruys Smith, *River of Dreams: Imagining the Mississippi Before Mark Twain* (Baton Rouge: Louisiana State University Press, 2007), 141–75; Headley, *Claiborne County*, 54–55 and 86–87. On domestication as an organizing concept for the political and economic development of the Deep South, see Adam Rothman, "The Domestication of the Slave Trade in the United States," in *The Chattel Principle: Internal Slave Trades in the Americas*, ed. Walter Johnson (New Haven, CT: Yale University Press, 2004), 32–54.

36. Rothman, *Slave Country*, 181; Olivarius, "Necropolis," ii, 16, and 216.

37. "Kidnapping," 41–42. Going after criminal traffickers like the Johnsons was also a means for officeholders like Stockton to address constituent concerns about fraudulent slave sellers. Planters constantly fretted about accidentally buying kidnapped slaves from itinerant "nigger jockeys." They believed that kidnapped free people were more likely to be unruly, or to contaminate other slaves with their ideas, or to run away, and knew that warranties and refunds were almost unheard of. Deyle, *Carry Me Back*, 137 and 162; Gudmestad, *Troublesome Commerce*, 98–100.

38. Lightner, *Slavery and the Commerce Power*, 58–59; Mason, *Slavery and Politics*, 79–80 and 138–39; Gudmestad, *Troublesome Commerce*, 73–74.

39. Ernest Obadele-Starks, *Freebooters and Smugglers: The Foreign Slave Trade in the United States After 1808* (Fayetteville: University of Arkansas Press, 2007), 46–74; Gudmestad, *Troublesome Commerce*, 74–100; Mason, *Slavery and Politics*, 168; Rothman, *Flush Times*, 11–12; Deyle, *Carry Me Back*, 51–55; Winfield H. Collins, *The Domestic Slave Trade of the Southern States* (New York: Broadway Publishing Company, 1904), 126–33. Every state in the Deep South debated regulating interstate imports of slaves in the decade after the War of 1812. An "act regulating the importation of Slaves," signed into law in 1819 by Mississippi governor David Holmes, a Pennsylvania migrant himself, required interstate traders to swear under oath before clerks of court as to the provenance of each chattel they imported into the state. The same act imposed five-hundred-dollar fines upon traders who failed to oblige, while an 1822 statute went further still, requiring traders to obtain sworn certificates of good character from the prior owners of their human property. By 1832, Louisiana, Alabama, and Georgia had also put such laws on their books, though they were regularly flouted by residents and interstate dealers alike. *Acts Passed at the First Session of the Second General Assembly of the State of Mississippi* (Natchez, 1819), 4–8.

40. Gudmestad, *Troublesome Commerce*, 148–68; Mason, *Slavery and Politics*, 168–69; Tadman, *Speculators and Slaves*, 186–89 and 247; Taylor, "Negro Slavery," 48. Northern papers rejoiced with word of each new (though usually toothless) restriction on slave trading in the southern states.

41. "Marine Register. Cleared," *Louisiana State Gazette* (New Orleans), May 29, 1826.

42. "For Philadelphia," *Louisiana State Gazette* (New Orleans), May 16, 1826; Survey of Federal Archives in Louisiana, *Ship Registers and Enrollments of New Orleans, Louisiana*, 6 vols. (Baton Rouge: Louisiana State University, 1942), 2: 24. Built in Bath, Maine, in 1824, the *Catharine* was lighter than the *Feliciana*, and displaced just 313 tons unladen.

Chapter 9: A LIVING WITNESS

1. Minutes, TCCC, March 12, 1827, 182–83.

2. Levina Johnson to Isaac Johnson, Loose Correspondence, incoming, 1820–1849, 1857, 1859–1863, reel 13, July 7, 1824, PAS. For another black-authored Mayday letter, see Aptheker, *Documentary History*, 1: 78–79.

3. In 1818, one African American mariner told PAS officers that during a recent voyage to New Orleans, "a black boy frequently came to the vessel of which Jones was the steward & cook" and informed him that he had been kidnapped from a home in Philadelphia. *Minute Book of the Acting Committee, 1810–1822*, reel 5, July 4, 1818, PAS.

4. Alton Lambert, *History of Tuscaloosa County, Alabama*, 3 vols. (Centre, AL: Stewart University Press, 1977), 1: 121; Tuscaloosa Genealogical Society, *Pioneers*, 1–5; Kelly M. Kennington, *In the Shadow of Dred Scott: St. Louis Freedom Suits and the Legal Culture of Slavery in Antebellum America* (Athens: University of Georgia Press, 2017), 52–58.

5. John W. Quist, *Restless Visionaries: The Social Roots of Antebellum Reform in Alabama and Michigan* (Baton Rouge: Louisiana State University Press, 1998), 8–9. The population of Tuscaloosa County rose from 7,339 in 1820 to 13,646 in 1830. One in three county residents were enslaved people of color; the statewide ratio was similar. Lambert, *Tuscaloosa County*, 1: 19.

6. Record of Pleas, TCCC, October 9, 1826, 388.

7. Randy J. Sparks, *On Jordan's Stormy Banks: Evangelicalism in Mississippi, 1773–1876* (Athens: University of Georgia Press, 1994), 1; Charity R. Carney, *Ministers and Masters: Methodism, Manhood, and Honor in the Old South* (Baton Rouge: Louisiana State University Press, 2011), 118; Cynthia Lynn Lyerly, *Methodism and the Southern Mind, 1770–1810* (New York: Oxford University Press, 1998), 47–48; Donald G. Mathews, *Slavery and Methodism: A Chapter in American Morality, 1780–1845* (Princeton, NJ: Princeton University Press, 1965), 5, 7, and 32; John H. Wigger, *Taking Heaven by Storm: Methodism and the Rise of Popular Christianity in America* (New York: Oxford University Press, 1998), 134–40; David T. Bailey, *Shadow on the Church: Southwestern Evangelical Religion and the Issue of Slavery, 1783–1860* (Ithaca, NY: Cornell University Press, 1985), 114.

8. Wigger, *Taking Heaven by Storm*, 139–40; Bailey, *Shadow on the Church*, 102–3.

9. Mathews, *Slavery and Methodism*, 24; Wigger, *Taking Heaven by Storm*, 142 and 144; Bailey, *Shadow on the Church*, 132, 136–37, and 141.

10. Lyerly, *Methodism and the Southern Mind*, 50–51; Sparks, *On Jordan's Stormy*

Banks, 69 and 124–25; Christopher H. Owen, "'To Keep the Way Open to Methodism': Georgia Wesleyan Neutrality Toward Slavery, 1844–1861," in *Religion and the Antebellum Debate Over Slavery,* eds. John R. McKivigan and Mitchell Snay (Athens: University of Georgia, 1998), 110–11. Despite this declension, full-throated biblical defenses of slavery did not emerge until the 1830s, and the denomination only finally split over the slavery question in 1844. Sparks, *On Jordan's Stormy Banks,* 115–18; Mathews, *Slavery and Methodism,* 31; Quist, *Restless Visionaries,* 349. For pockets of Methodist antislavery activity in the South in this period, see Mathews, *Slavery and Methodism,* 45–48 and 53–54; Bailey, *Shadow on the Church,* 138–39.

11. James B. Sellers, *The First Methodist Church of Tuscaloosa, Alabama, 1818–1968* (Tuscaloosa, AL: Weathersford Printing Company, 1968), 39 and 51; Anson West, *A History of Methodism in Alabama* (Nashville, TN, 1893), 325; Mario Elias Lazenby, *History of Methodism in Alabama and West Florida Being an Account of the Amazing March of Methodism Through Alabama and West Florida* (Nashville, TN: North Alabama Conference and Alabama-West Florida Conference of the Methodist Church, 1960), 69 and 144; "Recollections of Northern Alabama Methodism, No. 19," *Alabama Christian Advocate,* October 12, 1881.

12. West, *Methodism in Alabama,* 356, 457, and 568; Sellers, *The First Methodist Church,* 21, 25–26, and 45–46; Lazenby, *Methodism in Alabama,* 144; John G. Jones, *A Complete History of Methodism As Connected with the Mississippi Conference of the Methodist Episcopal Church, South. Written at the Unanimous Request of the Conference,* 2 vols. (Nashville, TN: Southern Methodist Publishing House, 1908), 2: 55–56; Tuscaloosa Genealogical Society, *Pioneers,* 377; Judson E. Crump and Alfred L. Brophy, "Twenty-One Months a Slave: Cornelius Sinclair's Odyssey," *Mississippi Law Journal* 86, no. 3 (May 2017): 470–71; William R. Smith, *Reminiscences of a Long Life; Historical, Political, Personal and Literary* (Washington, DC, 1889), 142–43. Kennon was also a talented preacher whose sermons burned with the sort of fire that left men's souls smoldering for days.

13. Wigger, *Taking Heaven by Storm,* 126–27; Sparks, *On Jordan's Stormy Banks,* 60.

14. West, *Methodism in Alabama,* 458.

15. The *Mirror*'s reporting is not extant but can be inferred from the contents of a later issue of a Mississippi paper that reprinted a related story. See "Tuscaloosa (Ala.) April 22," *Woodville Republican* (Mississippi), April 22, 1826. Similarly, the precise contents of the Tuscaloosa dossier, and which parts of it were printed in the pages of the *American Mirror,* are not known, though they certainly included copies of relevant items from the larger dossier Watson sent to Rocky Springs.

16. "Boy Lost"; Minutes, TCCC, March 12, 1827, 181–86; "Kidnapping," 37–39.

17. Record of Pleas, TCCC, February 17, 1827, 235–36; Crump and Brophy, "Twenty-One Months a Slave," 466.

18. Joshua Boucher to Watson, January 17, 1827, item 26, JWP; Record of Pleas,

TCCC, October 9, 1826, 388; Minutes, TCCC, March 12, 1827, 182–83. Most other enslaved petitioners were at least partially illiterate, so signed with the customary X. Lea VanderVelde, *Redemption Songs: Suing for Freedom Before Dred Scott* (New York: Oxford University Press, 2014), 8.

19. Kimberly M. Welch, *Black Litigants in the Antebellum American South* (Chapel Hill: University of North Carolina Press, 2018), 161–66 and 180; Judith Kelleher Schafer, *Becoming Free, Remaining Free: Manumission and Enslavement in New Orleans, 1846–1862* (Baton Rouge: Louisiana State University Press, 2003), 15–70 and 115–28; Kennington, *Shadow of Dred Scott*, 25–29 and 78–86; Anne Twitty, *Before Dred Scott: Slavery and Legal Culture in the American Confluence, 1787–1857* (New York: Cambridge University Press, 2016), 11–16.

20. Kelly Marie Kennington, "Law, Geography, and Mobility: Suing for Freedom in Antebellum St. Louis," *Journal of Southern History* 80, no. 3 (August 2014): 580–86; Welch, *Black Litigants*, 162–63, 183, and 263; Twitty, *Before Dred Scott*, 71–95; Kennington, *Shadow of Dred Scott*, 43–47. Welch's data is drawn from two Mississippi counties, Adams and Claiborne, and two parishes in Louisiana, Iberville and Pointe Coupee. Between 1815 and 1830, courts in Louisiana heard just ten cases brought by people of color claiming they had been kidnapped into slavery. Judges found in favor of only six of these plaintiffs. Race and Slavery Petitions Project, University of North Carolina at Greensboro, accessed July 1, 2018, https://library.uncg.edu/slavery/petitions/history.aspx, PARs 20881514, 20881603, 20881703, 20881705, 20881902, 20881903, 20882205, 20881603, 20882322, and 20882912. The pattern holds steady even when other grounds for petition are included. On the proslavery imperatives undergirding provision of freedom suits in the South, see Edlie L. Wong, *Neither Fugitive nor Free: Atlantic Slavery, Freedom Suits, and the Legal Culture of Travel* (New York: New York University Press, 2009), 5. The metaphor of the "escape hatch" is borrowed from Welch.

21. Loren Scweninger, ed., *The Southern Debate Over Slavery*, 2 vols. (Urbana: University of Illinois Press, 2001), 2: 18–19; John V. Denson, *Slavery Laws in Alabama* (Auburn: Alabama Polytechnic Institute Historical Studies, 1908), 24 and 29; Schafer, *Slavery, the Civil Law*, 220–22.

22. Tuscaloosa Genealogical Society, *Pioneers*, 318; Crump and Brophy, "Twenty-One Months a Slave," 471–72; Minutes, TCCC, March 12, 1827, 181–86.

23. Minutes, TCCC, March 12, 1827, 181–86 (quote on 182). For a similar petition lodged in the Tuscaloosa County courts in 1824, see Record of Pleas, TCCC, June 28, 1824, 441–44. John Boyd, a member of the Tuscaloosa Genealogical Society, has identified six more petitions for freedom in Tuscaloosa-area courts between October 1827 and October 1829. On claims for back wages or damages in other freedom suits, see Welch, *Black Litigants*, 188; Kennington, *Shadow of Dred Scott*, 38.

24. VanderVelde, *Redemption Songs*, 198–200; Schafer, *Becoming Free, Remaining Free*, 27; Kennington, *Shadow of Dred Scott*, 58–62; Smith, *Reminiscences*, 53–54.

On the ambivalence of white lawyers representing black litigants in freedom suits, see Welch, *Black Litigants*, 88–94; Twitty, *Before Dred Scott*, 102–25; Kennington, *Shadow of Dred Scott*, 69–78.

25. The letter itself does not survive, but was referenced in Watson's other letters and in PAS records. "Messrs. Crutcher & Stockton"; Boucher to Watson, January 17, 1827, item 26, JWP; *Minute Book of the Acting Committee, 1822–1842*, reel 5, June 23, 1826, PAS. See also Watson to Rawle, Loose Correspondence, incoming, 1820–1849, 1857, 1859–1863, reel 13, July 4, 1826, PAS.

26. Boucher to Watson, January 17, 1827, item 26, JWP. Members of the PAS Acting Committee were likely already aware of this requirement, having encountered it during activity in support of similar petitions in other southern states in 1819 and 1822. *Minute Book of the Acting Committee, 1810–1822*, reel 5, November 24, 1819, PAS; *Minute Book of the Acting Committee, 1822–1842*, reel 5, November 13, 1822, PAS.

27. "To the Editor of the African Observer. Just Reciprocity," *African Observer*, October 1827, 219–21; Boucher to Watson, January 17, 1827, item 26, JWP.

28. "Kidnapping," 37–39.

29. "To the Editor of the African Observer. Just Reciprocity"; "Kidnapping," 37–39; *Minute Book of the Acting Committee, 1810–1822*, reel 5, April 8, 1817, PAS; *Minute Book of the Acting Committee, 1822–1842*, reel 5, November 13, 1822, PAS. For an example of the legal agreements that the PAS sometimes struck with volunteers to set out their responsibilities and rights to reimbursement, see *Minute Book of the Acting Committee, 1822–1842*, reel 5, September 24, 1822, PAS. Missions into Maryland typically produced expense requests in the region of twenty dollars. But for missions to the Cotton Kingdom, expenses were dramatically higher, often more than one hundred dollars, and one mission to South Carolina required funds in excess of four hundred dollars. American Convention of Abolition Societies, *Fifteenth Convention*, 18; *Minute Book of the Acting Committee, 1800–1824*, reel 1, August 8, 1811, PAS.

30. "Kidnapping," 37. Traquair was never a member of the abolition society and held no role in Watson's municipal government beyond that of ward inspector on election days. Yet he was at the mayor's side on the day that Sam, Enos, and Alex finally arrived back in Philadelphia.

31. Matthew W. Clinton, Matt Clinton's Scrapbook, Tuscaloosa Public Library, Tuscaloosa, Alabama, 265. On the spectacle of court days in the Deep South, see Welch, *Black Litigants*, 31–32; Ariela J. Gross, *Double Character: Slavery and Mastery in the Antebellum Southern Courtroom* (Princeton, NJ: Princeton University Press, 2000), 35. Seth Barton, Cornelius's attorney, was involved in arguing several other cases before the court during its March 1827 term.

32. Minutes, TCCC, March 12, 1827, 181–86; VanderVelde, *Redemption Songs*, 1; Welch, *Black Litigants*, 10–11 and 34; Gross, *Double Character*, 66. Such tortuous time frames were not uncommon in freedom suits. Aaron Cooper labored on his master's plantation for three years while his own petition wound its

way through the Natchez courts. Herring, "Kidnapped and Sold," 352. Tuscaloosa's first purpose-built courthouse, a two-story brick structure, opened in 1830. Lambert, *Tuscaloosa County*, 1: 15.

33. Record of Pleas, TCCC, February 17, 1827, 235–36, October 9, 1826, 388; Crump and Brophy, "Twenty-One Months a Slave," 465–66.

34. Minutes, TCCC, March 12, 1827, 181–86; Welch, *Black Litigants*, 185; Kennington, *Shadow of Dred Scott*, 150–57. In a calculated move, Paul offered to free Cornelius there and then if Boucher or Kennon would cough up $300 to reimburse him for the money he had paid to Johnson. They declined. Crump and Brophy, "Twenty-One Months a Slave," 473. For the statute prohibiting the use of enslaved testimony except in freedom suits, see Harry Toumlin, comp., *A Digest of the Laws of the State of Alabama: Containing the statutes and resolutions in force at the end of the General Assembly in January, 1823* (Cahawba, AL, 1823), 627.

35. Minutes, TCCC, March 12, 1827, 181–86. Internal evidence gathered from the list of contents of the Rocky Springs dossier suggests that the smaller dossier Watson sent to Tuscaloosa contained at least eight items. Abstract of List of Documents, March 10, 1826, item 274, JWP.

36. Minutes, TCCC, March 12, 1827, 181–86; Samuel Garrigues, list of documents, November 3, 1827, item 7, JWC.

37. Gross, *Double Character*, 27; William Garrett, *Reminiscences of Public Men in Alabama, for Thirty Years with an Appendix* (Atlanta, GA, 1872), 458–59; Sarah Haynsworth Gayle, *The Journal of Sarah Haynsworth Gayle, 1827–1835: A Substitute for Social Intercourse* (Tuscaloosa: University of Alabama Press, 2013), xx and xxix–xxx. Gayle, a Jacksonian Democrat, resigned from the Third Circuit in 1828. He later served on the state's Supreme Court, as speaker of the state's lower chamber, and then as a two-term governor. His wife, Sarah Haynsworth Gayle, was eleven years his junior. They had seven children together, the first of whom, Matthew, was born in 1820.

38. Herring, "Natchez, 1795–1830," 234; Kennington, *Shadow of Dred Scott*, 134–41. On Paul's prior history as a litigant, see, for instance, Record of Judgments, TCCC, November 19, 1827, 164–65.

39. Welch, *Black Litigants*, 72–73; Gross, *Double Character*, 47–71; VanderVelde, *Redemption Songs*, 6. Putting slavery itself on trial would have been a losing proposition. On the limits upon public antislavery expression and action in the South in the 1820s, see James Brewer Stewart, "Evangelicalism and the Radical Strain in Southern Antislavery Thought During the 1820s," *Journal of Southern History* 39, no. 3 (August 1973): 379–80 and 394–95; Stanley Harrold, *The Abolitionists and the South, 1831–1861* (Lexington: University Press of Kentucky, 1995), 12–18.

40. "Tuscaloosa (Ala.) April 22," *Woodville Republican* (Mississippi), April 22, 1826.

41. Ibid. On the political repercussions of other freedom suits, see Kennington, *Shadow of Dred Scott*, 167–90.

42. Ibid.

43. Minutes, TCCC, March 12, 1827, 181–86; Record of Judgments, TCCC, December 24, 1827, 132–33. On jury selection, see Gross, *Double Character*, 37. For other successful Deep South freedom suits, see Herring, "Natchez, 1795–1830," 233–34; "The Habeas Corpus," *Niles Weekly Register* (Baltimore), April 24, 1819; Record of Pleas, TCCC, June 28, 1824, 441–44.

44. R. L. Kennon and Boucher to Watson, March 23, 1827, item 27, JWP. Traquair sent a similar letter to the officers of the Pennsylvania Abolition Society; "Kidnapping," 37.

45. *Minute Book of the Acting Committee, 1822–1842*, reel 5, March 22, 1823, PAS. The PAS sometimes imposed spending limits on rendition missions; for instance, the budget to liberate Thomas Fitzgerald was capped at seventy dollars. *Minute Book of the Acting Committee, 1810–1822*, reel 5, October 13, 1819, PAS; *Minute Book of the Acting Committee, 1800–1824*, reel 1, June 29, 1820, PAS; *Minute Book of the Acting Committee, 1810–1822*, reel 5, April 8, 1817, PAS. Surviving records show only a single twenty-five-dollar payment to Traquair for his trouble, though the costs associated with Cornelius's recovery topped $450, according to one estimate. "To the Editor of the African Observer. Just Reciprocity," 219; *Minute Book of the Acting Committee, 1825–1847*, reel 2, March 29, 1827, PAS. In May 1827, the PAS authorized another twenty-five-dollar payout, this time to Mayor Watson, to be used "towards obtaining [Cornelius's] release from unlawful bondage." Edwin Atlee to Henry Booth, Acting Committee: Treasurer, Accounts, Bills, Cancelled Checks and Receipts, 1784, 1810–1811, 1816–1817, 1822–1827, 1831, 1835, reel 18, May 24, 1827, PAS.

46. After returning to Philadelphia, Traquair held a number of modest public offices, including ward inspector and city commissioner. In 1833, he ran for superintendent of Girard College, but lost. He died on January 22, 1851, and is buried at Laurel Hill Cemetery.

Chapter 10: HUNTING WOLVES

1. Power, *Impressions of America*, 1: 189–90 (quote on 189); "Philadelphia, June 29," *Boston Commercial Gazette*, July 3, 1826; Isaac Harvey, diary entry, June 29, 1826, Harvey Papers; Finch, *Travels in the United States*, 94–95.

2. "Mayor's Office, Philadelphia, July 1, 1826," *New York Evening Post*, July 14, 1826.

3. Isaac Harvey, diary entry, June 29, 1826, Harvey Papers; Northup, *Twelve Years*, 215–17. When Sojourner Truth was reunited with her eight-year-old son following a similar illegal out-of-state separation, she stripped him down to count his wounds and then loudly cursed the men who had done this to her child. Stewart, *Narrative of Sojourner Truth*, 52–54.

4. Northup recalled talking with his family in those early days about "the thousand events that had occurred—the hopes and fears, the joys and sorrows, the trials and troubles we had each experienced during the long separation." Northup, *Twelve Years*, 215–17.

5. Watson to Hamilton and Henderson, March 15, 1826, item 276, JWP.

6. Kelli Lyon Johnson, "'If I Got a Chance to Talk to the World . . .': Voice, Agency, and Claiming Rights in Narratives of Contemporary Child Slavery," in *Child Slavery Before and After Emancipation: An Argument for Child-Centered Slavery Studies*, ed. Anna Mae Duane (New York: Cambridge University Press, 2017), 244. See also "To the Citizens of Georgia," *Georgia Journal* (Milledgeville), September 1, 1818; *Minute Book of the Acting Committee, 1810–1822*, reel 5, November 4, 1817, PAS. The very first thing Solomon Northup did after reclaiming his freedom in 1853 was to go to a magistrate to demand the arrest of the men who had abducted him. Northup, *Twelve Years*, 210–14.

7. "Kidnapping," 39–41.

8. Ibid. Corroboration with other surviving sources suggests that Sam made a few errors, the two most notable being the omission of Virginia and Tennessee in his account of the route and his recollection regarding the price for which Sinclair sold (it was $300, not $400).

9. "From the American Daily Advertiser," *Port Gibson Correspondent* (Mississippi), September 7, 1826; "Kidnapping," 39–41.

10. Watson to Rawle, Loose Correspondence, incoming, 1820–1849, 1857, 1859–1863, reel 13, July 4, 1826, PAS; "From the American Daily Advertiser"; Court of Quarter Sessions Docket and Index, PCA, 18: 321; John Schulze to Watson, March 29, 1846, item 478, JWP; Proceedings of the Governor and Council, 1821–1830, March 24, 1826, 617–18, Maryland State Archives, Annapolis, MD; *Governor's Register: State of Delaware*, 222–23; Joseph Tate to Watson, April 19, 1826, Joseph Watson Papers, Syracuse University Library, Special Collections Research Center, Syracuse, NY (hereafter cited as WPS). On July 3, Watson made payments of $115 to Captain Caleb Adams for the boys' passage from New Orleans and $6 to Benjamin Morgan's son, Samuel, for the expenses his father had incurred. Morgan to Watson, May 29, 1826, HSC.

11. Gaskins to Watson, February 19, 1826, item 176, JWP; Green to Watson, February 28, 1826, item 177, JWP; Garrigues to Watson, March 23, 1826, item 180, JWP; Watson to Hamilton and Henderson, March 10, 1826, item 275, JWP; "From the American Daily Advertiser."

12. Brown to Watson, July 5, 1826, item 72, JWP.

13. Brown to Watson, July 19, 1826, item 76, JWP.

14. "From the American Daily Advertiser."

15. Henderson to Watson, September 6, 1826, item 268, JWP.

16. Ibid.

17. "To the Editor of the Democratic Press," *Democratic Press* (Philadelphia), January 25, 1827. Its authors were Joseph Davis, a Natchez-area lawyer and the older brother of Jefferson Davis, and David Holmes, Mississippi's former governor (and a native of York, Pennsylvania).

18. "Kidnapping," 43–44. See also Winch, "Other Underground Railroad," 16–18.

19. "To the Editor of the Democratic Press"; "Kidnapping," 43–44.

20. "Kidnapping," 45; Samuel Garrigues, list of documents, November 3, 1827, item 7, JWC; Philadelphia Select Council, resolution, February 8, 1827, item 263, JWP. For press coverage of Watson's attempts to liberate members of this second cohort, see "To the Editor of the Democratic Press"; "Kidnapping," *Baltimore Gazette and Daily Advertiser*, January 26, 1827; "More Kidnapping," *Commercial Advertiser* (New York), January 30, 1827; "More Kidnapping," *Norwich Courier* (Connecticut), January 31, 1827; "Kidnapping," *Boston Spectator & Ladies' Album*, February 3, 1827; "More Kidnapping," *The Torch Light and Public Advertiser* (Hagerstown, MD), February 22, 1827; "Kidnapping," *Natchez Ariel* (Mississippi), March 2, 1827; "Kidnapping," *Baltimore Gazette and Daily Advertiser*, April 18, 1827; "Kidnapping," *Genius of Universal Emancipation* (Baltimore), April 28, 1827; "Kidnapping," 43. Watson also wrote to Duncan Walker, the Natchez lawyer who had taken Hook's deposition, directing him to "leave no stone unturned, no legal or humane effort unessayed," to locate and liberate as many of the cohort as possible and promising to reimburse him for all expenses after the fact. "Kidnapping," 45–46. In reply, Walker promised Watson to "leave no bayou unsearched for the restoration of the captives to their homes." "Kidnapping," 46–47.

21. "Mayor's Office—Forgery," *Eastern Argus* (Portland, ME), September 25, 1833. On Garrigues and his family, see Edmund Garrigues, comp., *A Genealogy of Matthew and Suzanna Garrigues, Who Settled in Philadelphia About the Year 1712, and Their Descendants; With Introductory Notes of Families of the Same Name with an Account of the Family in France, England, Holland, Germany, and Denmark*, 2 vols. (Oceanside, CA: R. C. Garrigues and M. L. Garrigues, 1982), 38–45; *Centennial Anniversary*, 59 and 63; "At an Annual Election," *Freedom's Journal* (New York), January 11, 1828. For Garrigues' career as high constable, see "From the Philadelphia Aurora," *Evening Post* (New York), February 16, 1825; "Philadelphia, March 18," *Evening Post* (New York), March 19, 1825; "The United States Gazette," *Ithaca Journal* (New York), March 2, 1825; "Elkton, Feb. 25," *Republican Star, or, Eastern Shore General Advertiser* (Easton, MD), March 7, 1826; Howard O. Sprogle, *The Philadelphia Police: Past and Present. Illustrated with Portraits and Etchings* (Philadelphia: Printed for the Author, 1887), 70–72.

22. "William Pettigon, alias Bill Paragee," *Washington Whig* (Bridgeton, NJ), June 2, 1827; "Kidnapping," *Freedom's Journal* (New York), June 22, 1827. See also "Kidnapping," *Providence Patriot & Columbian Phoenix*, June 23, 1827. Capital convictions against kidnappers were rare in antebellum America, but for exceptions, see "A Kidnapper," *Niles Weekly Register* (Baltimore), May 23, 1818; "Trial by Jury," *African Observer*, December 1827, 273.

23. James Porter to Watson, May 14, 1827, WPS.

24. "Kidnapper Caught," *Commercial Advertiser* (New York), June 5, 1827.

25. Ibid.; Boston Police Court Docket Books, Boston Municipal Court, Criminal Division, Suffolk County Court House, Boston, Massachusetts, May 28,

1827; Josiah Quincy to Watson, May 28, 1827, Josiah Quincy Papers, New-York Historical Society, New York, New York; "On Sunday Afternoon," *Connecticut Herald* (New Haven), June 5, 1827; Gertrude MacKinney, ed., *Pennsylvania Archives: Ninth Series*, 10 vols. (Harrisburg, PA: State Printer, 1931–1935), 9: 6635. Quincy later wrote to Watson requesting that Reed receive the reward, and there is circumstantial evidence that he did. On the procedures required to execute an executive warrant of rendition (also known as a governor's warrant), see John Bassett Moore, *A Treatise on Extradition and Interstate Rendition*, 2 vols. (Littleton, CO: Fred B. Rothman, 1996); James A. Scott, *The Law of Interstate Rendition, Erroneously Referred to As Interstate Extradition. A Treatise on the Arrest and Surrender of Fugitives From the Justice of One State to Another* (Littleton, CO: Fred B. Rothman, 1983).

26. "Kidnapping," *Providence Patriot & Columbian Phoenix,* June 23, 1827; Mayor's Court Docket, September 1827, PCA, 485; "No 6. Miliary Tubercles. Presented by Dr. Isaac Parrish," *Summary of the Transactions of the College of Physicians of Philadelphia* 3 (1849–1850), 24–25. The assault and battery charges against Garrigues were later thrown out.

27. Prisoners for Trial Docket, Philadelphia County Prison, PCA, June 11, 1827; "Kidnapping," *Freedom's Journal* (New York), June 22, 1827; "Kidnapping," *Providence Patriot & Columbian Phoenix*, June 23, 1827.

28. "Kidnapping," *Freedom's Journal* (New York), June 22, 1827; Edwin C. Surrency, "The Evolution of an Urban Judicial System: The Philadelphia Story, 1683 to 1868," *American Journal of Legal History* 18, no. 2 (April 1974): 97–102.

29. "Kidnapping," *Providence Patriot & Columbian Phoenix*, June 23, 1827; "Kidnapping," *Freedom's Journal* (New York), June 22, 1827; unidentified newspaper clipping, item 274A, JWP; Prisoners for Trial Docket, Philadelphia County Prison, PCA, June 13, 1827. In some of the legal documents and press coverage, writers also referred to Purnell by the aliases John Smith and Spencer Francis.

30. "Kidnapping," *Freedom's Journal* (New York), June 22, 1827.

31. Mayor's Court Docket, June 1827, PCA, 449; Smith, "Notes and Documents," 327; Court of Quarter Sessions Docket and Index, PCA, 19: 139–40.

32. "Kidnapping," 139–40; County Prison Receiving Description Docket, 1825–1828, PCA, 107; County Prison Sentence Docket, 1825–1835, PCA, 124; "Purnell," *Poulson's American Daily Advertiser* (Philadelphia), June 19, 1827. Prison intake inspections were standard procedure and useful in case of prison breaks or sudden death.

33. "A Kidnapper," *Niles Weekly Register* (Baltimore), June 23, 1827; "Exemplary Punishment," *Rochester Telegraph* (New York), June 25, 1827; "A Righteous Sentence," *Salem Gazette* (Massachusetts), June 22, 1827. The sentence was also reported in several southern papers; for instance, "Purnell, the Kidnapper," *Daily Georgian* (Savannah, GA), June 28, 1827.

34. H. V. Somerville to Watson, April 5, 1827, item 140, JWP; Watson to Philip

Hickey, April 20, 1827, item 2, JWC. See also "Kidnapping," 45–46; *Minute Book of the Acting Committee, 1810–1822*, reel 5, August 11, 1818, PAS.

35. Hickey to Watson, June 14, 1827, item 4, JWC; Watson to Hickey, October 2, 1827, item 5, JWC.

36. Watson to Garrigues, October 29, 1827, item 6, JWC; Garrigues to Watson, November 28, 1827, item 8, JWC; Garrigues to Watson, December 3, 1827, item 9, JWC.

37. Garrigues to Watson, December 3, 1827, item 9, JWC; "Kidnapping," 46–47.

38. "Horrors of Slavery," *Freedom's Journal* (New York), February 15, 1828; Watson to Duncan Walker and B. J. Walker, January 26, 1828, item 11, JWC. For a summary of these boys' testimony, see "High Constable Garrigues," *Baltimore Gazette and Daily Advertiser*, May 9, 1828. Garrigues and Lawrence returned to Louisiana in March 1828 so Lawrence could "stand trial as regards his freedom." During this second mission, Garrigues also secured a promise that Sarah Nicholson, "a yellow girl, shall be speedily sent home by sea, from New-Orleans." Garrigues to Watson, December 16, 1827, item 10, JWC; Henderson to Watson, January 2, 1826, item 262, JWP; Winch, "Other Underground Railroad," 20.

39. Medairy, *The Notorious Patty Cannon*, 152.

40. "Kidnapping," *New York Commercial Advertiser*, July 14, 1828; Watson to Walker and Walker, January 26, 1828, item 11, JWC; Hazzard, *History of Seaford*, 40; Medairy, *The Notorious Patty Cannon*, 170 and 181; Winch, "Other Underground Railroad," 21; Shields, *The Infamous Patty Cannon*, 9; Carter, *Sussex County*, 26; Green to Watson, March 12, 1826, item 178, JWP.

41. Mowbray and Rimpo, *Dorchester County History*, 53–54.

42. American Convention, *Twentieth Biennial American Convention*, 21–24; Medairy, *The Notorious Patty Cannon*, 160–64.

43. "Police Office," *Commercial Advertiser* (New York), October 6, 1828; Prisoners for Trial Docket, Philadelphia County Prison, PCA, October 7, 1828; Court of Quarter Sessions Docket and Index, PCA, 19: 385; Thomas Collins to Rawle, Loose Correspondence, incoming, 1820–1849, 1857, 1859–1863, reel 13, April 4, 1831, PAS; Medairy, *The Notorious Patty Cannon*, 168. Intake inspections records described Collins as a "White Man 5 feet 8 in." Another entry had him aged forty-four and "born in Delaware—dark com. Dark hair, hazel eyes, scar on the forehead." County Prison Sentence Docket, 1825–1835, PCA, 172; County Prison Receiving Description Docket, 1825–1828, PCA, 161.

44. "This Morning," *New York American*, October 22, 1828; "From the Phila Gaz," *New York Evening Post*, July 14, 1828.

45. "From the Phila Gaz." By the time of Watson's July 1828 speech, Garrigues had also arrested Henry Carr, a black oyster-shop owner who had been Purnell's accomplice in several of the abductions of members of the second cohort. Carr died of "Inflammatory Fever" in the Arch Street Prison on December 10, 1827, a month before Clem Coxe and Ephraim Lawrence returned from

the Deep South to give evidence against him. Prison Death Register, 1819–1830, PCA, December 10, 1827; Prisoners for Trial Docket, PCA, 84, 646, 663; "Domestic News," *Freedom's Journal* (New York), June 8, 1827; "Coloured Children," *Freedom's Journal* (New York), January 18, 1828; Winch, "Other Underground Railroad," 20–21; Watson to Walker and Walker, January 26, 1828, item 11, JWC.

Chapter 11: KIDNAPPERS ALL

1. "Murders in Sussex," *Delaware Gazette and American Watchman* (Wilmington), April 17, 1829; Medairy, *The Notorious Patty Cannon*, 171–76.
2. "A Horrible Development." One of the several newspapers to report the case suggested that the murdered trader had been killed by Henry Brevington, not by the Cannons and the Johnsons.
3. "Murders in Sussex."
4. Ibid.
5. "A Horrible Development"; "Patty Cannon," *Easton Gazette* (Maryland), May 23, 1829; Medairy, *The Notorious Patty Cannon*, 177–79; Hazzard, *History of Seaford*, 39; "Murders in Delaware," *Baltimore Patriot*, May 20, 1829; Session Dockets, CGS, 87–90. In this version of events, the lead officer on the Maryland side of the line was Thomas Holliday Hicks, the future governor of Maryland during the Civil War. Marks, *Moses and the Monster*, 3–4. For skepticism as to this and other details about the circumstances surrounding Cannon's arrest, see Roth, *The Monster's Handsome Face*, 77. Delaware attorney general James Rogers, who had been in close contact with Mayor Watson during early phases of the manhunt, signed each of the four indictments.
6. "A Horrible Development"; "Patty Cannon"; Medairy, *The Notorious Patty Cannon*, 180; Roth, *The Monster's Handsome Face*, 80–81. In his diary that day, Levi Sullivan, a local resident, wrote simply: "May 11th 1829 Patty Cannon deceased in Georgetown Jail said to have committed murder." Roth, *The Monster's Handsome Face*, 73. Over the years, many writers have suggested that Cannon committed suicide, perhaps by taking arsenic she had somehow smuggled inside. But the complications of advancing age and deteriorating health are surely the more likely culprits. None of the jail's small staff seem to have found her death suspicious—just disappointing. For the suicide claim, see Lanier, *Delaware Valley*, 71; Medairy, *The Notorious Patty Cannon*, 179–80; Carter, *Sussex County*, 25; Hazzard, *History of Seaford*, 39. For skepticism about it, see Roth, *The Monster's Handsome Face*, 78–79. On the sale of Cannon's small estate to clear debts after her death, see Medairy, *The Notorious Patty Cannon*, 183–89. Among the buyers of Cannon's property at public auction in October 1829 was Jesse Green, one of the men who had informed on her to Mayor Watson during his investigations. Roth, *Now This Is the Truth*, 130.

7. Sentence Docket, 1825–1835, County Prison, 124.

8. Collins to Rawle, Loose Correspondence, incoming, 1820–1849, 1857, 1859–1863, reel 13, April 4, 1831, PAS.

9. Ibid.; Collins to Thomas Shipley, Loose Correspondence, incoming, 1820–1849, 1857, 1859–1863, reel 13, May 9, 1831, PAS.

10. "A Kidnapper," *Niles Weekly Register* (Baltimore), October 18, 1828; Jen Manion, *Liberty's Prisoners: Carceral Culture in Early America* (Philadelphia: University of Pennsylvania Press, 2015), 50–59. He flattered Rawle shamelessly and crafted a sentimental story about victimhood, reformation, and familial dependence. It worked.

11. *Minute Book of the Acting Committee, 1825–1847*, reel 2, March 29, 1832, PAS; Sentence Docket, 1825–1835, County Prison, 172.

12. "Kidnapping," 139–40; American Convention, *Minutes*, 3: 989.

13. On the kidnapping of African American women and children during the Civil War, see Adam Rothman, *Beyond Freedom's Reach: A Kidnapping in the Twilight of Slavery* (Cambridge, MA: Harvard University Press, 2015), 2–4.

14. John M. Belohlavek, *George Mifflin Dallas: Jacksonian Patrician* (University Park: Pennsylvania State University Press, 1977), 29; Hazard, *Register of Pennsylvania*, 16: 269; "Died," *Philadelphia Inquirer*, August 20, 1835; "Joseph Watson, Esq.," *Daily Chronicle and General Advertiser* (Philadelphia), April 12, 1841. In addition to serving as a founding vice president of Philadelphia's Provident Society, a work-for-welfare charity that also oversaw the Asylum for Lost Children, between 1829 and 1834, he was also coauthor of a city report on female wages, the president of the Society for the Encouragement of Useful Domestics, a vice president of the city's Benevolent Society, and a manager of the Pennsylvania Society for the Suppression of Lotteries. *First Report;* Mathew Carey, ed., *Miscellaneous Essays* (Philadelphia, 1830), 267–72; *Philadelphia, July 20, 1830. Address to the Public of the Society for the Encouragement of Faithful Domestics* (Philadelphia, 1830); Pennsylvania Society for the Suppression of Lotteries, *Address to the People of Pennsylvania and the United States* (Philadelphia, 1834). On Watson's role on a commission to professionalize the Philadelphia police in the early 1830s, see Robert C. Wadman and William Thomas Allison, *To Protect and to Serve: A History of Police in America* (Upper Saddle River, NJ: Pearson, 2004), 12 and 23–24; *City Government*, 154; David R. Johnson, *Policing the Urban Underworld: The Impact of Crime on the Development of the American Police, 1800–1887* (Philadelphia: Temple University Press, 1979), 16–19. Watson funded these civic endeavors with income he derived as president of the Lehigh Coal and Navigation Company, a position held from 1830 until his death in 1841. Samuel Garrigues served as high constable until 1834. His younger brother, William Garrigues, who named one of his sons in Samuel's honor, was a longtime member of the PAS. He would later serve as the society's secretary, and in 1836 signed his name to a massive circular letter in support of immediate emancipation in the state of Pennsyl-

vania. Garrigues, *Genealogy*, 1: 266; "Whereas, this Society," *Liberator* (Boston), July 30, 1836.

15. Court of Quarter Sessions, Oyer and Terminer Docket, 1815–1833, PCA, 246. On Alberti's predations, see "Pennsylvania Kidnappers," *Genius of Universal Emancipation* (Baltimore), October 1837; "Arrest of Kidnappers," *Liberator* (Boston), November 17, 1837; *Minute Book of the Acting Committee, 1825–1847*, reel 2, January 26, 1838, PAS; Wilson, *Freedom at Risk*, 50–52. For other kidnappers active in Philadelphia, see, for instance, "Trial for Kidnapping," *Genius of Universal Emancipation* (Baltimore), May 1831; "Kidnapper," *Pennsylvania Freeman* (Philadelphia), May 9, 1844.

16. "Kidnapper," *Pennsylvania Freeman* (Philadelphia), May 9, 1844. On the Gap Gang, see Margaret Hope Bacon, *Rebellion at Christiana* (New York: Crown Publishers, 1975), 7; Thomas P. Slaughter, *Bloody Dawn: The Christiana Riot and Racial Violence in the Antebellum North* (New York: Oxford University Press, 1994), 44; James R. Robbins, *Report of the Trial of Castner Hanway for Treason* (Philadelphia, 1852), 109–16; R. C. Smedley, *History of the Underground Railroad in Chester and the Neighboring Counties of Pennsylvania* (Lancaster, PA, 1883), 107–8; Jonathan Katz, *Resistance at Christiana: The Fugitive Slave Rebellion, Christiana, Pennsylvania, September 11, 1851* (New York: Thomas Y. Crowell, 1974), 26. For other kidnappings in southern Pennsylvania before 1850, see "Kidnapping," *Genius of Universal Emancipation* (Baltimore), April 2, 1826; "Kidnapping," *Genius of Universal Emancipation* (Baltimore), July 28, 1827; Carl Douglas Oblinger, "New Freedoms, Old Miseries: The Emergence and Disruption of Black Communities in Southeastern Pennsylvania, 1780–1860" (PhD diss., Lehigh University, 1988), 91; David G. Smith, *On the Edge of Freedom: The Fugitive Slave Issue in South Central Pennsylvania, 1820–1870* (New York: Fordham University Press, 2013), 97–104; Lucy Maddox, *The Parker Sisters: A Border Kidnapping* (Philadelphia: Temple University Press, 2016), 17–18; William C. Kashatus, *Just Over the Line: Chester County and the Underground Railroad* (University Park: Penn State University Press, 2002), 29–30.

17. "Annals of Kidnapping and Slave-Trading in Our Free States," *National Inquirer, and Constitutional Advocate of Universal Liberty* (Philadelphia), January 14, 1837; Graham Russell Gao Hodges, *David Ruggles: A Radical Black Abolitionist and the Underground Railroad in New York City* (Chapel Hill: University of North Carolina Press, 2010), 93–94; Foner, *Gateway to Freedom*, 50–51; Leslie M. Alexander, *African or American?: Black Identity and Political Activism in New York City, 1784–1861* (Urbana: University of Illinois Press, 2008), 34–35. See also "Kidnapping," *Freedom's Journal* (New York), August 8, 1828; "A Young Colored Man," *Genius of Universal Emancipation* (Baltimore), January 15, 1830; "New York Morning Herald," *Genius of Universal Emancipation* (Baltimore), February 5, 1830; Leslie M. Harris, *In the Shadow of Slavery: African Americans in New York City, 1626–1863* (Chicago: University of Chicago Press, 2003), 208–9; Lois E. Horton, "Kidnapping and Resistance: Antislavery

Direct Action in the 1850s," in *Passages to Freedom*, 156. For kidnappings in nearby New Jersey, see, for instance, "Horrors of Slavery," *Genius of Universal Emancipation* (Baltimore), August 1831; "Kidnapping in New Jersey," *Genius of Universal Emancipation* (Baltimore), August 1831.

18. M. Scott Heerman, "Deep River: Slavery, Empire, and Emancipation in the Upper Mississippi River Valley" (PhD diss., University of Maryland, 2013), 179–80; "A Claimed Fugitive Gives Up," *Chicago Western Citizen*, April 6, 1843; "Kidnapping," *Brooklyn Daily Eagle* (New York), May 15, 1843 (quoting "Kidnapping," *Cincinnati Gazette*, May 1843). For kidnappings in the old Northwest, see "A Kidnapper," *Genius of Universal Emancipation* (Baltimore), April 21, 1827; "More of It," *Genius of Universal Emancipation* (Baltimore), August 1830; "Kidnapping," *Genius of Universal Emancipation* (Baltimore), May 1832; "Kidnapping," *Liberator* (Boston), May 18, 1849; Aptheker, *Documentary History*, 1: 245–46; Child, "Domestic Slave Trade," 104; Heerman, "Deep River," 182–96.

19. "Another Attempt at Kidnapping," *Genius of Universal Emancipation* (Baltimore), February 1831. For similar arguments about underreporting, see American Convention, *Minutes*, 3: 989; Weld and Thome, *Internal Slave Trade*, 272.

20. "Kidnapping," *Genius of Universal Emancipation* (Baltimore), October, 1830; R. W. Bailey to William McLain, February 11, 1850, American Colonization Society Papers, Library of Congress, Washington, DC; Weld, *American Slavery As It Is*, 140; Northup, *Twelve Years*, 217. See also "A Kidnapping," *Niles Weekly Register* (Baltimore), February 25, 1826; "Kidnapping," *Genius of Universal Emancipation* (Baltimore), July 28, 1827; Child, "Domestic Slave Trade," 101; Lydia Maria Child, *Anti-slavery Catechism* (Newburyport, MA, 1836), 14; Katz, *Resistance at Christiana*, 26–27; Wilson, *Freedom at Risk*, 9, 66, and 96–97.

21. Schermerhorn, *Money over Mastery*, 69. On Indian removal and the concomitant growth of the domestic slave trade, see Walter Johnson, *River of Dark Dreams: Slavery and Empire in the Cotton Kingdom* (New York: Cambridge University Press, 2013), 28–30. On slave sale prices in the Deep South in this period, see Deyle, *Carry Me Back*, 57.

22. Deyle, *Carry Me Back*, 100–112; Schermerhorn, *Money over Mastery*, 141; Weld, *American Slavery As It Is*, 142. On the integral relationship between the domestic slave trade and the market revolution, see Deyle, *Carry Me Back*, 6, 95–96, and 162. In his own memoir, Solomon Northup told readers that "hundreds of free citizens [that] have been kidnapped and sold into slavery" were "at this moment wearing out their lives on plantations" in Texas and Louisiana. Across the whole of the slave South that total likely topped several thousand. Northup, *Twelve Years*, 217.

23. Frederic Bancroft, *The Life of William H. Seward*, 2 vols. (New York: Harper & Brothers, 1900), 1: 57; Tadman, *Speculators and Slaves*, 141; Deyle, *Carry Me Back*, 248–52. On intrastate local sales, see Deyle, *Carry Me Back*, 157–61. For

further evidence of strong demand for child slaves in the slave South after 1830, see Lawrance, *Amistad's Orphans*, 5–7, 27, 35–36, 43, 121–22, 161–62, and 166. Seward was a future governor of New York and US secretary of state.

24. "Kidnapping," *Genius of Universal Emancipation* (Baltimore), March 24, 1827; James Silk Buckingham, *The Eastern and Western States of America*, 2 vols. (London, 1842), 1: 11–12; Horton, "Kidnapping and Resistance," 151–52; Wilson, *Freedom at Risk*, 14–15. On kidnapping into Texas and Florida, see Earl W. Fornell, "The Abduction of Free Negroes and Slaves in Texas," *Southwestern Historical Quarterly* 60, no. 3 (January 1957): 372–73; *Minute Book of the Acting Committee, 1825–1847*, reel 2, December 26, 1839, PAS; *Minute Book of the Acting Committee, 1825–1847*, reel 2, December 31, 1840, PAS.

25. Deyle, *Carry Me Back*, 96–141; Tadman, *Speculators and Slaves*, 200–204; Johnson, *Soul by Soul*, 78–133; Lightner, *Slavery and the Commerce Power*; Wilson, *Freedom at Risk*, 66 and 81–82; Manisha Sinha, *The Slave's Cause: A History of Abolition* (New Haven, CT: Yale University Press, 2016), 191. In 1828, Charles Miner, a Philadelphia-area congressman, denounced the black market in stolen people in a speech on the floor of the House of Representatives in which he also called for the abolition of slave trading within the District of Columbia. His words fell on deaf ears. The majority of southerners did not question the morality or legitimacy of the domestic slave trade—and several actively defended it in print or pointed to state-level regulations that they claimed deterred kidnapping and human trafficking. Gudmestad, *Troublesome Commerce*, 95–98 and 110–11; Tadman, *Speculators and Slaves*, 83–91 and 173–201; Deyle, *Carry Me Back*, 51–55 and 213–21; Rothman, *Flush Times*, 11–12. For activist outrage regarding congressional inaction to dismantle the Reverse Underground Railroad, see "Another Attempt at Kidnapping," *Genius of Universal Emancipation*, February 1831, 175.

26. Watson to Henderson and Hamilton, May 5, 1827, item 3, JWC; Watson to Rawle, Loose Correspondence, incoming, 1820–1849, 1857, 1859–1863, reel 13, July 4, 1826, PAS; Unknown to Henderson, note, no date, item 280, JWP; John J. Garvin, receipt, May 5, 1827, item 279, JWP. The plates were paid for by PAS members. For evidence of Hamilton's and Henderson's growing antipathy for each other, see "Kidnapping," *Port Gibson Correspondent* (Mississippi), June 8, 1826.

27. "Kidnapping," *Port Gibson Correspondent* (Mississippi), June 8, 1826; "Messrs. Crutcher & Stockton"; "Sherriff's Sales"; "T. Gibson vs. John W. Hamilton," *Port Gibson Correspondent* (Mississippi), March 31, 1827; "Same vs. Same and Richard White," *Port Gibson Correspondent* (Mississippi), August 30, 1828; Hamilton to Watson, May 17, 1826, item 277, JWP; Hamilton to Watson, July 12, 1826, item 278, JWP. Obviously strapped for cash, Hamilton had long angled for a financial reward for separating the Johnsons from their victims.

28. "Valuable Land for Sale," *Statesman and Gazette* (Natchez, MS), March 9,

1831; *John W. Bryan vs. John W. Hamilton*, Minutes 1824–1832, May 17, 1830, Supreme Court of Mississippi, Historic Natchez Foundation, Natchez, MS; *Richard White vs. John W. Hamilton*, Minutes 1824–1832, May 21, 1832, Supreme Court of Mississippi, Historic Natchez Foundation, Natchez, MS.

29. Henderson to Watson, July 16, 1826, item 269, JWP; "Mr. Stockton," *Port Gibson Correspondent* (Mississippi), June 16, 1827; "To the Citizens of Claiborne County," *Port Gibson Correspondent* (Mississippi), July 6, 1826; "We are authorized to announce," *Port Gibson Correspondent* (Mississippi), April 27, 1827; "Election Results," *Port Gibson Correspondent* (Mississippi), August 11, 1827; "Election Returns," *Natchez Ariel* (Mississippi), August 17, 1827; Antonio Rafael de la Cova, "Filibuster and Freemasons: The Sworn Obligation," *Journal of the Early Republic* 17, no. 1 (Spring 1997): 106 and 110. Henderson might have been behind a promotional piece timed to an upcoming election that appeared in the *Port Gibson Correspondent* in September 1826 that gushed about his good-heartedness and lavished praise upon him for his role restoring the lost boys to liberty "under circumstances which at once evince the purity of his motives, and the excellence and sublimity of his purpose." "Messrs. Crutcher & Stockton."

30. *Memoirs of Mississippi*, 1: 907; Ancestry.com, 1850 US Federal Census—Slave Schedules (Provo, UT: Ancestry.com Operations, Inc., 2004), Hinds County, Mississippi, 883; Gilles Vandal, *The New Orleans Riots of 1866: Anatomy of a Tragedy* (Lafayette: Southwestern Louisiana University, 1983), 112, 150, and 178–79; James G. Hollandsworth Jr., *An Absolute Massacre: The New Orleans Race Riot of July 30, 1866* (Baton Rouge: Louisiana State University Press, 2001), 50–51 and 113–14; *Report of the Select Committee on the New Orleans Riots* (Washington, DC, 1867), 15, 23, 299, and 389. John Henderson Jr. spent the war years in an insane asylum in Dixon, Mississippi. In 1871, five years after his death at the hands of the New Orleans mob, members of a Cercle Harmonique séance in New Orleans conjured his spirit. It spoke to them, saying: "In my new world, I am satisfied to have been a victim of the cruelty of fanatical enemies of Human Rights, for it has given me Light, and I am going forward toward Eternal Progress!" *New Orleans Riots*, 389; Melissa Daggett, *Spiritualism in Nineteenth-Century New Orleans: The Life and Times of Henry Louis Rey* (Jackson: University Press of Mississippi, 2017), 75–76 and 128.

31. Benjamin Fonatin, John Moore, and Dunstan Banks from James Paul, Book H, Deed Records, Tuscaloosa County Courthouse, Tuscaloosa, Alabama; Crump and Brophy, "Twenty-One Months a Slave," 508–9.

32. Sellers, *First Methodist Church*, 25; Smith, *Reminiscences*, 142–43; Quist, *Restless Visionaries*, 47 and 322. Another founding vice president of the Alabama Colonization Society was John Gayle, the judge who had heard Cornelius's freedom suit. Crump and Brophy, "Twenty-One Months a Slave," 477. Kennon died at home in Tuscaloosa in 1838 after a week's illness. He was buried three days later following a funeral before "a crowded and weeping assembly." West, *Methodism in Alabama*, 455–56. On colonization societies in the

Deep South, see Sparks, *On Jordan's Stormy Banks*, 71; Quist, *Restless Visionaries*, 314–16.

33. Jones, *Mississippi Conference*, 2: 115; Sellers, *First Methodist Church*, 41. Boucher would die in Missouri in obscurity and poverty. Lazenby, *Methodism in Alabama*, 144.

34. J. Thomas Scharf and Thompson Westcott, *History of Philadelphia, 1609–1884*, 3 vols. (Philadelphia, 1884), 1: 617; H. Robert Baker, *Prigg v. Pennsylvania: Slavery, the Supreme Court, and the Ambivalent Constitution* (Lawrence: University of Kansas Press, 2012), 65–81; Andrew K. Diemer, *The Politics of Black Citizenship: Free African Americans in the Mid-Atlantic Borderland, 1817–1863* (Athens: University of Georgia Press, 2016), 1–2 and 56–57; Drago, "Politics of Slavery," 89 and 105–9. On PAS lobbying, see *Minute Book of the Acting Committee, 1825–1847*, reel 2, June 10, 1826, PAS; *Minute Book of the Acting Committee, 1825–1847*, reel 2, June 11, 1826, PAS; Acting Committee: Treasurer, Accounts, Bills, Cancelled Checks and Receipts, 1784, 1810–1811, 1816–1817, 1822–1827, 1831, 1835, reel 18, February 17, 1827, PAS; Needles, *Historical Memoir*, 85. An editorial in the *African Observer* cheered this 1826 personal liberty law as having "very greatly increased the difficulty, of carrying away from the state of a free coloured person." "Trial by Jury," *African Observer*, 273.

35. Baker, *Prigg v. Pennsylvania*, 82–173; Diemer, *Black Citizenship*, 3 and 138–39; Christopher Malone, *Between Freedom and Bondage: Race, Party, and Voting Rights in the Antebellum North* (New York: Routledge, 2008), 81. For PAS lobbying in support of the passage of Pennsylvania's 1847 personal liberty law, see *Minute Book of the Acting Committee, 1825–1847*, reel 2, March 26, 1846, PAS.

36. Philip S. Foner and Ronald L. Lewis, eds., *The Black Worker to 1869*, 8 vols. (Philadelphia: Temple University Press, 1978–1984), 1: 109–13; American Convention, *Twentieth Biennial American Convention*, 53; American Convention, *Minutes*, 3: 1116. See also "Land of Liberty," *Freedom's Journal* (New York, NY), December 5, 1828; "Kidnapping," *Genius of Universal Emancipation* (Baltimore), April 1830, 14; Drew, *North-side View of Slavery*, 350, 363, and 372.

37. George M. Stroud, *Sketch of the Laws Relating to Slavery in the Several States of the United States of America* (Philadelphia, 1827), 73–74; J. D. Paxton, *Letters on Slavery; Addressed to the Cumberland Congregation* (Lexington, KY, 1833), 30; Child, "Domestic Slave Trade," 105; Weld and Thome, *Internal Slave Trade*, 272; Child, *Anti-slavery Catechism*, 14; Weld, *American Slavery As It Is*, 140. I have identified at least thirty-nine newspapers (and three magazines) that reported on the lost boys' case—often in multiple stories. *Freedom's Journal*, the nation's first black-owned and operated newspaper, and the *Genius of Universal Emancipation*, Benjamin Lundy's redoubtable antislavery paper, covered the story most aggressively, but big city papers in Philadelphia, New York, and Baltimore also closely followed its twists and turns.

38. Anna Mae Duane, *Suffering Childhood in Early America: Violence, Race, and the Making of the Child Victim* (Athens: University of Georgia, 2010), 14–15, 125–26, and 140–41; Hugh Cunningham, *Children and Childhood in Western Society Since 1500* (Harlow, UK: Pearson, 2005), 136. See, for instance, "Horrors of Slavery," *Freedom's Journal* (New York), February 15, 1828. Several antislavery activists noted that if traffickers had targeted free white children, the Northern outrage would have been "like the resistless Tornado, sweeping before it the slave-prisons and their keeper." They even printed a few spurious reports that this had happened in hopes that "the public may be brought to think a little more seriously on this awful subject." "Kidnapping in the District," *Genius of Universal Emancipation* (Baltimore), July 1831, 34; "Kidnapping," *Genius of Universal Emancipation* (Baltimore), March 24, 1827; George Bourne, *Picture of Slavery in the United States of America* (Middletown, CT, 1834), 119–20 and 144–45. For studies of portrayals of children in antislavery activism in other times and places, see Richard B. Allen, "A Traffic Repugnant to Humanity: Children, the Mascarene Slave Trade and British Abolitionism," *Slavery & Abolition* 27, no. 2 (2006): 219; Edward A. Alpers, "Representations of Children in the East African Slave Trade," *Slavery & Abolition* 30, no. 1 (2009): 27 and 32.

39. Philip Troutman, "Chronicles of Kidnapping in New York: Elizur Wright at the Borderlands of Slavery" (paper presented at the National Underground Railroad Conference, Cambridge, MD, May 18–21, 2017); Lawrence B. Goodheart, *Abolitionist, Actuary, Atheist: Elizur Wright and the Reform Impulse* (Kent, OH: Kent State University Press, 1990), 85–89. See, for instance, "For the Emancipator," *Emancipator* (New York), March 23, 1834. As Wright once explained, "It was enough for me to know that in the city of NY men, women, and children had been arrested and thrown into miserable dungeons, for no offense—but merely because they were claimed as property. If I understand my mother tongue, thus act, under whatever forms of law, or by whatsoever honorable agents it may be performed, is essentially kidnapping." On the activist deployment of kidnapping terminology in the Parker sisters case, see Maddox, *Parker Sisters*, 38–39. Peter Still and Samuel May were among the many others who deliberately refused to distinguish between kidnappers and slave catchers in their polemical work. Still titled his own account of being abducted and trafficked into slavery *The Kidnapped and the Ransomed* (1856). But a close reading reveals that Still's mother was a fugitive slave and that he had been apprehended by slave catchers working in compliance with federal law. In the same year, May offered up his own catalog of fugitive renditions in his opus *The Fugitive Slave Law and Its Victims* (1856, rep. 1861), but took care to describe many of them, especially those of young children, as kidnappings. See, for instance, Samuel May, *The Fugitive Slave Law and Its Victims* (Freeport, NY: Books for Libraries Press, 1970), 15, 23, 28, 39, 62, 81, 101, 102, and 120.

40. Henry Watson, *A Narrative of Henry Watson, a Fugitive Slave. Written by Him-*

self (Boston, 1848), 10; Edward E. Baptist, "'Stol' and Fetched Here: Enslaved Migration, Ex-slave Narratives and Vernacular History," in *New Studies in the History of American Slavery*, eds. Stephanie M. H. Camp and Edward E. Baptist (Athens: University of Georgia Press, 2006), 258; Bourne, *Picture of Slavery*, 16 and 35; "A Semi Kidnapper," *Genius of Universal Emancipation* (Baltimore), July, 1830, 61; Child, "Domestic Slave Trade," 101. Enslaved people, of course, had long thought of that second middle passage from the Upper South to the Lower South as legalized kidnapping. These epithets were not too distant from terms like "old robbers" and "pirates" by which a few coffle captains jokingly referred to themselves. Baptist, "'Cuffy,' 'Fancy Maids,'" 1626–27. Bourne addressed his illustrated 228-page pamphlet to "philanthropists who are opposed to man-stealing" and built his claims upon the premise that slaveholding violated God's commandment not to steal. Bourne, *Picture of Slavery*, 11–12 and 16. He also used similar language for comparable ends in George Bourne, *Slavery Illustrated in Its Effects Upon Woman and Domestic Society* (Boston, 1837).

41. Henry C. Wright, "Solomon Northup," *Liberator* (Boston), March 23, 1855. In one sense, these were old arguments. African Americans had long lived with the bone-deep conviction that bondage was theft and argued that the massive forced migration known as the transatlantic slave trade was the largest illegal abduction in human history. Frederick Douglass often repeated that claim, telling readers of each of his three autobiographies that many of the enslaved people among whom he had grown up on the Eastern Shore of Maryland had told him "that their fathers and mothers were stolen from Africa—forced from their homes, and compelled to serve as slaves." Baptist, "'Stol' and Fetched Here," 258. On the role of kidnapping in Atlantic slavery, see Rebecca Shumway, *The Fante and the Transatlantic Slave Trade* (Rochester NY: University of Rochester Press, 2011), 59–60; Anne C. Bailey, *African Voices of the Atlantic Slave Trade: Beyond the Silence and the Shame* (Boston: Beacon Press, 2005), 79–80; G. Ugo Nwokeji, *The Slave Trade and Culture in the Bight of Biafra: An African Society in the Atlantic World* (New York: Cambridge University Press, 2010), 131–32. On the presence of kidnapping in oral histories of enslavement in Africa, see Lawrance, *Amistad's Orphans*, 102; Bailey, *African Voices*, 80–82 and 108–13. George Bourne was one of several white activists to echo this argument. Bourne, *Picture of Slavery*, 44–46.

42. Maddox, *Parker Sisters*, 39; Wilson, *Freedom at Risk*, 5; Mason, *Slavery and Politics*, 142–43; Baptist, "'Stol' and Fetched Here," 258; Newman, "The Pennsylvania Abolition Society," 128. An n-gram search of printed material archived on the Internet suggests that usage of the word "kidnapper" and its cognates doubled between 1825 and 1835 and then doubled again by 1860. Over the same period, the use in print of "man stealing" and its cognates jumped threefold.

43. Mason, *Slavery and Politics*, 168–69; Gudmestad, *Troublesome Commerce*, 4 and 153–64; Wilson, *Freedom at Risk*, 5. In 1850 Seth Barton, the lawyer for

hire who had once represented Cornelius Sinclair, wrote a pamphlet accusing abolitionists of enticing away and ensnaring tens of thousands of enslaved people over the previous forty years. Barton estimated masters' losses at more than $20 million. Seth Barton, *The Randolph Epistles* (New Orleans, 1850), 3 and 9. On Barton's life and career after 1827, see Thomas Ray Shurbutt, "The Mission of Colonel Seth Barton, United States Chargé D'Affaires to Chile, 1847–1849" (AB thesis, West Georgia College, 1967).

Conclusion: THE FIRST LAW OF NATURE

1. Wilson, *Freedom at Risk*, 96–103; Foner and Lewis, *Black Worker to 1869*, 1: 109; Newman, "The Pennsylvania Abolition Society," 130–32; Sinha, *Slave's Cause*, 382; Minutes, 1827–1829, June 7, 1828, Baltimore Society for the Protection of Free People of Color, Friends Historical Library, Swarthmore College, Swarthmore, Pennsylvania (hereafter cited as BSP); Minutes, 1827–1829, January 3, 1829, BSP. For PAS antikidnapping work (including on behalf of several black seamen snatched during shore leave in New Orleans and Florida), see *Minute Book of the Acting Committee, 1822–1842*, reel 5, September 28, 1826, PAS; *Minute Book of the Acting Committee, 1825–1847*, reel 2, February 5, 1829, PAS; Loose Correspondence, incoming, 1820–1849, 1857, 1859–1863, reel 13, September 24, 1829, PAS; *Minute Book of the Acting Committee, 1822–1842*, reel 5, September 29, 1829, PAS; *Minute Book of the Acting Committee, 1825–1847*, reel 2, September 30, 1830, PAS; *Minute Book of the Acting Committee, 1822–1842*, reel 5, September 25, 1834, PAS; *Minute Book of the Acting Committee, 1822–1842*, reel 5, April 3, 1835, PAS; *Minute Book of the Acting Committee, 1822–1842*, reel 5, January 17, 1835, PAS; *Minute Book of the Acting Committee, 1822–1842*, reel 5, December 26, 1833, PAS; *Minute Book of the Acting Committee, 1825–1847*, reel 2, September 24, 1840, PAS; *Minute Book of the Acting Committee, 1825–1847*, reel 2, March 29, 1842, PAS; *Minute Book of the Acting Committee, 1825–1847*, reel 2, November 22, 1843, PAS; *Minute Book of the Acting Committee, 1825–1847*, reel 2, January 22, 1846, PAS. In 1840, members congratulated themselves for having rescued twenty people of color "from the relentless hands of oppression" over the previous six months. *Minute Book of the Acting Committee, 1825–1847*, reel 2, December 31, 1840, PAS. For similar summations, see *Minute Book of the Acting Committee, 1825–1847*, reel 2, November 2, 1837, PAS; *Minute Book of the Acting Committee, 1825–1847*, reel 2, March 29, 1842, PAS.

2. Nash, *Forging Freedom*, 174–83. For contemporary commentary on race prejudice in the labor market, see Andrews, *Domestic Slave Trade*, 30; "To the Editor of the Liberator," *Liberator* (Boston), February 12, 1831; Pennsylvania Abolition Society, *Present State*, 9–10. The formal disenfranchisement of Pennsylvania's free blacks would not be overturned until the passage of the Fifteenth Amendment in 1870 after the Civil War.

3. "Disgraceful," *Relf's Philadelphia Gazette*, November 28, 1835; Malone, *Be-*

tween Freedom and Bondage, 13, 20, and 59; Beverly C. Tomek, *Pennsylvania Hall: A "Legal Lynching" in the Shadow of the Liberty Bell* (New York: Oxford University Press, 2014), 36–39 and 77–82; Nicholas Wood, "'A Sacrifice on the Altar of Slavery': Doughface Politics and Black Disenfranchisement in Pennsylvania, 1837–1838," *Journal of the Early Republic* 31, no. 1 (Spring 2011): 79–80.

4. Sylviane A. Diouf, *Slavery's Exiles: The Story of the American Maroons* (New York: New York University Press, 2014), 72–129. Slavery in New Jersey would limp along in one form or another until the Civil War, though David Hill, Sam's legal owner, told census takers in 1840 that he no longer owned a single enslaved person. In Hunterdon County as a whole, the enslaved population plummeted from 178 in 1830 to just thirteen in 1840. Gigantino, *Ragged Road*, 116–73 and 194–212.

5. Isaac Parrish, *Brief Memoirs of Thomas Shipley and Edwin P. Atlee* (Philadelphia, 1838), 8.

6. Ibid., 9; Mayor's Court Docket, October 6, 1835, PCA, 315–16. My great thanks to Elliott Drago for sharing this citation.

7. Pennsylvania Abolition Society, *Present Condition*, 4–6; Nash, *Forging Freedom*, 211 and 273; Curry, *Free Black in Urban America*, 155 and 202; Tony Martin, "The Banneker Literary Institute of Philadelphia: African American Intellectual Activism Before the War of the Slaveholders' Rebellion," *Journal of African American History* 87 (Summer 2002): 305. An 1838 survey found that 2,776 of 3,330 black households in Philadelphia contained churchgoers, the vast majority of whom identified as Methodists (73 percent), Baptists (9 percent), or Presbyterians (7 percent); Herschberg, "Free Blacks," 194–204. On the sources, size, stratification, and spatial distribution of Philadelphia's free black community between 1825 and 1850, see Nash, *Forging Freedom*, 137–38; Winch, "Self Help," 78–79; Oblinger, "New Freedoms, Old Miseries," 181; Emma Jones Lapsansky, "'Since They Got Those Separate Churches': Afro-Americans and Racism in Jacksonian Philadelphia," *American Quarterly* 32, no. 1 (Spring 1980): 7; *Statistical Inquiry*, 30–32; Curry, *Free Black in Urban America*, 49 and 74–76; Herschberg, "Free Blacks," 185–93.

8. "Kidnapping in the City of New York," *Liberator* (Boston), August 6, 1836; "Kidnapping," *Freedom's Journal* (New York), August 8, 1828; Wilson, *Freedom at Risk*, 101 and 117. On vigilante violence against informants and kidnappers of color, see Bell, "Counterfeit Kin." On the Protecting Society, see Winch, "Other Underground Railroad," 22; "The Protecting Society," *Freedom's Journal* (New York), April 25, 1828; "Land of Liberty," *Freedom's Journal* (New York), December 5, 1828; Drago, "Politics of Slavery," 115–16; Foner, *Gateway to Freedom*, 61.

9. Wilson, *Freedom at Risk*, 111–12; Hodges, *David Ruggles*, 88–90 and 93; Foner, *Gateway to Freedom*, 65. Benjamin Quarles called the New York Vigilance Committee "the greatest" of the antebellum black self-defense organizations.

Benjamin Quarles, *Black Abolitionists* (New York: Oxford University Press, 1969), 150. Ruggles later claimed that in its first year of operation, New York's Vigilance Committee had saved "THREE HUNDRED PERSONS" from being carried into southern slavery. For more on Ruggles's Committee of Vigilance, see Hodges, *David Ruggles*, 86–97. In 1838, free blacks in Baltimore set up "The Relief Society in cases of seizure." Other vigilance committees sprang to life across southern Pennsylvania, including in Columbia, West Chester, Gettysburg, and York. On the Philadelphia vigilance group (and its successor, the General Vigilance Committee), see Newman, "'Lucky to Be Born in Pennsylvania,'" 426–27; Margaret Hope Bacon, *But One Race: The Life of Robert Purvis* (Albany: State University of New York Press, 2007), 78–81; Elizabeth Varon, "'Beautiful Providences': William Still, the Vigilance Committee, and Abolitionists in the Age of Sectionalism," in *Antislavery and Abolition*, 230–31.

10. R. J. Blackett, "'Freemen to the Rescue!': Resistance to the Fugitive Slave Law of 1850," in *Passages to Freedom*, 138; Bell, "Counterfeit Kin"; Stephen Kantrowitz, *More Than Freedom: Fighting for Black Citizenship in a White Republic, 1829–1889* (New York: Penguin, 2012), 66; Katz, *Resistance at Christiana*, 26–27 and 42; Wilson, *Freedom at Risk*, 115; Aptheker, *Documentary History*, 1: 245–46; Horton, "Kidnapping and Resistance," 155–57; Smedley, *Underground Railroad*, 29 and 94–96; Bacon, *Rebellion at Christiana*, 54–60; Foner, *Gateway to Freedom*, 70. On Christmas Eve 1836, David Ruggles sent a posse of armed men to the New York docks to liberate a dozen or so kidnapped Africans who had been smuggled into the United States for sale. Ruggles's men beat up several of the ship's Portuguese deckhands and pointed a pistol at another mate who tried to block them from entering its hold "and threatened to blow his brains out." Hodges, *David Ruggles*, 97.

11. Maddox, *Parker Sisters*, 69. Pennsylvania newspapers reported no less than a dozen abductions from a single rural county in the six months after the 1850 Fugitive Slave Act became law. Kashatus, *Just Over the Line*, 30. For a case study of one pair of kidnappings from Chester County, Pennsylvania, in 1851, see Maddox, *Parker Sisters*. On the black and white founders of the Anti-Man-Hunting League, see Sinha, *Slave's Cause*, 538–39.

12. Horton, "Kidnapping and Resistance," 166; Sinha, *Slave's Cause*, 500–542. Select cases include those of William and Ellen Craft, Henry Long, Shadrach Minkins, Anthony Burns, William Henry, Joshua Glover, and George and Rebecca Latimer. Radical abolitionists' many victories (and perhaps their many setbacks too) worked to broaden the base of white northern opposition to the Fugitive Slave Act by providing those on the fence with valuable proof of the power of grassroots antislavery activism.

13. Wilson, *Freedom at Risk*, 85–86 and 113–15.

14. *City Characters, Or, Familiar Scenes in Town. Illustrated with Twenty-four Designs* (Philadelphia, 1851), 15–16, 23–24, 83–84, and 99–110; Index of Depositors, 1816–1852, Philadelphia Saving Fund Society, October 1, 1836, entry 30824, Historical Society of Pennsylvania, Philadelphia; Nash, *Forging Free-*

dom, 144–49. In the antebellum era, only 4 percent of free black men engaged in white-collar jobs, usually as proprietors of secondhand clothing stores. Herschberg, "Free Blacks," 199. I am grateful to Reginald Pitts for pointing me to the PSFS record.

15. "$20 Reward"; Mayor's Docket, March 1828, PCA, 548. Enos had fallen into the orbit of Alexander Williams, a notorious thief who ran a squad of street kids, most of whom were too young to be tried as adults if caught. For a contemporary commentary that frames black criminality as a pragmatic response to job discrimination, intemperance, lack of job skills, and "early loss of parents," see Pennsylvania Abolition Society, *Present State*, 18–19. On the obstacles in the path of black men trying to achieve respectability after a conviction in this period, see Curry, *Free Black in Urban America*, 114. For an account of a young black boy who followed a similar path after his own return from Deep South slavery in the late 1820s, see Stewart, *Narrative of Sojourner Truth*, 73–74. The only possible reference to Enos Tilghman appears in the 1850 Federal Census for the town of Pottstown in Schuylkill County, Pennsylvania, where Enos "Tilman," a native of that state, appears as a fifty-year-old black male with no listed occupation; he is enumerated with Alice Hughes, an illiterate twenty-five-year-old native of Pennsylvania with no listed occupation. Ancestry.com, 1850 US Federal Census (Provo, UT: Ancestry.com Operations, Inc., 2004), Pottsville South Ward, Schuylkill, Pennsylvania, 377. I am grateful to Reginald Pitts for pointing me toward the Pottsville census.

16. Ancestry.com, *US Citizenship Affidavits of US-born Seamen at Select Ports, 1792–1869* (Provo, UT: Ancestry.com Operations, Inc., 2010), November 6, 1837. Alex, whose death certificate referred to him as "Manluff," died from an inflammation of the brain. Mary survived him. Ancestry.com, *Philadelphia, Pennsylvania, Death Certificates Index, 1803–1915*, April 21, 1869 (Provo, UT: Ancestry.com Operations, Inc., 2011). See also "Destructive Fire," *The Press* (Philadelphia), March 10, 1869.

17. Diemer, *Black Citizenship*, 4–7; Samantha Seeley, "Race, Removal, and the Right to Remain in the Early American Republic" (book manuscript); Wilson, *Freedom at Risk*, 40.

KEY SOURCES

Stolen is based on a treasure trove of small sources, from tax records to prison dockets, from medical bills to weather diaries, buried in archives across the United States. Three of the longest and richest sources are transcribed below.

The first is the letter sent from John Henderson, the lawyer from Rocky Springs, Mississippi, to Joseph Watson, the mayor of Philadelphia, informing him that John Hamilton had taken bonded custody of Sam, Enos, Alex, and Mary Fisher.

The second source, found in a Philadelphia newspaper, summarizes the testimony Sam gave to Mayor Watson at his office after his return to the city.

The third is a handwritten letter sent by Thomas Collins, one of the kidnappers, to William Rawle, the president of the Pennsylvania Abolition Society, in which Collins pleads for assistance in petitioning the governor of Pennsylvania for a pardon and early release from prison.

❖

JOHN HENDERSON TO JOSEPH WATSON
Rocky Spring Mississippi Jany. 2d. 1826

Sir

 I take the liberty to call your attention to the following statement of facts disclosing a most atrocious crime commited in your City.

 On the 21st. ult. a man by the name of Ebenezar F. Johnston stoped in this neighbourhood at the house of Mr. John W. Hamilton, he had with him five negroes that he offered for sale, namely three boys and two women, he had also in his wagon the body of a boy that died that day and which was buried in the evening. The following morning one of the boys sated to Mr. Hamilton that he and the other boys were stolen from Philadelphia in the latter part of sumer, and that Johnston had whiped him so much that he was then scarcely able to walk and beged of Mr. H to protect him. Mr. Hamilton striped off his cloths and found his body cut in a most cruel maner. He then sent for a justice of the peace for the purpose of having Johnston examined. on the examination Johnston produced a bill of sale for five boys and two women, signed Thomas Collins. he stated that his residence was in Acomack County Virginia, and that he had for some time past followed trading in negroes that last sumer he remained at home for the purpose of geting married, that he gave his money to said Collins in company with Joseph Johnston his Brother for the purpose of buying negroes, that they delivered these negroes to him and if they were stolen, his Brother and Collins had deceived him. There being no evidence but that of the negroes, the Magistrate did not think himself justified in commiting Johnston to prison, as by the laws of this State a negroe cannot give testimoney against a white person. Johnston appeared to be very much alarmed and perhaps did not know the law; at the request of some one present he agreed to place the negroes in the possession of Mr. Hamilton and let him keep them until he could procure from Virginia evidence of the correctness of his title He took from Mr. H an obligation to return them when proof was produced—

The oldest boy says his name is Sam, he appears to be fourteen or fifteen years old, Black complexion, says he belongs to David Hill, living in Ammel Township New Jersey about twelve miles from Princeton and twenty from Trenton, he does not know the name of the County. He says that he ran away from his master, was but a few days in Philadelphia, when a Mulatto man named John Smith met him in the Street and asked him if he would hire to carry watermelons from a boat, that he went to the boat, and that Smith said the watermelons were in a vessel lying out in the river, that he went on board of the vessel that a white man (Joseph Johnston) there drew a dirk threaten to kill him if he made any noise, tied his hands and put Irons on his legs, that one boy was then confined in the vessel and that they afterwards brought in three others in all five boys, that they then sailed to where Joseph Johnston lives, they remained a short time there confined and were again put on board of a vessel with the two women, that they were on the water about a week were then landed and proceeded by land to the State of Alabama, where they remained four weeks, and that Johnston there sold one of the boys named Cornelious, who is about ten years old of light black colour, and can read and write. He also says that Johnston treated them very cruelly, which is evident from their wounds, and that he beat the boy that died very severely about two hours before his death, that he knocked him down with the but end of his wagon whip stamped him and knocked his head against the wagon tire.

The second boy is black appears to be nine or ten years old, says his name is Enos Tilman, that he was bound to a coloured man by the name of Sam Murthry or Murray and followed the trade of Chimney sweep, that he lived in Shiping Street between sixth and seventh Streets, and that his Father's name is Elijah Tilman is a Sailor and sails to New Orleans, that his Mother's name is Hester Tilman. He says that when walking in the street in the night he met the above named Mulatto John Smith who said he would give him a fippeny bit [a silver coin] if he would go on board of a vessel and get some oranges that when he went on board he was confined in the maner described by Sam.

The third boy is a Mulattoe appears to be eight or nine years old, slim made, says his name is Alexr. Manly that his mother's name is Amy Manly, that he has a Step Father whose name is John Raymon and that he lives in Bedford Street near Seventh Street; that he was bound to a coloured man by the name of Caleb Carpenter, a mat-maker who lives in Market Street. He appears to be well acquainted with the Streets in your City says he knew Enos Tilman, and Corne-lious, (the boy sold in Alabama) there that he went to school to a man by the name of Kimbal that the Mulattoe above named asked him to go on board of the vessel to get watermelons and then confined him.

One of the women says her name is Mary Fisher that she was born free in Deleware State, that she lived some time in Smyrna and Wilmington, that she was hired near Elkton when she was stolen, that she was in the woods gathering lightwood when two men seised her, put her in a wagon and took her to North Fork near Cannon's Feiry where Joseph Johnston lives, that she remain some time with him afterwards lived with Johnstons sister or sister in law by the name of Patsey Cannon—

She says that the boy who died was black, and about fourteen or fifteen years old, that his name was Joseph and that he said he followed Chimney sweeping and lived in Mary Street Philadelphia—

The other woman acknowledges herself a slave says she was not stolen, beleves she was fairly purchased. She was consequently permitted to remain in possession of Johnston—

Johnston says he sold Cornelious, the boy mentioned above, to a man by the name of Paul living in Tuscaloosa, Alabama.

No doubt you will give this subject your immediate attention. With the aid of the Officers under your control and the benevolent Individuals of your City I trust you will be able to find the parents and masters of these children. If you find their statement correct would it not be well to publish it, that the coloured people of your City and other places may be guarded against similar outrages? Perhaps before publishing it would be well to endeavour to find the Mulattoe John Smith, and Joseph Johnston and have them arrested. I am sorry that Ebenezar F. Johnston was permitted to go at large as I have not the least doubt of his guilt. I was not present at his examination; the Magistrate before whom he was examined no doubt acted conscientiously Mr. John W. Hamilton is a very humane man and will no doubt take good care of these Children untill claimed by the proper authoroty—

I will take it as particular favour if you will inform the result of your enquiry. Any other information you may want or any assistance I can give in the business will be promtly rendered. It will be well to remember that any testimony to be offered in this State, must be that of white persons. Not having an opertunity to learn your name, I am compeled to address you by your title.

Very Respectfully yours
John Henderson

NARRATIVE OF SAMUEL SCOMP

City of Philadelphia, Commonwealth of Pennsylvania
Mayor's Office, June 30, 1826

Samuel Scomp, deposeth that he is about sixteen years of age; that he is the bound servant of David Hill of New Jersey, was to serve Mr. Hill until he was 25 years old, ran away from his said master and came to Philadelphia in the summer of the last year 1825, was at Market street wharf, in water melon and peach time; a small mulatto man named J. Smith, spoke to deponent to help him bring a load of water melons from the Navy Yard up to Market street wharf, for which Smith was to pay him a quarter dollar; they walked down town, below the Navy Yard and the Rope Walks, clear of all the houses, when a little boat came ashore from a small sloop at the anchor near the middle of the river; Smith asked the white man in the boat if he had water melons to sell, said he had plenty; when they got on board, a white man by the name of Joseph Johnson, asked them to go into the cabin to take a drink; they did so, no persons but themselves were in the cabin; Joe Johnson came down in a few minutes, crossed deponent's hands and tied them with rope yard, at the same time he tied Smith's hands in the same way, (this was about 8 o'clock in the morning,) Johnson said to the deponent, that deponent's father and himself were slaves and had run away from him in Maryland, that this was the first time he had seen him since; had a large Spanish knife and threatened to cut his throat if he resisted or made a noise.

John Smith sat still in the mean time, Joe Johnson then untied Smith and told him to be off, and not let him catch him there again; there was no peaches, melons, or corn, or other cargo on board the sloop, she was ballasted with stone; saw Smith in the boat going ashore, a white man lifted the hatch of the sloop and put him below and came down and put a round horse lock on his legs; thinks this man's name was Collins, for he heard Joe Johnson as they went afterwards through a corn field call him by that name. When deponent was put into the hold of the sloop, he found Enos Tilghman and Alexander Manlove already there, Enos was in irons, Alexander was not; these boys told deponent they had been caught the night before, by the same John Smith. The same day a boy, who called himself Joe Johnson, a sweep, about 16 years old, was also brought on board by John Smith, and was also immediately put in leg irons. Cornelius Sinclair, (who was sold at Tuscaloosa,) was the last one brought on board the sloop by John Smith, about an hour after the boy Joe Johnson; he also had leg irons put on him; Collins came down, and said to them, Now boys, be still make no noise or I'll cut your throats.

On the same night they got up the anchor and went down the river, and were on the water about a week, when they were landed, he don't know whether in Delaware or Maryland, about twenty miles from Joe Johnson's house, don't think the sloop was at sea on this occasion, they landed in a kind of pond about two hours after sun down, the irons were taken off their necks, they were then marched through marshes, corn fields, and brushwood, until they were taken up by a carriage drive by Joe Johnson, and carried to his house; they were confined in a garret there in irons 24 hours, then arrayed to Jesse Cannon's on a Sunday night, by him (Cannon,) and by Ebenezer F. Johnson; this was the first time the boys ever saw Ebenezer, they were kept at Jesse Cannon's about a week in irons in a garret.

On a Saturday night they were put in a wagon with Mary Fisher, (and another woman who said she was a slave named Maria Neal.) Mary Fisher declared she was a free woman, had been kidnapped, and carried to Patty Cannon's ; they rode about three miles in the wagon, which was drove by John Smith the mulatto; Ebenezer Johnson and his wife, were behind in a gig; they were put into a boat and rowed on board a larger sloop than the one they were first on the

Delaware; they were put into the hold in irons and kept so, the vessel went to sea for a week, when they again landed, he don't know where; he don't know either of the sloops' names, the last sloop was commanded by Robert Dunn, an old man who also cooked on board; Ebenezer Johnson and his wife and Jesse Cannon, were passengers on board, and helped to work the vessel.

Deponent and fellow prisoners were then marched through Alabama, with the irons off in the day time, and put on always when they stopt; Cornelius Sinclair was parted from them, and said to be sold in Tuscaloosa, for 400 dollars, as he heard Ebenezer Johnson tell his wife; they had a one horse wagon with some provision and baggage, it was generally drove by the little boys Enos Tilghman and Alexander Manlove; the wagon was followed by Ebenezer and his wife in the gig; the older and bigger prisoners walked as he believes 600 miles, until they arrived at Rocky Spring; believes they walked 30 miles a day without shoes; when they complained of sore feet and being unable to travel they were most cruelly flogged; that deponent has received more than fifty lashes at one time; that himself, Joe and Cornelius, were most frequently flogged; their feet became frosted in Alabama; that on one occasion this deponent attempted to escape while in the Choctaw nation, but was caught by an Indian, and returned to Ebenezer Johnson, who flogged him with a hand saw and with hickories in a most dreadful manner; (the back of this deponent and his head, were dreadfully scarred by the repeated beatings he had received,) the party of prisoners except Cornelius, remained near a month and a half, near a small town called Ashville, within 16 miles of the Cherokee nation, low down in Alabama; Ebenezer Johnson owned a log house and some land there; they then proceeded to Rocky Spring ; and when within 7 miles of Rocky Spring, John Johnson, one of the boys, died in the wagon in consequence of the frequent and cruel beatings he received from Ebenezer Johnson.

Deponent once heard Johnson's wife declare that it did her good to see him beat the boys; Joe was lame and frosted in the feet, was very weak, and for near three weeks fell frequently as he walked; the weather was very cold in Alabama; about one day before he died he was severely flogged with a cart whip, he died in the wagon; Mrs. Johnson was in the wagon when he died; Ebenezer had previously sold his horse and gig and one horse wagon, and traded for a four horse wagon; they were all except the slave woman, taken from Ebenezer Johnson by Mr. John W. Hamilton, a planter, about seven miles east of Rocky Spring, who kept them and provided well for them, and took care of them for four or five months, until he took them to Natchez, put them on board a steam boat and sent them to Benjamin Morgan at New Orleans, who procured them a passage to this port, where they arrived on the 29th inst. Mary Fisher, the woman, declined coming by sea, and preferred remaining with Mr. Hamilton, where she enjoyed the rights of a free woman; and further deponent sayeth not.

His mark

X SAMUEL SCOMP

Witness present, ADAM TRAQUAIR.

Sworn and subscribed before me, the day and year aforesaid,

JOSEPH WATSON, Mayor.

⋆⇥◉⇤⋆

THOMAS COLLINS TO WILLIAM RAWLE
Philadelphia, April 4, 1831, Penitentiary

Honored Sir,

As I have been imprisoned here at the instance of the Abolition Society I take the liberty (thro you who are the President of that Society) to address them. It may not have escaped your recollection, that on the seventh day of October, AD, 1828, I was sentenced to this Prison, to undergo a term of servitude of twenty one years for kidnapping.

As you, perhaps, are not acquainted with the whole of the circumstances attending this affair, allow me to give you a little detail of facts. I was arrested upon the information of a negro who had already been convicted and who had acknowledged himself to be an accomplice and this information was given under the expectation that he himself would be discharged. This negro is notoriously known been engaged in the business from childhood and he knew at the moment that he gave my name to the Police that I had been ?inveigled? into the affair (for which I was afterwards ?credited? by the artifices of others who had more understanding and cuning than I am possessed of, that I never had any connection with persons engaged in such concerns before, and that when I had leisure to reflect on the dangerous consequences and the wickedness of following up such a course that I immediately abandoned them. Thus the unprincipled man not only took advantage of the unfortunate circumstances which he knew I had been [illegible] to commit by the artful persuasions and representations of his wicked employers, but he also represented me in such colours to the Police officers as induced them to suppose that I was a most desperate and abandoned wretch. I was accordingly convicted without regard to my remonstrances and representations and without [illegible].

Had I been permitted I could have proved by very respectable persons that my character had been for some time at least unexceptionable, that I supported myself and family, not by kidnapping negroes, but by honest industry. But being a man without education (not being able even to read and write) and entirely ignorant of the laws and of the rules and forms of Courts, my friends and acquaintances being at such a distance as to preclude a possibility of their attendance at Court, and totally destitute of money, it is not wonderful that the court and the public should have looked in the light they did on my case and should have given me the extent of the law.

I now, Sir, after being confined for two years and six months, implore the mercy and the humanity of the Abolition Society. I beg them to reflect, that I was drawn into the commission of the offence by those who were more artful and more experienced than myself, that I never was engaged in the business but the once, and then only as a hand on board the vessel, that I have since repented of my folly, that it is my determination in future (should it please God to release me) to make all the amends to Society in my power, that I am a poor man, utterly destitute of money and friends who can release me and that I have a wife and children who [illegible] the consequences of this imprisonment are reduced to the most desolate and afflicted condition, being destitute of all support of even the necissaries of life and perhaps even now the wretched inmates of a Poor-house.

Will you please see to lay this letter before the Society at their next meeting, and tell them that I will do any thing to expiate my offence and to obtain their favour, if they will now have me released. And as you [illegible] serve as the President of the Society, the very [illegible] of which is to aid our kinship and protection to the unfortunate, and as I am informed, you are a kind hearted man, let me ask you to patronize my case. By doing so you will have the approbation of your own conscience and the gratitude of your unfortunate humble servant,

Thomas Collins

INDEX

ABOUT THE AUTHOR

RICHARD BELL teaches early American history at the University of Maryland. He has received several teaching prizes and major research fellowships, including a National Endowment for the Humanities Public Scholar award. His first book, *We Shall Be No More: Suicide and Self-Government in the Newly United States*, was published by Harvard University Press in 2012.

CPSIA information can be obtained
at www.ICGtesting.com
Printed in the USA
BVHW030538160522
636044BV00010B/8

9 781501 169441